Sharing Democracy

Sharing Democracy

Michaele L. Ferguson

OXFORD
UNIVERSITY PRESS

Oxford University Press is a department of the University of Oxford.
It furthers the University's objective of excellence in research,
scholarship, and education by publishing worldwide.

Oxford   New York
Auckland   Cape Town   Dar es Salaam   Hong Kong   Karachi
Kuala Lumpur   Madrid   Melbourne   Mexico City   Nairobi
New Delhi   Shanghai   Taipei   Toronto

With offices in
Argentina   Austria   Brazil   Chile   Czech Republic   France   Greece
Guatemala   Hungary   Italy   Japan   Poland   Portugal   Singapore
South Korea   Switzerland   Thailand   Turkey   Ukraine   Vietnam

Oxford is a registered trade mark of Oxford University Press in the UK and certain other countries.

Published in the United States of America by Oxford University Press
198 Madison Avenue, New York, NY 10016

Library of Congress Cataloging-in-Publication Data
Ferguson, Michaele L., 1973–
Sharing democracy / Michaele L. Ferguson.
    p.   cm.
Includes bibliographical references.
ISBN 978-0-19-992158-4 (hardcover: alk. paper)—ISBN 978-0-19-992160-7 (pbk.: alk. paper)
1. Democracy—Philosophy. 2. Group identity—Political aspects. 3. Identity politics.
4. Identity (Philosophical concept) 5. Agent (Philosophy) I. Title.
JC423.F433   2013
321.8—dc23   2012002811

9 8 7 6 5 4 3 2 1

Printed in the United States of America
on acid-free paper

To Bette, who has always had my back

CONTENTS

ACKNOWLEDGMENTS

I am proud, thrilled, and frankly relieved to be able to offer this book to you. This book has been many years in the making, and for several very dark years I truly did not know whether I would be capable of finishing it. I struggled, of course, with the typical anxieties of a first-time book author and a former graduate student trying to find her own voice. But I also struggled with illness that made it an exhausting challenge for me to hold on to one relatively concrete thought long enough to speak it in a sentence. It seemed impossible only a few years ago that I would be able to hold a series of complex, abstract ideas in my head for long enough to compose this book. And yet, here it is, in happy defiance of my old fears.

I am most grateful for the friends who stood by me through all the challenges I faced and who never lost their faith that I would someday share this book with the world. Lori Marso stubbornly insisted that I could do it, and she was right. She read drafts, she gave me loving and critical feedback (which is the hardest kind to give—but also the most valuable), and she supported me intellectually and emotionally through the hardest days. Patchen Markell helped me to triage the manuscript in January 2010 and was always at the ready with professional advice and encouragement. I was sustained by his belief in the project and his steady support for me as a scholar and a friend. I am glad to call him one of my oldest and best friends.

I benefited enormously from the individual and collective support of a group of friends all at work on their first books: Karen Zivi, Jill Locke, and Holloway Sparks. We have shared so many drafts, so many heartaches and joys over the years, that this book is in many ways theirs just as much as mine. Karen has patiently and generously read many, many versions of this project dating back to the dissertation. She inspired me to make the project better, to finish the book, and to be gentle with myself in the hard times. Jill is a great reader and an uncompromising pillar of strength. I am grateful to have her on my side as a friend. She gently but firmly pointed out weaknesses in my writing, and I am indebted to her for my growing awareness of my own voice. Holloway has given her time and her love to me so freely. I am continually inspired by the political engagement of her scholarship to bring my own work back to the present and to my own political commitments. Her support and her example have helped me to stay connected to my work and my politics. I am truly lucky to have these three amazing women in my life.

I have also learned a great deal about my ideas, my writing, and sharing by presenting my work at conferences and workshops. I am grateful to the brown bag series in Political Science, the Women and Gender Studies Program speaker series, and the Rhetoric Workshop at the University of Colorado at Boulder for giving me the opportunity to present parts of this book along the way. I am especially thankful for Sam Fitch's comments on what later become chapter 4. Steven Johnston's comments as a discussant on chapter 6 helped me to see some of the strengths of my argument. That chapter also benefited from the great and critical discussion of it at the Political Theory Workshop at UNC Chapel Hill. Thanks to Jeff Spinner-Halev and Susan Bickford, as well as the other participants, for an incredibly thoughtful conversation about my work.

I was supported in 2005–2006 by a Tanner Fellowship at the University of Utah. The participants in the research workshop there helped me to think through the book project as a whole and to refine an early version of chapter 3 that was published as "Sharing without Knowing: Collective Identity in Feminist and Multiculturalist Theory," in *Hypatia: A Journal of Feminist Philosophy*, 22,no. 4 (Fall 2007): 30–45. Thanks to John Wiley and Sons for permission to reprint this material. That chapter also benefited from critical feedback from the editors of the special issue of that journal, Claire Snyder-Hall and Noëlle McAfee. I am also grateful to my department for arranging a partial research leave during 2011 to support finishing the manuscript, and then completing revisions in response to reader feedback. I owe a special debt to my colleague Jennifer Fitzgerald for her conversations and suggestions for reading for chapter 4.

I also thank Courtney Berger for her helpful and detailed feedback on the first book manuscript, as well as the four anonymous readers who gave me generous, supportive, and truly helpful comments. Every book author should be lucky enough to have such insightful, careful readers. I hope I have done at least some of your comments justice with my revisions. I am also grateful for Angela Chnapko's advocacy of the book, as well as her patience and understanding as my acquisitions editor with Oxford University Press, and for Leslie Johnson's willingness to work through all the details of the publication process with me.

I would not have made it through the last few years without the support of colleagues and administrators at the University of Colorado. I am especially grateful for the support I received from Lorraine Bayard de Volo, Anne Costain, Jeff Cox, Elissa Guralnick, Ruchi Malhotra, and Patricia Rankin.

Finally, there are many others whose support, whether they knew it or not, gave me the strength to finish this book. I would not have been able to do it without them. Wendy, Elizabeth, Dana, Stefanie, April, Cleo, Susan, and Norm: I cannot thank you enough for what you have done for me, and what you have shown me I can do. Ginger, Jamie, Mike, Mom, and Dad, thank you for being there for me through it all. Last, but not least: Tara, Emily, Perry, Trixie, Cleo, and Pompeii, thank you for all of the cuddles, the licks, the purrs, and the love.

Sharing Democracy

Introduction

"We Are All Egypt"

The essence of the protests in the Arab Spring is that people can imagine an alternative.
—Anthony Shadid and David D. Kirkpatrick[1]

Because the Obama team never found the voice to fully endorse the Tahrir Square revolution until it was over, the people in that square now know one very powerful thing: They did this all by themselves. That is so important. One of the most powerful chants I heard in the square on Friday night was: "The people made the regime step down."
—Thomas L. Friedman[2]

The spring of 2011 was hailed as the Arab Spring because it appeared to mark the rebirth of democracy in North Africa and the Middle East. Yet as the headline of a front-page analysis in the *New York Times* ominously declared that May: "Promise of Arab Uprisings Is Threatened by Divisions." Only a few months after the Arab Spring began, the optimism brought on by early democratic successes in Tunisia and Egypt had waned in the face of the brutal tribal and sectarian repression of rebellions in Yemen, Syria, and Bahrain, and the beginnings of what became a bloody civil war in Libya. Even in Tunisia and Egypt, old divisions had resurfaced with sometimes violent results, as conflicts broke out between religious groups. Shadid and Kirkpatrick, the authors of the analysis, question whether these Arab peoples possess the sense of common purpose necessary to make a successful transition to democracy, in spite of their differences. As they see it, "The question of identity may help determine whether the Arab Spring flowers or withers." While the uprisings offer "a new sense of national identity built on the idea of citizenship," this unifying identity "is being tested as the enforced silence of repression gives way to the cacophony of diversity."[3]

Shadid and Kirkpatrick articulate a familiar anxiety about democracy: that without some kind of commonality unifying the people, democracy will fail. Diversity is unavoidable in contemporary democracies, whether it is a matter of racial and ethnic difference, ideological or religious disagreement, or class cleavages. Insofar as diversity sets citizens against one another, it can make sharing democracy between them difficult, if not impossible. How might democracy flourish among the countries touched by the Arab Spring when their populations are deeply divided by religion, sect, tribe, class, and gender? Will such diverse groups of people actually be able to share democracy together? Will they be able to overcome legacies of suspicion and trust one another enough to be willing to share power? Will members of one group be able to accept leadership by members of another group? The anxiety driving these questions is that if the people who share a democracy are too divided, they will not be able to identify as one self-governing people, to cooperate and trust one another, or to accept the decisions of democratic institutions as legitimate if their own group has been outvoted. And so Shadid and Kirkpatrick make a familiar move: they suggest that the answer lies in "a sense of self that transcends the many divides."[4] That is, they presume that the antidote to the centrifugal pull of diversity is the countervailing, unifying force of commonality.

Commonality, it seems, is the glue that binds together diverse persons into a single people capable of democratic self-government. It transcends our differences, it gives us a "sense of a collective destiny," it ensures "stability and security," and it "unites, not divides."[5] As one Syrian intellectual quoted in the article states, without a unifying sense of national identity, "The costs otherwise would be disintegration, strife and civil war."[6] This fear of fragmentation is not unique to the Arab world. It shows up regularly in comparatively stable, established democracies in the West. Arthur Schlesinger Jr., for example, famously expressed the concern that identity politics in the United States risked tearing the country apart. "If separatist tendencies go on unchecked," he warned in 1992, "the result can only be the fragmentation, resegregation, and tribalization of American life."[7] This fear of division and disintegration drives us to grasp ever more tightly to the belief that we must have something in common in order for democracy to work.

But what must be true about the world in order for commonality to be able to make diverse individuals into a unified people? First, it must be the case that political community is a product of its members having something in common, such as a national identity. Where people do not have commonality, they must be unable to form a community. Further, commonality must be able to generate bonds of trust. That is, the recognition that we have something in common must have some kind of psychological effect on us, such that it can generate affective connection where there previously had been suspicion and mistrust. Finally, commonality must be able to confer legitimacy on democratic institutions and decisions. It must be able to make us more willing to accept rule by those who differ from or disagree with us, because we know that at the end of the day, we still share something important in common.

Yet is this really how we share democracy? Do we need commonality to have a sense of community, to trust one another, to accept decisions we ourselves would not have made? While many political theorists (especially over the past thirty years) have been preoccupied with rethinking democracy's relationship to diversity, they have left curiously unexamined its relationship to commonality. This omission is all the more remarkable because, like Shadid and Kirkpatrick, democratic theorists—even as they seek to accommodate diversity—regularly assume that democracy will only be stable and sustainable among a population that shares in some kind of commonality. Theorists disagree about what citizens should have in common; but they are largely in agreement that citizens must have something in common. Yet this position is typically assumed, rarely made explicit, and has not been the focus of critical investigation in democratic theory. In this book, I seek to address this gap by offering an analysis of the assumption that we *must* have something in common, or we could not constitute a democratic people. In this book, I reveal how pervasive this assumption is in our thinking about democracy, I give an account of why it is so appealing to us, and I offer an alternative account of the relationship of commonality and democracy that aims to loosen its power over our thinking.

Whereas theorists often presume that we need commonality in order to produce shared identity, affective bonds between citizens, and a sense of collective agency, I take a phenomenological turn to look and see what it is that we do when we share. I argue that when we look at what we do, it turns out that whether we actually have anything in common is not essential to our ability to share. When we describe ourselves as sharing something in common, we are expressing a *belief* that we have about the world, a belief that does not need to correspond to some empirical truth in order to be meaningful. Human beings make sense of the world in part by claiming commonalities and assigning meaning to them. We understand objects with four legs and a flat surface to be tables, for example, or we understand people who carry certain kinds of passports to be Americans. Yet we could imagine tables and Americans differently, as defined by different commonalities, or perhaps as not defined by commonalities at all. To think of commonality in this way is to reveal that humans do the work of making sense of the world; its meaning is not simply out there waiting to be discovered by us. While we typically do this meaning-making work without even realizing it, we can make it a critical, self-conscious activity: we can take responsibility for how we make sense of the world, and we can imagine new ways of understanding it. In this capacity to make sense, I find the basis for an alternate conception of democracy, one grounded in our ability to shape the meaning of the world in which we live. This is an understanding of democracy based in our ordinary political freedom to remake the world, in how we share the world together, rather than in what (or whether) we share.

From this perspective, the idea that democracy requires commonality appears to be not a necessary truth but one partisan way, among others, of making sense of the world. It is a part of a worldview that has a significant, antidemocratic effect on what those captivated by it can and cannot perceive. It occludes human agency in making sense of the world, and it consequently disavows our responsibility for how we imagine democratic community. In its insistence that the people must have something in common, or else democracy will fail, it risks ignoring or pathologizing those voices that challenge the presumption of commonality. Most important, it prioritizes the passive possession of commonality over the active exercise of political freedom.

These two visions of democracy competed in the coverage of the uprising in Cairo's Tahrir Square in early 2011. Much of the reporting expressed either celebration or concern over the degree of commonality expressed in the protests. One strand, for example, emphasized the diversity of the protesters as a sign of the widespread convergence of Egyptians on a common agenda: to oust President Hosni Mubarak and usher in democratic institutions.[8] People who would not ordinarily have interacted with one another before the revolution erupted on January 25 were now able to interact peacefully and cooperatively, despite differences of class, a culture of widespread sexual harassment, and deep ideological divides.[9] As one protester interviewed said, "You see all these people, with no stealing, no girls being bothered, and no violence. . . . [Mubarak's] trying to tell us that without me, without the regime, you will fall into anarchy, but we have all told him, 'No.'"[10] Some interpreted this harmony as a sign of an underlying Egyptian national identity, and of a newfound commitment to civility and democratic power sharing. Another strand characterized this same diversity as a sign of the lack of coherence of a political movement that was essentially leaderless and ill-equipped to assume the reins of a new Egyptian democracy.[11] Moreover, some reflected skepticism that the goodwill of Tahrir

Square would survive the transition to democracy.[12] Both of these strands of reporting operate within the logic of commonality: either the protests are a hopeful sign of a democratic future for Egypt because the protesters share a common agenda and identity, or they reveal how very far Egyptians are from possessing the unity they will require to share in self-government. In either case, the emphasis on commonality orients our attention to an imagined democracy in the future: Do the Egyptians have the commonality it will take to build and sustain democratic institutions?

A competing narrative of the occupation of Tahrir Square stressed a vision of democracy understood in terms of present political freedom rather than institutions to come. The revolts in Tunisia and Egypt offered the protesters a firsthand education in self-government. As a Lebanese columnist said, "This is a historic moment, and it is teaching the Arab world everything. They are learning that if they take to the streets they can accomplish their goals."[13] Egyptians learned from the Tunisian experience that they did not have to accept Mubarak's rule as necessary or inevitable. Once freed from their belief that they could do nothing to change their situation, they discovered that they had the capacity to rule themselves. Rami Khouri, a journalist and scholar at the American University in Beirut, expressed the euphoria of Tahrir Square this way: "We are witnessing an epic, historic moment of the birth of concepts that have long been denied to ordinary Arabs: the right to define ourselves and our governments, to assert our national values, to shape our governance systems."[14] This vision of democracy stresses the human capacity to shape the world—available to all of us, and not only to those already in power. This is democracy not as found only in institutions but as expressed in the desire to make the world anew. As Friedman writes in the epigraph here, "The people made the regime step down." The Egyptian protesters shaped their own reality, and in so doing, they governed themselves.

What if democracy ordinarily looks like Tahrir Square? On the morning of January 25, the protesters took action without knowing how things would turn out. They made claims in the name of Egypt, without knowing whether other Egyptians, and enough Egyptians, would agree with them. They occupied Tahrir Square, without knowing how long they would need to hold onto it, without knowing whether the police or the military would use force to displace them, without knowing whether they would be successful. They called on others to join with them, even though they had their differences and disagreements, without knowing whether those others would join them, without knowing whether they would be able to work together, without knowing whether their movement would be overtaken and thwarted by an organized and established opposition. They demanded democratic institutions, without knowing whether they would get them, and if so what they would look like and whether they would indeed be democratic.

I propose that acting without knowing—far from being the rare province of courageous protesters risking their lives—is the ordinary condition of democratic politics. We ordinarily act into a world of others without knowing in advance who will show up, and even whether anyone will show up to support us. We ordinarily act without knowing whether the people we address with our political claims will agree with us. We ordinarily act without knowing what we have in common, and whether we have anything in common with one another. And we ordinarily act without knowing whether we will achieve our goals or, if we do, whether the results will be what we had hoped for. Democracy involves acting together with people we do not know, to pursue goals we cannot know in advance that we share, in the hope of a future we cannot control. This is sharing democracy in a world inhabited by plural others. The allure of commonality is that it appears to offer us a kind of knowing to allay some of the uncertainty of interacting with others: it promises that we can know with whom we share democracy, that we can therefore trust them and accept letting them make some of the decisions. Yet to orient ourselves to political freedom is to acknowledge that the outcomes of democratic action cannot be controlled, that they are and always will be uncertain. This is the at once exhilarating and terrifying promise of Tahrir Square: that, as many signs at protests around the world since have read, "We are all Egypt."

CHAPTER OVERVIEW

In chapter 1, I examine the curious fact that the belief that democracy requires some kind of commonality repeatedly shows up in the works of those contemporary democratic theorists who would seem most likely to eschew it: those who are concerned to acknowledge the inevitability and even the desirability of difference in democracy. These theorists are themselves often quite critical of particular kinds of commonality—such as shared ethnicity, centralized institutions, and a common culture—that they believe are unjustly at odds with diversity. Yet, rather than rejecting commonality altogether, they simply modify the kind of commonality that they believe democracy requires. What is the allure of commonality, I ask, such that they are so unwilling to let go of it? I argue that democratic theorists are drawn to commonality because they believe it is necessary to satisfy three requirements of democracy: the requirement that the people have a distinct identity; the requirement that the people have a horizontal, affective attachment to one another; and the requirement that individuals understand the will of the people as their own. In order to let go of the belief that democracy requires some kind of commonality, we must also be able to let go of the corollary assumptions that commonality is necessary to produce shared identity, affective ties, and collective agency.

When democratic theorists believe that democracy requires some kind of commonality, they are captivated by what I call an objective mental picture of sharing. In chapter 2, and by way of a critical reading of Danielle Allen's analysis of the integration of Little Rock Central High School in 1957, I offer an account of two different pictures of how sharing takes place. The first is the objective picture of sharing: we share when we have some objective thing in common. Sharing, on this view, is passive: we can share something in common without doing anything, and without even knowing that we share it. Consequently, this picture of sharing can be depoliticizing: it occludes human agency and responsibility for sharing.

The second—an intersubjective picture of sharing—I develop through an engagement with Hannah Arendt. In this picture of sharing, a common thing is neither a necessary nor a sufficient condition for us to share. Rather, sharing is a matter of how we stand in relation to others: it is a first-person awareness of living in a world inhabited by other people, who are themselves subjects like ourselves. We share when we interact with other people to try to make sense of the world together; this meaning-making activity is what Arendt calls "world-building." In this picture, sharing is active: it takes human beings actively interpreting and communicating with one another about the world. This intersubjective picture of sharing is the basis for the account of democracy that I develop over the remainder of the book as an alternative to accounts of democracy grounded in commonality.

Chapter 3 is the first of three central chapters addressing the three democratic requirements identified in chapter 1: identity, affect, and agency. Here, I turn to debates within feminist theory over "the category of women" in order to shed some light on the problem of democratic identity. Feminist theorists have long been explicitly preoccupied with the relationship between commonality and feminist politics, although they, too, have been caught up in a version of the objective picture of sharing: "women" must have something in common, or else the category is incoherent and a problematic basis for a political movement. Drawing on Linda Zerilli's recent critique of feminist theory, I argue that identity is improperly conceived as grounded in objective, knowable commonalities. Instead, I argue that identity is a matter of belief, held in place by multiple, overlapping, yet not entirely contiguous social practices. I substantiate this claim by working through the case of

Indochinese identity discussed by Benedict Anderson in *Imagined Communities*. In conclusion, I argue that we need to reconceptualize the identity of the demos as the product of human imagination, and therefore as a matter of the intersubjective human activity of world-building.

Chapter 4 begins with a critical reading of Robert Putnam's recent survey of social capital in the United States, which he claimed reveals that diversity undermines relationships of trust and solidarity between citizens. His essay highlights a tension between two logics that I identify as present in democratic theory as well. On the one hand is a causal logic that claims commonality produces trust and solidarity, while difference produces distrust and anomie. On the other hand is a constructivist logic that claims for scholars, if not also for ordinary citizens, the ability to shape identities and allegiances so as to redirect trust and solidarity to their proper referents. I show through readings of David Miller, Jürgen Habermas, and Charles Taylor how this tension typically gets resolved in a way that bolsters the appeal of the assumption that democracy requires commonality. In particular, commonality appears to offer democratic theorists a way to address the perceived affective deficit of the modern state, and to address the problem that we cannot have knowledge of what our fellow citizens actually think and feel: theorists need only locate the right commonality, and the appropriate affective ties will follow. However, I argue that affective ties are grounded in belief, not in knowledge of others. This means that theorists cannot secure the kinds of affective ties they should like to construct. Nonetheless, while affect is not fully within our control, insofar as it is a matter of belief, it is a product of human imagination. I argue that this makes claims about affective ties inherently political exercises of power, and that consequently we bear responsibility for reflecting critically on how we imagine our relationships to others.

In chapter 5, I turn to Taylor both to illustrate how democratic agency is often conceived in terms of commonality and to develop an alternative. On the one hand, Taylor seems to subscribe to the idea that the people who govern a democracy must have something in common in order to share a will. In his writings on democracy, he argues that we can and must correctly identify what the demos has in common in order to motivate citizens to feel included in decisions made in the name of the people. Without sharing in some commonality with one another, citizens are likely to feel excluded from the demos. On the other hand, the account of collective agency Taylor offers in his philosophical and historical writings presents collective agency as a product of the imagination. We moderns, he argues, imagine democratic collective agency in two forms: as the agency of a prepolitical "people" and of a self-constituting "public." Drawing critically on his work, I develop an opposition between two kinds of democratic agency: sovereign democratic agency, which is located in the demos of state institutions; and democratic interagency, which is the dialogic agency that emerges in the interactions between persons engaged in making claims about how we should imagine our shared world, wherever these interactions should occur. Democratic interagency enables me to reframe democratic inclusion not as inclusion in and identification with the popular sovereign but as the intersubjective exercise of one's political freedom to shape the world in which one lives. This is to move beyond the state and to pluralize the demos of democracy.

In the final chapter, I offer a positive vision of what democratic theory and practice might look like beyond commonality. In particular, I turn to protests as a model for a democratic imaginary that captures the features of democracy without the insistence that we have something in common. I couple a reading of the 2006 immigrant rights protests in the United States with a critique of the literature in feminist theory on "coalition politics" to show the limits of commonality as a framework for making sense of protests. Protests—far from embodying agreement and unity of purpose—are often cacophonous events that include disagreement, dissent, and counterprotest. What they do embody is the first-personal quality I call "democracy sense": the awareness that humans exercise agency together with others in shaping the world in which we live, the understanding that we can imagine the world differently than we do now, and the sense that each of us has that capacity for world-building freedom within us. Protests are expressions of a self-authorizing democratic freedom to shape the world in which we live—a freedom that can only be exercised together with others, and whose outcome cannot be guaranteed.

CHAPTER 1

The Allure of Commonality

Consider for example the proceedings that we call "games." I mean board-games, card-games, ball-games, Olympic games, and so on. What is common to them all?—Don't say: "There must be something common, or they would not be called 'games'"—but *look and see* whether there is anything common to all.
—Ludwig Wittgenstein[1]

This book is about two different ways of seeing democracy. You might think about them as a version of the duck-rabbit image: when we look at the image in one way, we see it as a duck; when we look at it in another way, we see it as a rabbit. The same lines that seem to depict the duck's bill, if we just look at them differently, appear instead to indicate the rabbit's ears. We can see the image as either the duck or the rabbit, but somehow we are unable to see the image in both ways simultaneously. And sometimes when we are able to see the duck, we simply cannot shift our way of seeing to make out the rabbit, or vice versa. The two ways of seeing democracy are like these two ways of seeing the duck-rabbit.

The first way of seeing democracy is oriented toward commonality. We focus on what, if anything, the people in a democratic community have in common. We might see a shared language, a set of institutions, an ethnicity, or a particular history, for example. The commonality gives the democracy its structure and definition.

The other way of seeing is oriented toward activity. In this case, looking at the same phenomena, we focus instead on the exercise of political freedom in acts of self-government. We might see a congressional debate, a protest march, a person publishing a book or a blog post, or a consciousness-raising group. Democracy here emerges in the interactions between people.

Each way of seeing significantly affects how we conceptualize democracy, politics, and human agency. Each way of seeing impacts what we do, what we value, and how we relate to one another. How we see democracy matters.

Ironically, when we see democracy in terms of commonality, we take an antidemocratic view of politics. What is occluded from view is our very ordinary human agency—our capacity to shape the world in which we live through active interaction with one another. We focus instead on characteristics or things that the citizens of a democracy share with one another passively. In this view, these commonalities seem to be what grounds a given democracy; the activity of self-government appears at best secondary in importance, at worst irrelevant to democratic politics.

When instead we see democracy in terms of activity—as I will argue we should—we take a more democratic view of politics, one that highlights the active exercise of political freedom. This is a view of democracy that places at its center our ordinary human agency to shape the world in which we live together. It orients us to thinking of democracy not as a form of government but as the activity of self-government, whether expressed within or beyond democratic institutions.

In contemporary democratic theory the commonality view dominates, at the expense of the view oriented toward activity. In fact, commonality so dominates our seeing that we theorists are often like the person so captivated by the image of the duck that she finds it impossible, or even nonsensical, to see the image of the rabbit. The dominance of this commonality orientation comes at a significant cost: it generates false and misleading problems for theory and practice, and it directs us on a never-ending search for the elusive commonality that could unite everyone in a democracy.

What I seek to do in this book is to help us shift our way of seeing so that we can more clearly see democracy as an activity—a view that is obscured when we focus on commonality, just as the rabbit is obscured when we think of the drawing as depicting a duck. My first step in effecting this perceptual shift is to argue that the focus on commonality in democratic theory is contingent and unnecessary. This argument will challenge different readers in different ways. Some of us simply have a hard time imagining democracy without commonality: it seems self-evident that democracy requires it. Others of us, including some prominent democratic theorists, believe that we have rejected commonality—usually in favor of diversity and difference—when in fact we have not rejected it altogether. Once we have become accustomed to seeing democracy as a duck, it can be difficult for us to even realize that this is just one way of seeing.

In order to loosen our attachment to commonality, we need to understand why this way of seeing is so alluring. I propose that its appeal derives from the belief that commonality makes possible three requirements of democracy: a collective identity, an affective attachment between citizens, and the capacity to act as a singular, collective agency. I will argue that commonality never truly satisfies any of these requirements. Far from securing democracy, it perversely undermines our pursuit of democracy by occluding political freedom.

Simultaneously, I will gradually bring to the forefront the activity-oriented view of democracy: a view that orients our attention to political freedom, to the capacity of human beings to shape a shared world. Just as it may be difficult to sustain the view of the rabbit when you are first able to see it—the image keeps frustratingly slipping back into the duck—the glimpses that I will show of an orientation to activity may be difficult to sustain. But I aim to increase your fluidity in moving between the two ways of seeing until, by the final chapter, it feels just as familiar to see democracy in terms of activity as it once did to see it in terms of commonality. I will show that the dominance of the commonality orientation has significant costs for democratic theory and practice, and I hope by the end of the book to persuade you to see democracy instead in terms of political freedom.

DEMOCRACY AND COMMONALITY

It may seem counterintuitive to some readers for me to suggest that most contemporary democratic theorists are committed to the view that democracy requires commonality. After all, the dominant trend over the past thirty years or so has been for theorists to try to revise our understanding of democracy in order to acknowledge diversity, to reject homogeneity and assimilation, and to find ways to accommodate and even celebrate differences among citizens. We could say that political theory of late has been moving steadily away from the idea that a democratic people must be united by commonality, and toward acceptance of the ineradicability (and even desirability) of difference.

Although I grant that democratic theorists today tend to be more critical of commonality and more open to acknowledging a wider range of difference than in the past, they typically do not take the radical step of rejecting commonality altogether. Rather, they remain attached to the belief that democracy requires a citizenry that shares something in common. Consequently, what they reject is not commonality as such, but only specific sources of commonality. Here, democratic theory follows the course of political developments, social movements, and demographic shifts over the past century that have called particular forms of commonality into question without thereby challenging our underlying way of seeing democracy in terms of what we share in common. To illustrate this point, let us briefly consider some of the classes of commonality that have been challenged in political practice.

The most striking example of a commonality that has been discredited on both empirical and ethical grounds is the idea of a *common ethnicity*. Empirically, the ideal of the homogeneous nation-state has been in tension with demographic reality since it first emerged. Over the twentieth century, it became even more implausible as waves of non-Western migration significantly broadened the ethnic, linguistic, religious, and racial diversity in Western democracies.[2] Even where the idea of a homogeneous community may have had some credibility in the past as fact, and not merely as retroactive fiction—as perhaps in a country like Sweden—it is no longer empirically convincing to describe contemporary democracies as ethnically pure nation-states.[3] Ethically, moreover, the means that would be required to ethnically homogenize a population are widely regarded as repugnant, to put it mildly. And where ethnic groups and immigrants have intermarried and reproduced, such methods could never result in homogeneity anyhow. The legacy of the Holocaust, and its echoes in the Rwandan genocide and the Balkan conflicts in the 1990s serve as a strong reminder that democracies must accept ethnic diversity as a fact, rather than seek a way to eliminate it or nostalgically wish it away.[4]

Many national minorities, immigrants, and aboriginals have gone further and argued against the necessity of a *common culture* in democracy, to which all citizens are expected to assimilate. They have organized to preserve their cultural and linguistic diversity in the face of long-term state policies of voluntary and involuntary assimilation. Second- and third-generation immigrants in the midcentury United States rejected the need for complete assimilation when they sought to publicly reclaim the cultural and linguistic heritage that their parents and grandparents had shunned. In response to Canadian policies dating back to the nineteenth century that disadvantaged francophones and Catholics in the worlds of business and politics, Quebecois nationalists established language laws and cultural programs to forestall assimilation to a Protestant, English-language norm. Aboriginal groups exposed reeducation projects aimed at dismantling traditional cultures that involved relocating young children in adoptive white families, and organized to preserve communities and ways of life at odds with majority society. Democracies, these different movements claim, have demanded of their populations a degree of cultural homogeneity that is neither necessary nor achievable by ethical means. They contend that democracy does not require a common culture but is compatible with the flourishing of diverse languages, religions, and ways of life.

Political and social movements have also challenged commonality in the form of *common institutions*: uniform codes of law, shared structures of government, and inclusive public spheres. Many national minorities and aboriginal groups have argued for local sovereignty on the grounds that they cannot protect their unique forms of life within state-level institutions in which they are outnumbered. As a result of historical treaties as well as more recently negotiated forms of local rule, common institutions as a practical matter do not exist in many democracies: there is no single set of laws or procedures that apply equally to all of their citizens. Additionally, cultural and religious minorities have claimed that the institutions they share with the majority are biased against them, and so are not truly the same for all. States abdicate neutrality when they recognize specific holidays, celebrate particular cultural traditions, restrict only some forms of religious dress, and declare certain languages to be official. Relatedly, feminists and antiracism activists have called out how the rights-bearing individual of liberal democracies, far from being a universally valid account of human subjectivity, is in fact a particular conception of the political subject—one that is presumed to be white, male, and middle-class. And some aboriginal and minority religious groups (such as the Amish) have charged liberal democracies with privileging modern individualism and capitalism, at the expense of traditional and communal values.[5] These groups argue that our institutions, far from being common to all, reflect and perpetuate the dominance of those already in power.

In response to these perceived biases, many activists have called for the formal recognition of group differences, which in turn challenges another source of commonality: *common citizenship*. Citizens, they argue, should have differentiated rights based upon group membership, rather than having a single set of rights common to all. In some cases, this conviction has manifested in a call for the state to formally recognize diversity—for example, the demands that Sikh men serving as Canadian Mounties have the right to wear their religiously mandated turbans, that state services and documents be provided in multiple languages, and that the government preserve and encourage diversity by providing funding and legal protections for minority cultural groups. In other cases, it has manifested in a call for structural and institutional changes in order to give previously excluded and disadvantaged groups fairer access to political and economic power such as affirmative action programs, educational programs and scholarships targeted at minority populations, demands for quotas on party lists or in legislative assemblies, and the creation of advisory boards like the

Muslim Council in France to give minority groups a formal voice on policy matters that affect them.[6] According to this line of argument, true equality among citizens can only be achieved by recognizing, accommodating, and even cultivating difference.

Theorists often group together the variety of movements that challenge existing conceptions of commonality under the headings of "the politics of difference,"[7] "the politics of recognition,"[8] "the politics of cultural recognition,"[9] or multiculturalism,[10] despite the variety of issues, demands, and identities at stake—not all of which have to do with cultures or cultural groups.[11] For some, these developments are met with nostalgia for a mythical past when our democracies were not troubled with conflict about difference,[12] or with a hope for a future in which economic issues might once again trump the distracting and largely epiphenomenal issues of identity.[13] However, while some have dismissed these phenomena as irrelevant to or dangerous for democracy, the general trend over the past thirty years in democratic theory has been toward the view that democracy as practiced today needs to be revised in light of these new political claims, social movements, and demographic changes. Diversity is widely taken to be an unavoidable—if not desirable—feature of contemporary democratic life. Different theorists adopt different attitudes—from merely acknowledging, to trying to accommodate, to celebrating and even promoting diversity. They disagree about which kinds of difference matter to democratic politics, which kinds can be overcome in keeping with liberal and democratic principles, and which are intractable and must be either accommodated or excluded. Yet they share the presumption that democracies are now and ever will be composed of diverse populations.

This acceptance of diversity—whether begrudging or enthusiastic—leads contemporary theorists to challenge assertions that democracies require certain kinds of commonality. Not every theorist attacks the same conception of what the demos should have in common, of course. Yet taken together, democratic theorists have criticized a variety of sources of commonality: religious and moral agreement;[14] ethnic or cultural homogeneity;[15] a shared, supposedly neutral legal system that treats all citizens equally;[16] thick, national identity;[17] and a strong patriotism that overpowers other affective attachments.[18] The grounds on which they criticize commonality also vary, and echo the concerns of political and social movements. Some are concerned that an emphasis on ethnic, cultural, or national homogeneity leads to objectionable policies, such as ethnic cleansing and forced migration, forced assimilation, the production and reproduction of structurally disadvantaged groups through the elevation of one group to the norm, and the unjust denial of local autonomy under uniform and centralized government.

Some argue that an emphasis on commonality denies empirical reality; it is idealistic, naive, and ultimately based on false presumptions about demographic homogeneity.[19] Some contend that calls for commonality are grounded in a view of equality as sameness: those who are equal must be alike; in its place, they argue for rethinking equality as compatible with difference.[20] Some suggest that an emphasis on what we have in common makes us resistant to acknowledging our historical and moral obligations to others in our community.[21] Some are concerned about how an emphasis on commonality constitutes a hegemonic norm and misleadingly presents it as neutral.[22] Finally, some criticize commonality for simply failing to acknowledge what these theorists themselves have come to accept: that diversity is an unavoidable, even desirable, part of democracy.

Yet while contemporary theorists tend to be quite critical of specific kinds of commonality in the name of difference, they do not reject commonality as such. Instead, they are typically concerned to find a way to accommodate difference, but within the limits of a new understanding of what the people should have in common. They are willing to alter democratic theories in order to acknowledge differences, but not to such an extent that citizens in a democracy are left with nothing to unite them. The assumption that democracy requires some kind of commonality—while seemingly called into question—is not jettisoned; it is merely modified.

COMMONALITY AS A THOUGHT IMPEDIMENT

Allow me to illustrate democratic theory's investment in commonality by showing how it manifests in Charles Taylor's work. Taylor is an interesting figure for me because he is one of the rare theorists who has explicitly (albeit briefly) examined the persistence of a commonality orientation in democratic theory and practice. As I will show, he is both critical of the tendency to insist that we must have something in common in democracy and curiously susceptible to it himself. I contend that he lapses back into a commonality orientation because what he criticizes turns out to be not commonality as such but only specific kinds of commonality. And so Taylor at once reveals that our stubborn attachment to commonality is an unnecessary "thought impediment" and demonstrates how difficult it is to break free of its hold on our thinking.

Taylor's complicated relationship to commonality emerges in his analysis of the secession crisis in Canada in the early 1990s. Quebecois nationalists were frustrated by a long history of discrimination and cultural imperialism, and distrustful of federal political institutions they believed disadvantaged Quebec. Liberals, however, resisted granting concessions to Quebec that they perceived to be at odds with the protection of the rights of individuals living in that province. Repeated rounds of constitutional negotiations over the previous fifteen years had failed to produce a solution acceptable to both groups. In response, the nationalist Parti Quebecois proposed in a referendum in 1995 to reclaim Quebec sovereignty and renegotiate political and economic relations with the rest of Canada.[23] Secession, it seemed, was the only way out of the impasse.

Taylor argues that Canada's political stalemate was the result of a "thought impediment."[24] While liberal democrats and Quebecois nationalists disagreed about how to recognize and accommodate difference in their constitution, both sides stubbornly insisted that diverse Canadians need to have a uniform conception of citizenship. Liberal democrats, for example, conceptualized difference only as individual. They sought to recognize this difference through the protection of individual rights and freedoms; difference could be accommodated by treating each person in the same way. Quebecois nationalists demanded instead that Quebec be recognized as a "distinct society" within Canada—a nation with its own unique history, language, and culture, all deserving of recognition and promotion. Then, compelled by the idea that there should only be one conception of citizenship for all, these nationalists applied the "distinct society" model to the rest of Canada—suggesting that the country be understood as conglomerate of national societies: francophone, anglophone, and aboriginal. For the nationalists, difference could best be recognized by treating each distinct society in the same way. While both sides aimed to recognize difference, each succeeded at recognizing only one particular kind of difference, which they then assumed applied generally to all Canadians. Because they were unable to think of difference as complex and multidimensional, their proposals for ways to recognize difference all amounted to proposals that paradoxically recognize only sameness.

The impediment to their thinking, according to Taylor, is that both sides were captivated by the idea that all Canadians need to understand their citizenship in the same way: either as liberal individuals or as members of distinct nations. Consequently, once they identified one kind of difference, they were compelled by a very strong impulse to generalize it and turn it into a kind of sameness. Taylor presents this impulse in the text as an insistent, parenthetical imperative: "(Hurry! declare everybody uniform again!)"[25]

In the place of a uniform sense of citizenship, Taylor advocates embracing the multiplicity of ways that Canadians relate to their community: some might conceive of their citizenship as that of liberal individual rights-bearers, while others might conceive of their citizenship as mediated by their membership in a distinct, national society.[26] He believes the tendency of liberal and nationalist uniformity thinking to reduce all difference to just one kind is what brought Canada to the brink of secession in the 1990s. Taylor aims to avoid this reduction by simultaneously acknowledging multiple dimensions of difference—what he calls "deep diversity."[27] His hope is that, by replacing an insistence on uniformity with an acceptance of deep diversity, Canadians might be able to rekindle their sense of common citizenship.

From one perspective, Taylor is a critic of commonality. He exposes how contemporary politicians are often gripped by a way of seeing that drives them to insist that Canadians must have something in common. He notes how this way of seeing the world created the perception of an impasse that fueled talk of secession: if Canadians could not agree on what they had in common, then they could not share a democracy. Yet he identifies the thought impediment as the expectation that Canadians must have a uniform sense of citizenship. It is commonality in the specific form of uniformity—and not commonality more generally—that is the subject of his criticism.

And so, from another perspective, Taylor is an advocate of commonality. Indeed, he argues that the need for commonality arises from democracy itself.[28] "A democratic society requires a certain kind of unity," he writes, "because its people supposedly form a unit of collective decision."[29] Because we make decisions together that affect all of us as a democratic people, we "have to be able to trust one another and have a sense of commitment to one another, or the whole process of common decision will be poisoned by division and mutual suspicion."[30] In order to trust one another, he argues, we require "a sense of common citizenship, that is, a common understanding of what it is to be a member of this society."[31] This is why, he claims, modern democracies have sought to locate and cultivate national identities, in order to unite diverse populations to form a cohesive popular sovereign. Indeed, Taylor believes that this need for unity is so central to a well-functioning democracy that he assures us that "there is nothing wrong with this enterprise. On the contrary, in some form it is indispensable."[32]

If democracy requires a sense of common citizenship, then it seems we cannot do without commonality. Taylor can reject uniformity as the wrong way to achieve democratic unity, but he cannot reject commonality as a whole without rejecting democracy itself. Therefore, he modifies the commonality required for democracy, shifting it from the same sense of common citizenship to merely some sense of common citizenship, which diverse citizens may feel in different ways. It is as if the need to locate a commonality were a kind of mental tic, a stutter, or perhaps a thought impediment: an involuntary move that Taylor makes despite his best intentions, not even realizing it. He cannot tolerate the vacuum left by his criticism of uniformity and must rush to fill it with something new. (Hurry! declare that we have something in common again!)

THREE STRATEGIES

As I suggest throughout the book, this same pattern is repeated over and over in contemporary democratic theory. Far from being an exception, Taylor is typical of contemporary democratic theorists who are critical of certain claims to commonality because they view them as incompatible with the diversity of our political communities, and who nonetheless remain committed to the idea that democracy requires some kind of commonality. As each theorist rejects one form of commonality, she fills the void with another. To paraphrase Ludwig Wittgenstein's imagined interlocutor, it is as if democratic theorists were saying, "We *must* have something common, or we could not be called 'Canadians' or 'Americans' or so on."

Of course, democratic theorists do not agree on how to reconcile their commitment to accommodating diversity with their persistent belief that some kind of commonality is necessary to democracy. Let me briefly introduce here the three broad strategies theorists use to reconcile diversity with the perceived need for commonality. I will go into more detail about specific examples of these strategies in later chapters.

The first is the *minimal strategy*. This approach tries to identify the most minimal commonality that a demos needs to share in order for democracy to work, leaving the maximum room possible for diversity. Those who adopt this strategy are often critical of theories that call for the necessity of comparatively "thick" commonalities—like shared genealogical descent, religion, culture, history, language, or political values. States overextend their authority when they demand that citizens share more than what they need to in order for democracy to work, leading to abuses of individual rights, or to gross injustices such as ethnic cleansing and forcible assimilation. The state's authority must therefore be limited to what democracy requires. Indeed, this approach to commonality in democracy is a manifestation of a kind of liberalism in that it calls for limitations on the role of government in order to allow for maximum liberty for individuals (and, for some theorists, for groups as well).

Whereas the minimal strategy limits the thickness of commonality, the *civic strategy* restricts its location.[33] That is, it locates commonality in the political realm alone—for example, in common political institutions, a single political culture, shared political values, a common good, or participation in a shared public sphere. Elsewhere—in associations, in the workplace, in private, anywhere people do not appear as citizens—diversity is allowed to flourish. The civic approach, then, insists on the necessity of *political* commonality—as opposed to, say, cultural, moral, or linguistic commonality. For some who take this approach, political commonality is necessary by definition: a community is a collective of persons who by virtue of forming a political unit have a common good or a common interest, or share a set of institutions or laws. For others, political commonality is a functional necessity: without it, there is nothing to hold the diverse members of the community together as a unit. Moreover, as a practical matter, some see agreement on the basic rules governing the community and conflict resolution as necessary. Finally, for some, political commonality is a matter of democratic legitimacy: all citizens must be able, at least hypothetically, to agree on fundamentals or procedures for decision making in order for the government to have the legitimate authority to rule. Civic thinkers understand democracy's need for commonality as a strictly political one; where we are not primarily citizens, it is not important for us to have things in common. As such, this strategy allows a great deal of room for the flourishing of diversity and difference outside of those institutions and activities that have to do with democratic politics, such as in religion, home life, and the workplace.

Where theorists who adopt the first two strategies are concerned with determining what kind of commonality we should share, theorists who adopt the third approach—the *perspectival strategy*—are more concerned with redescribing how we experience sharing what we share. They delimit commonality not by minimizing it or confining it to the political sphere but by showing that what we actually can share is much less than theorists often suppose. Each person, according to this view, has a unique, particular perspective that may be shaped by her membership in particular social groups. That every individual has a different perspective might seem to imply that we can have nothing in common with one another. However, the very use of the metaphor of perspective suggests that perspectivists do not reject commonality altogether: the common thing is that which is "seen" from the multiplicity of different perspectives. People, then, are individually distinct, but the things that they perceive from their different standpoints are common. The implication of this view is that in order to share something, we must not only have it in common but also be able to understand that our different perspectives are actually perspectives on that same thing. Accommodating diversity on this model requires acknowledging and attending to how multiple people may see the same thing differently.

Each of these three strategies enables theorists to accommodate difference in some way without having to let go of commonality. This enables them to criticize certain claims to commonality—those that are too maximal, or that extend beyond the political sphere, or that ignore differences of perspective. Yet it also enables them to hold on to the assumption that democracy requires commonality by modifying it rather than challenging—let alone unseating—it. It is as if democratic theorists, like Taylor, were compelled to hold on to some kind of commonality, and so had to fill the void left by their own critiques.

THREE DEMOCRATIC REQUIREMENTS

I find it curious that many political theorists take such pains to make commonality compatible with accommodating diversity in democracy. After all, they have access to a long history of political and philosophical arguments against a variety of sources of commonality. They could call the whole enterprise into question. Why instead do theorists by and large persist in thinking that a diverse democracy still requires commonality? As I suggested in the opening of this chapter, my answer is that they are captivated by a particular way of seeing democracy: they assume that democracy requires some kind of commonality. As a consequence, theorists stubbornly try to hold on to some form of commonality despite their critiques: they are motivated by the fear that, if we did not have anything in common, democracy would fail.[34]

But why might theorists think that democracy would fail in the absence of commonality? I claim this is because they take commonality to be essential to meeting three democratic requirements: the requirements that the people in a democracy share identity, affect, and agency. We have already seen this in Taylor's case: he declares that some kind of commonality is indispensable because the people in a democracy need to have a "common understanding of what it is to be a member of this society" (identity), and they need "to be able to trust one another and have a sense of commitment to one another" (affect), so that they can "form a unit of collective decision" (agency). I develop an account of how theorists take commonality to be related to meeting these three requirements in chapters 3, 4, and 5, but let me begin to sketch its outlines here.

Democracy, in its most basic definition, is the rule of the demos, or the people. Yet every demos is composed of a multiplicity of individuals. The first requirement of democracy is to constitute from this multiplicity a cohesive group. This is the requirement for a *collective identity* that unites disparate persons into a people that can be the subject of its own self-government. In addition, this identity distinguishes members of the people from others, who have no claim to rule. In more modern conceptions of democracy, collective identity justifies the boundaries of democratic sovereignty: we should rule ourselves, and not be ruled, because we constitute a distinct community. It is important to establish the identity of the demos because this determines who rules what community.

Moreover, in order to rule together, the individuals who make up the demos must actually want to share rule with one another. They need to be willing to give up complete sovereignty over their own affairs and to let their fellow citizens have some say. In order to rule together, then, citizens must be able to trust one another. Additionally, they need to care enough about the community to participate in the activities of self-government and to make personal sacrifices for the group. Democracy's second requirement is thus for some kind of *horizontal affect*, a bond between the individuals who make up the demos that sustains their commitment to sharing in rule with one another.

Finally, for the people to govern itself, the many individuals that make it up, each with their own individual wills, must be able together to constitute a single, *collective agency*. Sharing in self-government with others means that individuals will not always get the outcomes that they want. And yet, in order for democracy to function, citizens must be able to accept the decisions of the collective as their own. That is, they must be able to see themselves as a part of a larger agency: the people. That agency must be able to rule cohesively, even when the persons who make it up do not agree on a single course of action. Democracy therefore needs to create from a disparate collection of individuals a clear, coherent agency.

Commonality functions in democratic theory as a way to address these three requirements.[35] If "we, the people" are not just an arbitrary set of individuals but a group of individuals with something in common, then we have a way of responding to each of these problems. Who is the people? The people is the collection of individuals who share this x in common. The shared thing clarifies the boundaries between those who belong to the community and those who do not. Why should we trust one another enough to make decisions together? Our trust arises from knowing that we have something in common; we can assume that we share an interest in preserving the community defined by that commonality. How do we come to accept collective decisions we disagree with as legitimate? The commonality we share with our fellow citizens is the basis for imagining ourselves as together forming a collective agency, even with strangers. We can understand decisions we disagree with as "our" decisions insofar as they are decisions made by this imagined agency. Having something in common, it seems, is what produces and secures democratic identity, affect, and agency.

Difference, then, can be expected to challenge our ability to meet these requirements: if the others with whom I share in democracy do not seem to value what I value, do not act or look the way that I do, or do not share in the same institutions and rights as me, then it will be that much harder for us to identify with one another, to trust each other with collective decision making, and to act as one. It is no surprise that—faced with the challenges of demographic shifts and political movements demanding change—theorists would find themselves repeatedly returning to the seeming security of commonality as they wrestle with how to accommodate difference. How could we have democracy if we had nothing in common? The thought is perhaps too terrifying to bear. (Hurry! declare that we have something in common again!)

Yet in order for commonality to secure shared identity, affective bonds, and collective agency for democracy, a number of corollary assumptions about how commonality works in politics and psychology must be true. That is, the belief that democracy requires commonality is held in place by a series of related beliefs about the world. First is the belief that collective identity is a product of commonality. A group of individuals can constitute a collectivity only when its members have something in common with one another. If the individuals do not share anything in common, the group will lack cohesion and definition. Commonality is what marks off one collectivity from another, what distinguishes "us" from those who are not us.

The second corollary belief is that affective bonds are a product of commonality. That is, the assumption that commonality can generate horizontal bonds between citizens in a democracy is based in an assumption about human psychology: that people care more or feel sympathy for those who share something in common with them, and correspondingly they care less or feel antipathy for those who do not. If a collection of individuals does not have anything in common, then they will not feel attachment to one another. Yet even if they are strangers to one another, if they have something in common, then the belief is that this commonality can generate an affective bond between them.

The final corollary assumption is that collective agency is a product of commonality. That is, a group of individuals can act together as a singular agent only when they have something in common. Without commonality of interest or intention, the individuals' actions would be at cross-purposes to one another, and so they could not be properly understood to constitute a collective agency with a coherent will. Multiple persons can only become a plural agent, a "we," when they share the same agenda. In democratic theory, this is often characterized in terms of having a common good, a common interest, or a public thing.

The view that democracy requires sharing something in common persists in democratic theory despite the many criticisms of commonality because it is held in place by these related assumptions about the causal relationship between commonality and shared identity, affect, and agency. These corollary assumptions are supported in turn by other beliefs about language, epistemology, and metaphysics, as I will show in chapter 2. In short, the belief that democracy requires commonality is just one piece of a larger worldview. It is difficult to alter our way of seeing democracy because so many other ideas and mental pictures would have to change as well. Yet this is precisely what I argue we need to do.

SEEING THE RABBIT

In this chapter, I have taken the first step toward shifting how we see democracy: raising the awareness that we have a particular way of seeing democracy. Theorists tend to view democracy in such a way that commonality comes to the forefront. Commonality defines democracy: its borders, its distinctive character, its reason for being. It produces the demos of democracy as a distinct political subject, capable of and willing to govern itself. It provides a stable framework within which democratic activity can take place. I will show over the course of the book that this is a contingent, rather than a necessary, way of seeing democracy. That is, we can see democracy differently than many of us do now.

In the following chapter, I will sketch out the basis for an alternative way of seeing democracy that I have only begun to hint at here: one in which activity comes to the foreground, while commonality recedes into the background. In this view, the causal logic of commonality is reversed: it is human activity that produces the framework in which commonalities appear to be meaningful, and not the other way around. Through their interactions with one another, people do the work to bring the demos into being, create affective ties with one another, and act together. To some readers this may seem like I am simply suggesting that we produce commonality, that commonality is a social construction rather than an objective fact. However, as I develop throughout the book, there is more to this alternative way of seeing democracy than that. If we are responsible for producing commonality, this is because as human beings we have the capacity to intersubjectively make sense of the world we share. Yet this is a capacity that we must presume *all* humans possess. We inhabit a world together with plural meaning-making subjects. And so, any attempt one of us makes to produce commonality is uncertain and unstable: it can be contested, misunderstood, or simply fail to reach those to whom it is addressed. From this view, therefore, it is the intersubjective activity of meaning-making in a world of other people who are themselves also engaged in meaning-making that is the basis for democracy, rather than the uncertain and unstable outcome of that activity.

This activity-oriented way of seeing democracy thus takes political freedom rather than commonality as its focal point. Political freedom is the freedom to engage in this ordinary capacity for meaning-making (or what Hannah Arendt calls world-building), the freedom to shape the world we share together with others. Democracy, on this view, is the activity of political freedom rather than a form of government or set of institutions. It arises whenever and wherever this freedom is exercised. Consequently, democracy is threatened when this ordinary capacity is occluded: when we accept the contours of our world as given, as natural, or as simply beyond our ability to affect. And so, the aim of democratic politics must be to open up our awareness of this capacity for freedom, to encourage its exercise by ourselves and others, and to proliferate competing claims about how we should make sense of the world we share.

I contend that this activity orientation to democracy is phenomenologically superior to the commonality orientation. That is, it offers a more compelling account of how we share identity, affect, and agency in practice. In the chapters that follow, I take Wittgenstein's advice and look and see what we do when we share.[36] It turns out that we ordinarily generate collective identity, affect, and agency without knowing in advance whether we have anything in common. Rather than being a pathological sign of the incoherence or instability of democracy, being suspended in uncertainty about whether and what we share with others is an ordinary feature of human existence. We act together without knowing whether or what we have in common. We act without knowing what the outcome will be, whether others will join with us in collective action, whether others will prove worthy of our trust. We act anyhow.

Further, I contend that this activity orientation to democracy is normatively preferable to the commonality orientation. The belief that democracy requires some kind of commonality comes out in theory and practice in antidemocratic ways. First, it directs our attention as theorists and actors to trying to locate what we share, a project that accords a privileged position to academics and other elites who are taken to be in the best position to observe and identify commonalities. Furthermore, by insisting that we must have something in common, this orientation pathologizes uncertainty and disagreement, viewing these as threats to democracy. And so, rather than opening up greater spaces for difference, this approach to conceptualizing democracy has the opposite effect: it cannot tolerate forms of diversity and disagreement that defy commonality. Difference can only be tolerated insofar as it is compatible with our having something in common. Finally, this view of democracy as arising from commonality conceals and thereby inhibits political freedom: our ordinary human capacity to shape the world in which we live.

By contrast, the activity orientation that I advocate in this book is radically democratic. It locates the capacity for producing commonality in all of us rather than just among elites. A freedom-centered democracy is therefore a nonhierarchical one in which the power to shape the world is dispersed and shared intersubjectively. Moreover, on this view, disagreement about what and whether we share in common, far from being a problem, is simply the expected expression of living in a world together with other meaning-making subjects. That is, this view embraces the qualities of plurality and nonsovereignty that characterize the human experience: we share in the ability to shape the world with others who see matters differently. Thus, this way of seeing democracy opens us up more fully to difference: to appreciating and accepting a plurality of perspectives, and to living within the tension of disagreement. Finally, rather than occluding freedom, this vision of democracy cultivates and aims to proliferate its expression among us all.

My aim in this book is to shift our way of seeing democracy so that we take political freedom rather than commonality as our focal point. This is to move from thinking of democracy as a form of government to thinking of democracy as an ordinary activity available to us all acting within, without, and against formal institutions. The cost of adopting a commonality orientation is that we occlude this everyday capacity that humans possess to shape the world they inhabit together. That is, a focus on commonality obscures our democratic capacity to share in governing ourselves. Yet, just as when we see the rabbit in the duck-rabbit image, it may still be possible for us to switch back to seeing the duck, I do not expect that simply showing you a freedom-centered way of seeing democracy will forever displace commonality. The appeal of the commonality orientation is very strong, as I will show in the following chapters by engaging with thinkers who themselves begin to articulate an activity-oriented account of democracy but nonetheless slide back into a concern with what we have in common: Danielle Allen, Robert Putnam, and Charles Taylor, as well as numerous feminist theorists. We may never be able to fully rid ourselves of our tendency to think in terms of commonality. What I aim for, then, is to increase awareness that this is just a contingent way of seeing democracy, that it has significant democratic costs, and that we can see things otherwise. By the end of the book, I hope you have become more fluent in moving back and forth between the duck and the rabbit, commonality and activity. Even more, I hope to persuade you to try to hold political freedom in view when you think of democracy, despite the persistent allure of commonality.

CHAPTER 2

Sharing the World in Common with Others

A picture held us captive. And we could not get outside it, for it lay in our language and language seemed to repeat it to us inexorably.
—Ludwig Wittgenstein[1]

TWO PICTURES OF SHARING

Philosophers, according to Wittgenstein, are captivated by certain mental pictures: ways of "seeing" the world that direct them to puzzles and problems that would simply disappear, if only they were able to see things differently. When democratic theorists assert that we need to have something in common in order for democracy to work, they are captivated by such a mental picture and by the unnecessary problems it generates for their thinking.

As a case in point, let us consider the mental picture that captivates one particular theorist, Danielle Allen, as she responds to some very material pictures: the photographs taken on September 4, 1957, of Elizabeth Eckford, a fifteen-year-old black girl, as she attempted to integrate the all-white Little Rock Central High but found her way blocked by the bayonets of the Arkansas National Guard. Allen treats these photographs as objects common to all Americans: objects whose true meaning is fixed and independent of the people who view them. In doing so, she invokes an *objective picture of sharing*—the mental picture that I believe captivates us when we think that commonality is necessary to democracy.

Yet, without even noticing a shift in her thinking, Allen occasionally invokes a different mental picture: one in which meaning is not attached to objects but instead is shared intersubjectively—that is, it is manifested in social interactions. In this view, humans create and contest the meaning of the photographs, whether directly by offering interpretations of them or indirectly by altering their patterns of behavior in response. Moreover, people can exercise this capacity to make and communicate meaning with one another without being focused on the same photograph—indeed, without being focused on any common object. At moments, Allen's account of the Eckford photos offers us a tantalizing glimpse of this different mental picture, one in which we share by interacting with others in ways that create and contest meaning: an *intersubjective picture of sharing*.

Although Allen urges her readers to see the photos as shared intersubjectively, she is unable to keep that mental picture in view herself. Instead, like the person looking at the duck-rabbit who catches a glimpse of the rabbit but cannot hold it in her mind long enough to displace the image of the duck, Allen quickly lapses back into an objective picture of sharing. Her struggle suggests that it may be extremely difficult for us to free ourselves from our captivity to this objective mental picture. Yet even so, her effort inspires my attempt, later in this chapter, to trace out an alternative.

First, a bit of background about the photographs.[2] Eckford was one of ten black students selected by the Little Rock school board in 1957 to enroll in the previously all-white Central High.[3] This was the first stage of the Little Rock School District's plan to integrate its schools in compliance with the US Supreme Court's unanimous decision, in *Brown v. Board of Education* three years earlier, that segregated schools were unconstitutional. Arkansas governor Orval Faubus, however, saw a political opportunity in taking a stand against racial integration. Ostensibly to protect white and black students alike from the threat of racial violence, he called in the National Guard on Labor Day, declaring ominously on television that "'blood will run in the streets' if Negro pupils should attempt to enter Central High School."[4] The next day, the school was surrounded by 250 rifle-bearing troops and a menacing mob of at least several hundred white civilians, all intent on maintaining segregation.

The black students sat out the first official day of school while the district superintendent tried to find a way to guarantee their safety. He advised the students' parents to send their children to school the next day unaccompanied, arguing that it would be "easier to protect the children if the adults aren't there."[5] But Daisy Bates, the president of the Arkansas NAACP, asked a group of white and black ministers to go with them, out of concern that the students would be vulnerable if they faced the mob alone. She alerted the parents about this new plan by phone, thus missing the Eckfords, who did not have one. Bates intended to go to Elizabeth's house early the next morning to let her know when and where to meet up with the ministers, but she forgot.

So Elizabeth followed the original plan: she went to school by herself. She walked up to an entrance that was some distance from where the mob had gathered, but her way was blocked by members of the National Guard. In the meantime, the mob had caught sight of her trying to get into the school and surrounded her as she walked away. People in the crowd shouted racist epithets, and some called for lynching her on the spot. She sat down at a bus stop, where she was joined first by a Jewish *New York Times* reporter, who put his arm around her, and then by other sympathetic adults, who kept the mob at bay until she was safely aboard a bus. Elizabeth's confrontation with the National Guard, her walk surrounded by the mob, and her wait at the bus stop were all captured in a series of photographs taken by Will Counts, a local, white photojournalist. These pictures, as well as others taken by Counts throughout the school year, were circulated widely by the Associated Press in newspapers across the United States and around the world.

Allen, in her book *Talking to Strangers*, designates one of these photographs of Elizabeth as "a national icon of our interracial distrust" and "an icon too of the basic problems involved in democratic citizenship generally."[6] This is the picture of Elizabeth walking away from the school, her head slightly bowed, calmly moving forward as she is surrounded by the white mob. One person in the crowd—another student from Central High, a white girl named Hazel Bryan—is shouting at Elizabeth with a look of anger and disgust on her face, brandishing a rolled-up newspaper gripped tightly in her right hand.[7] In Allen's reading, this photo possesses a remarkable truth-telling agency: it "rendered visible democracy's 'public sphere,' as it existed in 1957," "stripped away idealized conceptions of democratic life," and "dr[e]w back the veils that had previously hidden the inner workings of this country's public sphere."[8] It did this by simply recording what happened in Little Rock.[9] According to Allen, those who look at the picture have immediate access to its truth: "In one quick instant, looking at photos of Elizabeth and Hazel, viewers saw, as we still do too, the skeletal structure of the public sphere, and also its disintegration."[10] By revealing the racialized nature of citizenship, the photo "elicited" and "provoked" an "epiphanic awareness" in its viewers, thereby turning "the inner workings of public life" into "the highly scrutinized subject of the public sphere."[11]

This photo exposed, according to Allen, a social structure common to all American citizens: one characterized by racial inequality and the corresponding habits of white domination and black submission.[12] This common social structure existed prior to that day in September when Elizabeth tried to attend Central High. Yet for most Americans, it was not the conscious object of public scrutiny. It simply lay in the background, shaping the "deep rules" governing how citizens interacted with one another.[13] For Allen, phenomena like racial hierarchy make up the "shared life" of citizens, whether we are conscious of them or not. The "shared elements" of our lives include "events, climates, environments, imaginative fixations, economic conditions, and social structures,"[14] which Allen treats as *objective commonalities*. That is, Allen takes it to be an objective fact about American citizens that they have these things in common. For her, Americans in 1957 shared a racialized social structure, whether or not they were aware of sharing any such thing.

However, Allen is not a naive objectivist, believing that people have unmediated access to the truth that inheres in these common objects. She is a perspectivist: she believes that our access to the objective truth is filtered through our different subjective perspectives on our shared world. The life we share in democracy, she writes, is one "in which each citizen and noncitizen has an individual perspective on a set of phenomena relevant to all."[15] This explains, for example, why racial hierarchy might have one set of meanings for whites and another for blacks. Or how some of us could immediately come to see the truth of inequality, while others might take longer to become conscious of it.[16] Yet no matter how diverse our perspectives may be, the object that each of us perceives remains identical for Allen. She explains, "Some live behind one veil, and others behind another, but the air that we all breathe carries the same gases and pollens through those veils."[17] In other words, what we share in common—even though we may perceive it differently—is, like the air we breathe, objectively the same for us all. It exists independently of whether we perceive it, and remains unchanged by how we perceive it. What is "unveiled" by the photos, then, is the objective truth of what Americans share, despite their different subjective positions: namely, a racialized social structure that governs citizenship and relations among citizens.

Allen's commitment to an objective reality underlying our different perspectives emerges again in her evaluation of Hannah Arendt and Ralph Ellison's disagreement over school desegregation. Arendt controversially argued in her essay "Reflections on Little Rock" (1959) that the US government was wrong to pursue racial integration first and foremost through the forced desegregation of public schools.[18] The civil rights movement, she contends, should have prioritized securing more fundamental liberties, such as voting rights and the "right to marry whoever one wishes."[19] For Arendt, school desegregation not only was less important than other issues, it also placed the burden of fighting for racial progress onto children. Arendt believed this displacement entailed irresponsible cowardice on the part of the black students' parents and the NAACP.[20] Ellison countered that Arendt misunderstood the black experience. In his view, black parents were not shifting any uniquely adult burden onto their sons and daughters. Instead, they were exhibiting their understanding that their children, by confronting the white mob, would experience a necessary "rite of initiation" into the terror of racial inequality, an experience they had to master in order to survive in racist America.[21]

Allen presents these two perspectives, then poses the question, "Which account of democracy or citizenship, Arendt's or Ellison's, is the more accurate analysis of the events at Central High and their political significance?"[22] In framing the question as one of accuracy, Allen implicitly argues that the validity of these different perspectives depends upon their correspondence to objective reality. According to Allen, "[Arendt] and Ellison surely were focused on the same object but from different perspectives."[23] Yet Arendt could not make out what Ellison could see clearly: that black parents were willing to sacrifice their children as a courageous political act for the sake of future progress. Thus, for Allen, Ellison prevails because of his "accuracy in analyzing the events in Little Rock."[24]

But were Arendt and Ellison actually focused on the same object, as Allen presumes? It is unlikely. Despite the title of her essay, Arendt's reflections on desegregation are general in character: she makes little reference to "the events in Little Rock" at all.[25] Her comments, though *occasioned* by the events in Little Rock, do not *focus* on them. As Arendt notes in her "Reply to Critics," a photograph served merely as "the point of departure of [her] reflections."[26] This is "the photograph reproduced in newspapers and magazines throughout the country, showing a Negro girl, accompanied by a white friend of her father, walking away from school, persecuted and followed into bodily proximity by a jeering and grimacing mob of youngsters."[27] Arendt's readers often take this description to refer to the classic photo of Elizabeth being harassed by Hazel, which, if true, could suggest that she was indeed focused on the events at Little Rock.[28] However, the photo that Arendt describes, as Allen perceptively notes, does not correspond to any of the photos Counts took of Eckford, who had gone to school alone. Instead, it is likely another photo published on the front page of the *New York Times* on the same day as a photo of Elizabeth, this one a picture of Dorothy Counts (no relation to Will Counts) walking to school in Charlotte, North Carolina. Allen's discovery about the photograph strongly suggests that Little Rock was not the specific object of Arendt's focus. And yet Allen interprets the evidence to mean that Arendt mistakenly "thought she was writing about the photo of Elizabeth Eckford."[29] Arendt, on this reading, had the same object in mind as Ellison, only she confused the photograph of one black girl with another—a confusion that epitomizes her inaccurate view of race in America.

Oddly enough, there is no textual evidence to support Allen's reading, since Arendt never claimed that the photograph depicts events *in Little Rock*. Rather, Allen projects onto the text her belief that Arendt must mean to describe a picture of Elizabeth. But why would she need Arendt to intend to focus on the same events as Ellison? I suspect that Allen is motivated by a desire to insulate her perspectivism against the charge of subjectivism. Perspectivism, after all, can slide into pure subjectivism easily. If each of us sees the world from our own, unique perspective, then our viewpoints are incommensurable: we have no way of knowing whether we share the same world, because all we can know is our first-person experience. For the charge of subjectivism to be neutralized, our different perspectives must be perspectives on the same, objective world. The objective existence of the world guarantees that our perspectives are not merely subjective, that when we communicate we are talking about a common world, and that we can make judgments about the relative accuracy of different perspectives. Under the circumstances, it seems likely that the fear of subjectivism holds Allen captive to the objectivist mental picture: Arendt and Ellison *must* have something in common, or we could not judge between them.

For my part, I see this fear as misplaced. In particular, unlike Allen, I see the exchange between Arendt and Ellison as evidence that:

• We are able to communicate meaningfully with one another without having a common object.
• We are able to communicate meaningfully with one another without *knowing* whether we have a common object (and, if so, what it is).
• We are able to communicate meaningfully with one another even when we openly disagree about whether there is a common object.

It is factually the case that Arendt and Ellison are not focused on a common object (the events in Little Rock), yet this difference in focus does not mean that they cannot communicate. Similarly, Arendt's readers are likely focused on a different object (a photo of Elizabeth) than she was (a photo of Dorothy), yet this disconnect does not render their interpretations of her work meaningless.

Interestingly, there are moments when Allen, too, admits that communicability and meaning may not depend on objective commonality. Elsewhere in *Talking to Strangers*, for example, she notes that facts are uncertain, that we can reasonably disagree about the meaning of what facts we can be certain of, that facts alone cannot determine what course of action we should take, and that a speaker's factual accuracy is just one criterion among many that we should use to assess his trustworthiness, and therefore to evaluate what he has to say.[30] What is more, in a separate and longer comparison of Arendt and Ellison published a few years earlier, Allen acknowledges that the difference between the two was not a simple matter of how they perceived the facts. Allen claims that their disagreement was instead a matter of "a deep theoretical dispute about how to conceptualize disagreement, law, and political action."[31] In comparing their arguments, she asks: What does each thinker help us to see? How do they help us to think? What do their ideas occlude, and what do they make visible?—questions that cannot be decided solely or primarily in terms of accuracy because they are questions of interpretation.[32] In this essay, Allen seems to understand Arendt's and Ellison's different perspectives as competing claims about how to make sense of the world, rather than truth claims about what simply is. Our perspectives, she implies, are not positions from which we innocently observe an objective world; they are positions from which we make sense of and imagine the world. We are not passive observers of reality; we are active participants in creating meaning out of what we observe.

Consider that when the pictures of Elizabeth circulated throughout the United States, what changed were not the objective facts of racial inequality but rather how these facts were perceived by Americans, now that they could be perceived. What changed in 1957, Allen claims, was "how citizens of the United States imagine[d] their political world."[33] The alteration, in other words, was hermeneutic, not factual. Allen refers to the role humans play in making sense of their shared world as a "communicative power to establish reality." She observes that our choices to adopt certain perspectives, our "collective decisions, including laws, *produce* our realities, our shared world."[34] Even while declaring that we all breathe the same air through our different veils, she offers in the very next sentence the provocative thought that "our shared elements . . . are made out of the combination of all our interactions with each other. We are all always awash in each other's lives."[35] Thus, the commonness of our world, far from being an objective characteristic of it, is a first-person experience produced through interactions between people, through the exchange of perspectives, and through the prominence or even hegemony of certain perspectives over others. Sharing a life together is an active practice of laying claim to how we should make sense of our common reality, of rendering some things visible and others invisible, of imagining and reimagining our shared world.

I propose that we understand Allen to be vacillating between two different mental pictures of sharing: one objective, the other intersubjective. This vacillation can account for some of the apparent contradictions in Allen's claims about the Eckford photos: on the one hand, that they unveil an already existing reality, which we can perceive more or less accurately; and on the other hand, that disagreements about the import of these photos can be deep, theoretical, and reasonable. She is at once committed to the idea that we share an objective world, which we perceive from different perspectives, and to the idea that our different perspectives, when shared with others, may help bring into being a common world that is "made out of the combination of all our interactions with each other." She describes our varied perspectives as veils that simply filter what each of us does and does not see; and she describes our varied perspectives as ways of imagining that shape, create, and produce what we perceive.

The first mental picture to which Allen subscribes is an *objective picture of sharing*. According to this picture, we share in common only when something is objectively common to us. This shared thing is independent of the people who share in it; in fact, we may not even know that we share it. Even so, we must actually have something in common in order to share. In this view, without an objective world in common, it would be incoherent to say that we share a world. Therefore, claims about what we share are descriptive, truth claims: they are claims about facts. Either we do share this thing in common, or we do not; there is no room for disagreement or interpretation. Finally, when we share something in common, we do not have to do anything in order to share. Sharing, in other words, is passive.

This objective picture of sharing is perhaps most apparent in the writings of perspectivists like Allen, whose choice of words evokes the image of a group of viewers oriented toward a shared focal point. Yet I believe this mental picture captivates more than just those who adopt a perspectivist approach. The picture holds many, perhaps most, democratic theorists captive, making us think that we *must* have something in common, or else we will slip into the abyss of subjectivism. In the following section, I offer an outline of this objectivist picture and show how it manifests itself in the way some prominent theorists conceptualize and describe democracy. In addition, I examine the political stakes of our continued commitment to this mental picture and find that it has deeply antidemocratic effects on our thinking. The objective picture of sharing encourages a preoccupation with what citizens passively share in common rather than with what they actively do. It paints a flattering self-portrait of the theorist as a neutral producer of knowledge that justifies an elitist (as opposed to a bottom-up) approach to addressing political problems. And it discourages theorists' curiosity about and openness to disagreement, conflict, and discord, as these can challenge the validity of claims about what the people share in common. My wager is that, if we can dislodge the mental picture that often underlies our thinking about democracy, then we will be less likely to fall into these antidemocratic patterns. But even if, like Allen, we can never fully let go of this objective mental picture, my hope is that by becoming aware of the costs to democracy of the objective way of seeing, we can mitigate some of these negative effects.

I believe that we can see democracy differently with the aid of the second mental picture, invoked yet unexplored by Allen: the *intersubjective picture of sharing*. In this mental picture, sharing is a quality of our first-person experience rather than an objective characteristic of the world. Yet to say that sharing is a matter of first-person experience is not to say that it is purely subjective, valid only for the individual. On the contrary, sharing is a first-person experience of relating to others: I experience that I inhabit the world together with other persons who are themselves subjects. Therefore, I am not isolated in my subjective experience; I live instead in the company of others, each of whom experiences matters from her own perspective. In this view, without my awareness of the existence of other subjects, it would be meaningless to say that I share: With whom could I share, if there were no others? Sharing requires plural subjects rather than singular objects.

With this picture in mind, we can read the iconic photo of Elizabeth differently. Rather than revealing a social structure common to all Americans in 1957, I suggest that we take the photo as a depiction of plural subjects inhabiting public space together. Elizabeth's presence among the mob is a dramatic enactment of the reality that the white people who surrounded her lived in the company of black people, despite practices of segregation. Her figure demands an acknowledgment that we share this existence with other people who are themselves subjects. It is as if the photo were saying to us: we already do share the world together—but is this really *how* we want to share it with one another?

Later in this chapter, I develop this account of an intersubjective picture of sharing by working critically through Arendt's work. Here, I turn not to her essay on Little Rock but to her many reflections on "sharing-the-world-with-others."[36] In order to share the world together, she believes that we need to accept and cultivate the human condition of *plurality*—the idea that each human is unique. Furthermore, since humans are plural, sharing the world with others entails accepting our *nonsovereignty* as well: if each of us sees things from a unique vantage point, then no single perspective can be sovereign. Our perspectives are partial in the dual sense that they are nonobjective and incomplete. To accept human plurality, then, is to accept that we will disagree, miscommunicate, and conflict with one another, and further, to accept that this is an expected part of sharing the world with others. Having something objectively in common turns out to be neither necessary nor sufficient for sharing because sharing is instead a matter of how we experience ourselves in relation to other subjects. This intersubjective picture underlies the alternative account of democracy that I develop in the chapters to come.

THE OBJECTIVE PICTURE OF SHARING

When theorists claim that commonality is necessary to democracy, I believe they are captivated by the objective mental picture of sharing: the picture that insists that when we share, we must share some *thing* in common. Such theorists may disagree about what people must share in common: it might be an environment, a culture, a social structure, a set of values, a common good, or a historical reference point. They may believe that these commonalities are a prerequisite for building democracy, or they may believe that these commonalities only come into being as the product of democratic politics. They may believe that citizens must share an understanding of what they share, or they may believe, like Allen, that each of us views the thing we share from a unique perspective. However different the specifics of their theories, they agree that the people in a democracy must share some same thing. Now we could take this widespread agreement as an indication that democracy truly does require commonality to function: so many smart people would not agree on such a fundamental point if there were not some truth to it. But I want you to entertain the possibility that democratic theorists converge on commonality not because democracy actually requires it but because they are caught in the logic of a particular picture of sharing. This is the picture of sharing articulated by Wittgenstein's stubborn interlocutor, who insists about "board-games, card-games, ball-games, Olympic games, and so on" that "there *must* be something common, or they would not be called 'games.'"[37] In this view, sharing—in this case, sharing a name—is only coherent if there is something in common. Let me sketch out some of the assumptions implicit in this mental picture before turning to reflect on its implications for democratic theory.

According to this picture, when we share, we share some *thing* in common. In order to be common, the shared thing must have an objective existence, independent of the people who share it. Indeed, those who share do not even need to be aware that they have anything in common. The commonality of the shared thing—the quality of its being common to us—is independent of how and whether it is perceived by the persons said to share it. It is objectively real.

Consequently, in this picture claims about what we share operate simultaneously on an ontological and an epistemological level. They are first of all claims about what is, about a state of affairs: it is the case that there is an x such that it is shared by us. Accordingly, they are *truth claims* whose validity derives from their correspondence to the world. It either is or is not the case that we share x. We can test claims about what we share by looking to see whether we do, in fact, share x in common; we can disprove claims about what we share by providing evidence to the contrary. While theorists may disagree about whether and what we can know about the things we share, the claims generated by this mental picture are epistemological claims to knowledge of an objective world.

Sharing commonality, then, is passive in this mental picture: we can share something in common with one another without doing anything. In fact, the people who share a common thing need not even know that they have it in common in order to share it. In other words, sharing does not require a first-person experience of sharing; indeed, an independent observer may have better knowledge about what a collection of people shares in common than they have about themselves. What is shared stands apart from human activity and subjective experience. Some of the things we share may themselves be the product of human activity, of course: for example, we might share institutions, a collective will, or ideas. Yet these socially produced things can have the quality of being shared by us without our having to do anything special to share in them.

The English language reflects this objective picture of sharing, reinforcing its hold over our thinking.[38] Our ordinary usage of the verb "to share" refers to a thing that is shared, whether explicitly or implicitly, and so repeats to us the idea that sharing entails sharing some *thing*. Consider this definition of sharing in the *Oxford English Dictionary*: "To divide (what one has or receives) into portions, and give shares to others as well as one's self."[39] And another: "To participate in (an action, activity, opinion, feeling, or condition); to perform, enjoy, or suffer in common with others; to possess (a quality) which other persons or things also have."[40] We never share as such; to say that we share is always to imply that we share some thing, even if the object is not expressed along with the verb. We share possessions, actions, feelings, performances, experiences, and qualities. And as these two definitions suggest, the common things we share are of two kinds: things each one of us shares in individually, and things we share in collectively.[41]

The first kind of commonality I will indicate throughout the book as *sameness*. In this kind of sharing, we have something in common with one another when we are alike in some way: each individual who shares does so in the same way.[42] For example, we might share a cake: the cake is sliced into portions that may vary in size, but each of us has a piece of the same thing.[43] Or each of us may have a particular characteristic that the others also have—blue eyes, dark skin, a zip code, a Buddhist practice, a Volkswagen Jetta. In such instances, nothing has been partitioned among us, yet each of us has the same thing. We share not by being entirely the same but by being individually the same in some respect.

I call the second kind of commonality *commons*.[44] We have something in common when we share a thing that cannot be individually possessed. Commons, historically speaking, were plots of land that belonged to the community as a whole. Similarly, with this kind of sharing, what is shared is collective and indivisible. We share not by dividing the commons into smaller, individually owned plots of land but by caring for it and using it together. Some examples of this kind of commonality are public things that belong to a collectivity and could not belong to any single individual: territories, institutions, cultures, histories, or common interests, wills, and goods.[45] Other indivisible commonalities are shared experiences that are, to borrow Charles Taylor's language, "irreducibly social." These are experiences that we could not have singly or alone, such as laughing about a joke together, having a conversation, or listening to a symphony in the company of a large audience.[46]

I stress that the things we share can be individually *or* collectively shared because this is a detail that democratic theorists tend to overlook when they offer critiques of commonality. Many theorists reject commonality as sameness, while leaving commonality as commons untouched. For example, some argue that an emphasis on homogeneity is at odds with diversity, and instead advocate that we should share in irreducibly collective things, which do not demand that we be the same. Because these theorists see homogeneity as the problem, rather than commonality as such, they do not interrogate their own investment in an objective picture of sharing. Yet this interrogation is precisely what we require.

OBJECTIVE DEMOCRACY

How does this objective picture of sharing affect how we theorize democracy? Most immediately, it shapes the kind of sharing that theorists believe is necessary to democracy. Theorists captivated by this mental picture will tend to focus on the objective things that the people have in common, at the expense of examining the first-person experience of sharing a world with others. Moreover, such theorists will believe that people *must* have something in common in order to constitute a demos, and correspondingly they will be concerned when it appears that citizens lack commonality altogether.

Consequently, this mental picture motivates theorists to try to locate what the people have (or at least should have) in common in a democracy. We can see how this comes out in practice in a variety of ways. For some theorists, the objective picture manifests itself in the empirical verification of claims to commonality. Acting like demographers, theorists observe populations to determine what people do or do not share. They then use this empirical data to support or reject the truth of claims to commonality. For example, Will Kymlicka appeals to survey data to support his contention that the commonality uniting Puerto Ricans with Americans is a sense of belonging to the United States, even though the data suggest that only "91 per cent of the residents of Puerto Rico think of themselves as Puerto Ricans first, and Americans second."[47] Kymlicka's use of these data implies that the greater the portion of the population that demonstrably shares in a commonality, the stronger the validity of the claim.[48] The 9 percent of Puerto Ricans who do not identify as Americans do not pose a problem for Kymlicka, since his aim is to show that the commonality is shared by *most*.[49] This example illustrates how, from the perspective of the theorist-as-demographer, political theorists treat claims about commonality as if they were truth claims that could be empirically verified or disproved by their degree of correspondence with objective reality.

Another way that the objective picture manifests itself is in the guise of a Rousseauian legislator, who observes what potential sources of commonality are latent in a given community and then seeks to cultivate these. In some communities—especially those marked by histories of conquest or immigration—it is impossible to locate any single commonality that is already shared by the population. In such a case, the theorist-as-legislator looks to the objective world for evidence of qualities that could be nurtured and developed among the people, so as to make them into commonalities. For example, Jürgen Habermas's proposed constitutional patriotism for Germany is not so much an already observable commonality shared by Germans as it is a potentially shareable form of attachment that as yet is only manifest among subgroups. His hope is that this form of attachment could be cultivated in the present so that it could become common to all Germans in the future.[50] As for the demographer, for the theorist styled as a kind of Rousseauian legislator the presumption is that these claims to even only potential commonality have the status of verifiable epistemological claims: we can observe now that this commonality is latent and has the potential to be shared, and we can track over time the extent to which with the proper nurturing it becomes widely shared.

The objective picture of sharing orients democratic theorists not only to discovering what the people *do* or *could* share in common but also—and more significantly—to what the people *should* share. Contemporary democratic theorists are concerned to locate sources of commonality that are ethically more palatable than those that were invoked in the past. It is not sufficient for a commonality to be widely shared in a population: it also needs to be the *right* kind of commonality, one that is normatively acceptable. For example, it may be empirically true for a particular democracy that 93 percent of its population shares a common ethnic identity. Yet ethnic identity is widely rejected as a basis for commonality for ethical reasons, and so theorists would likely refuse it as a source of commonality despite its empirical reach. Habermas, for one, offers constitutional patriotism as an alternative to blood belonging for Germans, despite the fact that a significant majority of citizens are ethnically German. The role of the democratic theorist that follows from the objective mental picture is thus twofold: first, to locate commonalities that are empirically shared or at least realistically shareable within a given population, and second, to locate among those available options the ethically preferable commonality that could come to or already does unite a democratic people. We might think of these as concerns with identifying the "right" and the "best" commonality that does or could unite a people.

Whether she is concerned with empirical or normative questions of commonality, the objective picture of sharing positions the theorist as a kind of expert, a neutral producer of knowledge.[51] Theorists present the question of what a people does or should have in common as a matter that could be resolved through philosophical reflection and argument, perhaps occasionally supplemented by empirical data. In this way, the objective picture of sharing generates a powerfully self-validating narrative for the political theorist. The theorist has a special role to play in making democracy work: we need him to identify what we share, which we need to know in order to produce collective identity, affect, and agency—especially under contemporary conditions of increasingly complex diversity. This account of the importance of political theory is perhaps even more compelling to us today, with the humanities under attack within the university, and the subfield of political theory under pressure within the discipline of political science to demonstrate its usefulness.[52] How reassuring to discover that political theory turns out to be necessary to democracy itself!

Furthermore, this self-presentation of the theorist as a much-needed, neutral knowledge producer serves to disavow any political responsibility theorists themselves might have for the claims they make. Democratic theorists regularly present claims about what we do or should share in common as facts and truths, or as the outcome of rational, philosophical argument. In so doing, they disavow their own political agency; they obscure how these claims are partisan exercises of power. Consider again Kymlicka's claim that Puerto Ricans share in common with other US citizens a sense of belonging to America. What is he doing when he makes this claim? He appears to be presenting a neutral fact: the results of a recent poll. Yet he is not merely presenting the poll data; he is also interpreting it—and interpreting it to be consistent with the political position he advocates. The 91 percent of respondents who identify as Puerto Ricans first, and as Americans second, he reassures his readers, "do see themselves as Americans, but only because this does not require abandoning their prior identity as a distinct Spanish-speaking people with their own separate political community." Here, he is far removed from simply reporting poll data. He offers a narrative that explains the poll data in the way most sympathetic to his view that differentiated citizenship is compatible with a shared sense of solidarity: it is because they have their own separate political community that Puerto Ricans are able to feel solidarity with other US citizens. Then he concludes this paragraph by stating that "the United States, for [the 91 percent of Puerto Ricans], is a federation of peoples—English, Spanish, Indian—each with the right to govern themselves"—a peculiar inference to draw from a narrow piece of poll data. This way of glossing the poll sounds remarkably familiar: it echoes a narrative about Canadian belonging that Kymlicka references later on the same page. Canada, according to this way of thinking, is a federation of English, French, and aboriginal peoples, each deserving of their own, separate political or cultural institutions. On his reading of the poll, the Canadian model conveniently turns out to be the American model, too![53] Far from neutrally presenting factual knowledge, Kymlicka is framing and interpreting the poll data so as to support his advocacy of a particular political position.[54] Yet he presents his interpretation not as a contestable claim about what he thinks US citizens share in common, not as an argument about how he thinks US citizens should imagine themselves as a federation of peoples, but as if it were an innocent reflection of the truth clearly revealed by the poll.

In lieu of owning their own agency in identifying and selecting sources of commonality, theorists often project agency onto the common thing itself. Theorists frequently (and perhaps unintentionally) attribute to the common thing the capacity to unite, to give coherence, even to grant legitimacy to a political community. Habermas, for example, is concerned that "the binding force of the common political culture . . . remain strong enough to prevent the nation of citizens from falling apart."[55] A common political culture, he implies, can have force enough to bind together a nation of citizens. Similarly, Chantal Mouffe declares the paradox of democracy to be "how to envisage a form of commonality strong enough to institute a demos but nonetheless compatible with certain forms of pluralism."[56] Commonality, she suggests, could be strong enough not just to keep a nation together but to actually bring it into being. If pressed, both Habermas and Mouffe might find these locutions to be peculiar and at odds with many of their views. Maybe they would concede that it is imprecise to attribute to political culture or to commonality the capacity to bind and found community—surely they would acknowledge that the people themselves who found communities, and who produce and reproduce political culture, have at least some responsibility of their own for generating political unity.[57] Yet why is it so easy and familiar for otherwise careful theorists to make statements like this? Maybe these phrases do not ordinarily strike us as unusual because it is second nature for us to speak as if commonality does the work of founding and binding. That is, we are so captivated by an objective picture of sharing, so used to its focus on things and its corresponding occlusion of the experience of the people who share them, that we do not notice when we assign agency to commonality.

The attribution of tremendous agency to commonality has the effect of further depoliticizing the theorist's claims about what we do or should have in common. If it is commonality that does the work of founding or binding—and its absence that correspondingly makes communities fall apart—then the theorist himself is innocent in the matter. His claims about what we do or should have in common are in themselves ineffectual: claims about commonality are not responsible for holding communities together, nor for tearing them apart; only the presence or the absence of *actual* commonality can do that. The relationship between commonality and political unity is therefore presented in these moments as natural, causal, and inevitable: if we have something in common, then these things will follow; if we do not have anything in common, then these things will not follow. Since the theorist does not cause us to have or to not have commonality, his actions can be seen as separate from and independent of this process.

If we take these statements about the agency of the common to their logical conclusion, moreover, it is not just theorists whose actions appear to have no impact on political unity or disunity; ordinary persons are also occluded as agents whose actions matter. Locutions like those quoted earlier attribute the capacity to unite, to bind, to legitimize, and to found to the presence of commonality, to the fact of having something in common—but not to the actions of the people who purportedly have this thing in common. The objective picture of sharing, then, puts the emphasis on what is shared as the agent in sharing: we share when x is common to us, and not because of anything that you or I do. Sharing is fundamentally passive; it is not an activity that any of those who can be said to share have to be involved in doing in order to share. Insofar as what is shared is taken to be a fact of the matter, this mental picture occludes how we come to share this particular thing in common: what the politics are that have determined that it is significant that we share this, and not that; whether the shared thing is simply a background feature of a given population, or whether it is meaningful to the people who share in it. What we miss in this way of thinking about sharing is how sharing appears to the agents who do the sharing, how ordinary persons are political agents in the production and reproduction of commonality.

Insofar as contemporary democratic theorists are captivated by this picture of sharing, then, what they are doing is at odds with what they profess to be doing: the effect of this way of theorizing is to close down, rather than open up, to difference and democracy. If what we do or should share in common is conceptualized as a question that can be answered by a theorist, then the claims that democratic actors make about what they do or do not share are irrelevant to theory. From this perspective, commonality is a matter that can be settled by experts; it is not something that theorists typically expect to be settled through some kind of democratic decision making. Consequently, democratic theorists usually disregard popular claims about what we have in common, preferring instead to argue among themselves.

Moreover, even when they do take into account what nonexperts say they share, if they are captivated by an objective picture of sharing, theorists are less likely to hear claims that challenge the view that democracies require commonality to function.[58] If we are looking for confirmation that a people really does share x in common, we will be less open to hearing that the people themselves do not agree. If theorists do hear challenges to their claims to commonality, these can easily be dismissed as unreasonable: either because those who make opposing claims refuse to see the facts or because they are unwilling to adopt the beliefs or practices that they should have in common with their fellow citizens. Think of how Kymlicka presents his evidence that 91 percent of Puerto Ricans think of themselves as Americans second: what of the other 9 percent? He is eager to tell us that the poll results must mean that Puerto Rican identification is facilitated by differentiated citizenship (a detail he reads into the poll without checking to see whether this is how the 91 percent sees it), yet he is curiously silent about how the minority identifies.

What if we were to think of the nonconforming remainder not as the symptom of a lack of actual commonality, not as a threat to democratic unity, but instead as the expected outcome of sharing the world with others? I propose that we take the plurality of claims that democratic citizens (and democratic theorists) make about what we do or should have in common not as a symptom of our failure to have located the right or best source of commonality—but rather as indicative of what it looks like to share the world in common with others. This is to shift our mental picture of sharing from an objective to an intersubjective one. In the intersubjective picture of sharing, sharing does not depend on singular objects possessed in common but rather on ongoing interactions between plural subjects who need not ever come to agreement on what they share in order to share a world in common.

THE INTERSUBJECTIVE PICTURE OF SHARING

While the objective mental picture may often captivate us, it is not the only way we have of thinking about how we share: we also have ordinary experiences of this different, intersubjective picture of sharing. Consider what we are doing when we tell one toddler to share with another. When we urge children to share, what we are teaching them is a way of seeing themselves in relation to others that we hope will guide their behavior into adulthood. More specifically, we aim to teach children that they live in the company of other people who are subjects just as they are—in this instance, the other children with whom they play. When we teach children to share, our focus is not so much on the things we want them to share in common (such as their toys) as it is on their developing a particular, first-person understanding of how they relate to others. We are teaching them, in other words, an intersubjective mental picture of sharing.

In this section, I sketch in some details of this intersubjective picture by taking inspiration from Arendt. I find in her work an account of sharing the world in common with others that contrasts with the objective mental picture: whereas in the objective picture of sharing, it is the *presence* of the common thing that makes it shared, for Arendt what matters is the *appearance* of the common thing to plural subjects. That is, a thing is common only when subjects experience it as appearing to themselves and to others. Things are not objectively common to us. Rather, for Arendt, commonness is a quality of the human experience of the world: things are common only when we experience them as shared with other subjects.

The first distinctive feature of this mental picture, then, is that it is first-personal rather than objective. This is a picture of sharing as seen from a participant's perspective. From this first-person point of view, this picture depicts a world inhabited by multiple subjects. That is to say, when I adopt an intersubjective mental picture, I experience myself as one subject among many others, each of whom has her own first-person perception of the world we inhabit together. For Arendt, this basic belief that we live in a world with other subjects arises from what she calls *sensus communis*, or common sense. The classic concept of *sensus communis* is that of a sixth sense "needed to keep my five senses together and guarantee that it is the same object that I see, touch, taste, smell and hear."[59] In this formulation, common sense is merely a private, subjective sense like sight or hearing. However, Arendt understands this sixth sense somewhat differently. Following Immanuel Kant, she takes common sense to include the presumption that all human beings possess these same six senses. As such, the *sensus communis* orients us toward a public, nonsubjective world shared with other similarly sensing subjects.[60] Common sense therefore does more than just integrate the data from our five senses; it "fits" these data into a perception of an intersubjectively shared reality.[61] That is, it integrates my subjective sensations of a thing with my perception that other subjects also have their own subjective sensations of that same thing.

In this picture, our access to a nonsubjective world is mediated through this awareness that we share the world with others; we cannot have direct knowledge of an objective world. When a person sees something—say, a table—her perception is subjective. That is, she senses that there is a table in front of her, but this perception alone cannot give that table the sense of being real. After all, her vision might not be good, or she could be halluci-nating, or perhaps she is dreaming. She can confirm that what she senses is *real* only when she perceives other beings who seem to sense it, too. As Arendt explains, "To men the reality of the world is guaranteed by the pres-ence of others, by its appearing to all."[62] The confirmation of others shows that a person's subjective perception of the table has intersubjective valid-ity: the table is not just for her but for all perceiving subjects.[63] In this way, common sense entails a sensitivity to the presence of other subjects in the world, whose reactions to what we see and hear can confirm that what we sense is not merely subjective.[64] Arendt claims that this "recognition and acknowledgement" of others gives us a sense of the reality of our selves "as well as that of the world. In both cases, our 'perceptual faith,' as [Maurice] Merleau-Ponty has called it, our certainty that what we perceive has an existence independent of the act of perceiving, depends entirely on the object's also appearing as such to others and being acknowledged by them.

Without this tacit acknowledgment by others we would not even be able to put faith in the way we appear to ourselves."[65] In the intersubjective picture, then, we have faith and certainty, rather than objective knowledge, that the things we perceive have an existence independent of our perceptions. Our capacity to believe in the reality of a nonsubjective world is thus grounded in our sense that we inhabit it together with other subjects. Indeed, we only have access to the idea of an objective reality by virtue of having this common sense.[66] Our sense of reality depends upon the presence and confirmation of others.

Yet for Arendt, sharing the world in common with others requires not only common sense but also what she calls "community sense": "an extra sense—like an extra mental capability . . . that fits us into a community."[67] While she does not elaborate further, I take her to mean that we humans fit into a community when we are aware that we share the world with *plural* others; community sense, in other words, is a sense of human plurality. Arendt defines plurality as "the twofold character of equality and distinction": humans are like one another (e.g., in that we each possess the same six senses), yet each person is unique.[68] Unlike other species whose members have "immediate, identical needs and wants," humans have different desires, tastes, thoughts, and judgments.[69] Consequently, we require the complex medium of language to interact with one another: we aim not merely to express basic needs or emotions but to communicate something of ourselves to others.[70]

Arendt illustrates this point by citing Kant's distinction between the sane and the insane: only the sane have community sense, and therefore only they are able to communicate with others.[71] The madman, according to Kant, acts according to his subjective sensations and thoughts, without checking them against those of others: he "*talks aloud* to himself" or "hears a voice that no one else hears."[72] He is a kind of solipsist, "abandoned to a play of thoughts in which he sees, acts, and judges, not in a common world, but rather in his own world (as in dreaming)."[73] By contrast, a person with community sense is sensitive to the subjectivity of her thoughts and sensations; she is aware that they do not as such have validity for others. Just as she seeks confirmation that the voice she hears is real in the reactions of others around her, she seeks confirmation of the validity of her thoughts and judgments by making them communicable to others. That is, she does not merely express herself; she is sensitive to what might be understood (and possibly agreed to) by others. To have a sense of what is and is not communicable, a person must be aware that other people see things from different perspectives. As Arendt puts it, "One can communicate only if one is able to think from the other person's standpoint; otherwise one will never meet him, never speak in such a way that he understands."[74] Surely this is an overstatement: we do not think from our interlocutor's actual standpoint when we communicate.[75] Nonetheless, a person with community sense is sensitive to her audience. She thinks about how the words she uses might come across to others, and she is willing to rephrase or edit what she has to say in order to communicate more effectively. When we have community sense, we are sensitive to what is communicable—to the difference between what is only subjectively valid and what could have intersubjective validity if confirmed by others.

Moreover, community sense makes us want to interact with other people. A person with community sense is aware that she shares the world with plural subjects. She is aware that her experience of reality and meaning— even her sense of self—requires the presence and confirmation of others. And so she wants to be around other people, to communicate with them, and to exchange thoughts and judgments with them. She is, in Kant's terminology, *sociable*—drawn toward the company of other human beings.[76] The presence of others enables us to experience things differently than we could on our own: it gives things the sense of reality, and it enables us to see whether what we subjectively experience has meaning for others. When a person with community sense makes a judgment that she thinks has intersubjective validity, she wants other people to agree with her, and so she seeks the company of others and shares her views with them. This, Kant notes, is the point of publication: "We advance [our own thoughts] in public in order to see whether they also agree with the understanding of others."[77] Just as a person with common sense is aware of how other subjects respond to appearances in the world they share in common, a person with community sense is aware of how other subjects respond to the claims she makes; she seeks confirmation of the validity of her political and aesthetic judgments by communicating them with others.

The picture of intersubjective sharing that comes out of my reading of Arendt, then, depicts humans relating to one another as plural subjects. When I adopt this mental picture, I have a particular experience of myself in relation to others. I see myself as a perceiving subject who inhabits the world together with human beings who are also subjects who perceive as I do. I experience a nonsubjective world as real because I see other subjects relating to what I perceive in ways that confirm that the world is not for me, but for us. Further, I am aware that other human beings are different from me: they have their own subjective experiences, and they also have different desires, tastes, thoughts, and judgments. As a consequence of this human plurality, we need to communicate our differences with one another; I cannot presume in advance that others will desire, like, think, or judge as

I do. And since we differ, I can expect to encounter disagreement, conflict, and misunderstanding even when we do try to communicate. Sharing the world with others, then, is a matter of seeing myself as living in the company of plural subjects, each with their own unique experience.

COMMONALITY AS POLITICAL CLAIMING

When we shift from an objective to an intersubjective picture of sharing, this does not mean that we must forgo making claims about what we have in common. On the contrary, noticing and naming commonality are important ways in which humans make sense of their world. What shifts, then, is not whether we make claims to commonality but how we understand what we are doing when we make such claims. From within this intersubjective picture of sharing, claims about what we have in common appear to be political claims rather than neutral observations about the world. In the objective picture of sharing, claims about commonality are claims to direct knowledge of an objective world that exists independently of us. In the intersubjective view, however, they are hermeneutic claims about how we should make sense of and understand the world that we share. Such claims seek the agreement of others, seek to persuade others, and seek to shape the way others see the world that we share intersubjectively. That claims to commonality are political is a central argument of this book, so let me take some time to explain this point.

Identifying commonalities is an important way in which we humans create order and structure out of the extraordinary complexity of our sense perceptions. Without the capacity to notice what particulars have in common with one another, each thing that we sensed would seem to be entirely unique and unrelated to what we had sensed previously. We would not be able to recognize tables, but only "this," and "this," and "this." That is to say, humans must *interpret* their perceptions of the world in order to see tables. One table might objectively share certain features in common with other tables: a flat surface, legs, solidity. However, simply having some of the same characteristics in common with other tables does not make this table a table. The table is a table only when it appears to be a table to a perceiving subject. I synthesize my sense data (that this object has a flat surface, legs, and solidity) in order to understand what I perceive to be a table, like other tables I have encountered before. I decide which of its many features to focus on as relevant to identifying what kind of object this is. In perceiving the table, I could focus on its other material properties—the stuff of which it is made, for example, or its color and texture; or I could focus on its function—that it is used as a piece of ornamentation or furniture; or I could focus on its location, age, history, ownership, style, price, or portability. Each of these different ways of thinking about the table brings into focus a different set of properties that it shares in common with a different set of objects. "This" appears as a table only when I focus on a certain subset of features that this object has in common with only a certain subset of other objects (and even only a certain subset of objects we call "tables"). For Arendt, our ability to understand "this" to be a table depends upon being able to relate the particular table that we perceive right now to a schema of "table" she believes is present in our minds, which we do by means of the faculty of imagination. We recognize this as a table by noting what qualities this particular table shares in common with the general concept we have of a table.[78] Whether or not we follow Arendt in committing ourselves to a Kantian notion of schemas, we humans require some ability to recognize commonalities in order to identify patterns, develop knowledge, and ultimately make sense of the world we inhabit.

We do more than just recognize commonalities, however; we also name the things that share them: we call objects like these "tables," for example. Language, according to Arendt, "gives an object its common name," that is, a name that is public, and therefore can be part of an intersubjectively shared world. In other words, by naming an object we turn it into something that can be talked about with others. She explains that the commonness of names is "the decisive factor for intersubjective communication—the same object being perceived by different persons and common to them."[79] This ability to name and talk about things enables us to make sense of and humanize our experience of our common world.[80] Naming makes it possible for us to recognize familiarity in what would otherwise be strange and entirely unique (that's a table!), and in this way it helps us to orient ourselves in a world that we share intersubjectively with other linguistic subjects.

Consequently, language adds another dimension to our sense of reality: meaning. As I noted earlier, I experience the world as real when other subjects behave in a way that indicates that they perceive what I perceive. But as linguistic beings, we intersubjectively share a world that is made up of more than just material objects we can perceive with our senses, like tables and trees. Language makes it possible for humans to make the immaterial common as well: words, concepts, categories, ideas, and histories through language can become a part of our intersubjectively shared world. That is, language enables us to express that which cannot be perceived. Through communication, our otherwise imperceptible desires, thoughts, tastes, and judgments become public. This is meaning-making. Arendt writes, "Implicit in the urge to speak is the quest for meaning."[81] We make ourselves at home in the world by naming things and talking about them with one another. That is, through talking with others about the world, we experience it not only as real but as meaningful. When we give the world communicable meaning, we endow it with a kind of permanence and immortality that can outlast the life of any single human being. A humanized world, for Arendt, requires a built material environment coupled with the construction of immaterial meaning: "Without being talked about by men and without housing them, the world would not be a human artifice but a heap of unrelated things to which each isolated individual was at liberty to add one more object."[82] Our linguistic capacity to communicate and create meaning is thus central to what Arendt calls "world-building": building a world that we experience as shared in common with plural subjects.

It would be very easy here to slide back into an objective picture of sharing to make sense of how we share the world in common. We could imagine that the word "table" makes sense to us as English speakers because each of us shares the same concept of what a table is. We can communicate with each other, then, because we have the same definitions in mind when we speak. Our common world is made up of material, conceptual, and linguistic objects that are the same for all. Arendt herself often writes in a way that encourages such a reading of her work. In "The Crisis in Culture," for example, she describes "the world itself" as "an objective datum, something common to all its inhabitants."[83] This world, moreover, seems to have an existence independent of those who share in it, such that each of us has a different relation to it. "The stage is common to all who are alive, but it *seems* different to each species, different also to each individual specimen."[84] We each see the world and the things in it from our own unique perspectives, yet what we see in the world is "sameness in utter diversity": we are all looking at "the same object" from within the same context.[85] Indeed, the metaphor of the table that she famously uses to explain her concept of the world repeats the idea that what we share is a distinct, identifiable thing: "To live together in the world means essentially that a world of things is between those who have it in common, as a table is located between those who sit around it."[86] Even when Arendt describes the sharing of ideas, her words often seem to reify what we share, treating it as one selfsame thing common to all, as when she writes that "all single agreements or disagreements presuppose that we are talking about the same thing—that we, who are many, agree, come together, on something that is one and the same for us all."[87] Sharing the world, having something in common, being able to communicate—all of these, Arendt seems to say, require that we have in advance the same material, conceptual, and linguistic objects. Without settling the question of how we should interpret Arendt on this matter, I want to resist the temptation to slide back into an objective mental picture here and instead think about how we share language intersubjectively.

To that end, let me briefly invoke the intersubjective account of meaning in Wittgenstein's later works. He notes that when we learn our mother tongue, we do not learn the meaning of words in isolation the way we might when studying a foreign language. Rather, as children we learn the meaning of words as a part of an overall world picture that we inherit from adults.[88] Kids do not learn the meaning of "table" by learning the definition of the word. They learn to behave a certain way when eating at the kitchen table, to watch out for their heads when playing around tables with sharp corners, and to talk about tables as inanimate objects rather than as persons. They learn, that is, a whole way of life, a more or less complete world picture.[89] Accordingly, "this" appears to us as a table only in the context of intersubjective practices of naming objects like it "tables" and interacting with this object as one has learned to interact with a table. The meaning of "table," in the classic paraphrase of Wittgenstein, is its use: it is used in the context of an intersubjectively shared world in which there are things called tables, and in which communicating about and interacting with tables has significance for other subjects. Just as our sensation of reality depends upon the confirmation of other subjects, the meaning and communicability of our words depend upon it as well. To say that a meaning is shared, then, is to say that other people appear to me to use the same words in a way that suggests they understand them as I do. To say that a meaning is communicable is to say that others respond to my speech in a way that suggests that my meaning was successfully communicated to them.

On this intersubjective view, communication does not require that we have the exact same definitions of our words in mind when we speak; indeed, it does not depend upon us having any precise definition of our words at all. Rather, as Arendt puts it, I "*presuppose* that we are talking about the same thing" when I talk to you—which is decidedly not the same as *knowing in advance* that we are talking about the same thing. When I speak, I do so in the belief that you will be able to understand me because I presume that you think and use these words as I do. Yet this is a first-person belief not an objective fact. Think about the readers of Arendt's "Reflections on Little Rock" who presume that she must mean to refer to a picture of Eckford. Although Arendt seems to have a different photo in mind, this does not make their readings of her incoherent or incomprehensible. It may change how we evaluate and interpret the claims that they make, but it does not render those claims meaningless because it turns out that they are not talking about the same thing as Arendt. Communication does not break down because we do not have the exact same objects or meanings in mind. In the process of communicating with others, we may come to the realization that we are talking about different things, or using the same words but with different understandings of their meaning. At such a point in a conversation, we may stop and try to clarify our terms. But we do not need to define all our terms in advance in order to get the conversation off the ground in the first place. Communication does not depend on our *knowing* that we are talking about the same things using the same linguistic objects but on our socialization into a set of practices from within which we can make some sense of one another.

That is to say, our use of words to communicate has the same kind of validity as an aesthetic or political judgment. Rather than being fixed and the same for all, the meaning of our words is created and sustained in our intersubjective interactions. The validity of my use of the word "table" to mean objects that share these commonalities, but not those, is not guaranteed by some facts about tables in the world but is instead a function of other language users (whether implicitly or explicitly) accepting my use of the word in this way and responding as if they have understood it.

When humans aim to make sense of the world by making claims about what certain things have in common, or by using words that presuppose a schema that unites the particulars to which they are applied, they are engaging in a kind of *political* practice. When I call these activities "political," I do not mean to refer to some kind of institutionalized, formal practice of collective government. Rather, I mean to invoke Arendt's distinction between truth claims and political claims.[90] I develop this distinction in more detail in chapter 3, but here let me just briefly note that truth claims have a different kind of validity than political claims. Truth claims are coercive: "They are beyond agreement, dispute, opinion, or consent. For those who accept them, they are not changed by the numbers or lack of numbers who entertain the same proposition; persuasion or dissuasion is useless, for the content of the statement is not of a persuasive nature but of a coercive one."[91] Political claims, by contrast, are claims that—like Kant's aesthetic claims—do not have validity in advance of persuading others to agree. They are contestable, they "woo" the consent of others, they seek agreement. As we saw earlier with Kant, we make our "political" opinions public in order to see if others will agree, in order to try to persuade them to agree, in order to establish whether they have intersubjective validity.[92]

Yet meaning, interpretation, and claims about commonality are also political in another sense: they have the effect of shaping the world that we share with others. Insofar as claims about meaning seek intersubjective validity, they seek agreement on how we should interpret the world. Every interpretation makes some possibilities visible and occludes others. When we make claims about how to interpret the world, as Linda Zerilli argues, we "alter our sense of what is common or shared: we alter what Arendt calls the world."[93] When we interpret the world, when we share our interpretations with others, and especially when we seek to have them share our interpretation, we are participating in building the world we share in common with others. Making claims about what kinds of things share which commonality, making claims about what is or should be common to us all—this is a matter of world-building: trying to make sense of the world, trying to generate agreement about how to make sense of it, making some possibilities visible, and occluding others.

Assertions about what we do or do not have in common in democracy are, then, ways of making sense of our experience of the world. Far from being a matter of mere neutral description, claims about commonality are very much political. When theorists like Kymlicka and Habermas lay claim to what we share, they do so as political actors. Theorists are not neutral knowledge producers. They are political partisans advocating for a particular position. They aim in their arguments to try to persuade others to agree with them. They aim to shape how we see things, and what it is that we see. As such, theoretical claims to commonality have no greater validity than the claims of other political actors; theorists are no closer to "the truth" of what we share in common.

Consequently, from within an intersubjective picture of sharing it is impossible to disavow our human agency in making sense of the world. Recall that the objective picture attributes to the commonalities that we share the capacity to found and bind communities. However, if we do the work of making sense of our world in terms of these commonalities, rather than those, then it is we humans who are ultimately doing the work of founding and binding. Humans do the work of imagining their world in a particular way. To say that this is something that humans do is not to say that any one of us is sovereign over the world, that I could imagine the world to be whatever I wish it to be. Rather, our way of making sense of the world arises from our relation to other subjects and to the material world. We are constrained by the physical properties of the world in which we live; we are limited in our capacity to share meaning by how other people respond. We would be like Kant's solipsistic madman if we sought to imagine the world in a way that could not be communicated to others. Moreover, to say that we do the work of making sense of the world is not to say that it is a matter of free choice how we make sense. Our worldview may have been passed down to us through inheritance or education, or otherwise imposed through some form of coercion. Our ability to name things or to communicate, for example, is limited by the existing grammar of the language we use. We exercise this capacity to make sense of the world within the limits of nonsovereign subjects born into an already existing material, linguistic, and intersubjective reality. Even within these limits, however, we have the capacity to imagine and reimagine our world through our interactions with one another.

I am not the first theorist to maintain that claims to commonality are political. Others have also argued that commonality is the product of human interpretation and meaning-making, and that we should therefore understand claims to commonality as exercises of political power. I am indebted here to the work of Chantal Mouffe and Ernesto Laclau in *Hegemony and Socialist Strategy* and Zerilli in *Feminism and the Abyss of Freedom*, who have made these points compellingly, albeit in different ways.[94] By drawing attention to the politics of commonality, their work resists the objectivist tendency to naturalize claims to commonality, shows that these claims are contingent and therefore contestable, and calls on each of us to own our political freedom by engaging in contestation over what we have in common. I find myself deeply sympathetic to their arguments, and yet I believe they do not go far enough in moving us beyond a politics oriented toward commonality.

My concern is that the view that claims to commonality are political remains compatible with the objective picture of sharing. From this perspective, what we share is not objectively common to us but rather is the product of intersubjective activity. Yet this is only to alter our understanding of its provenance: rather than being independent of us, the common thing is our creation. We can still share a social construction as if it were an object common to us all. It is possible, then, to determine that commonalities are produced through political action between subjects and still remain focused on *what* we share in common. Consider how Zerilli, even as she advocates a freedom-centered politics, has a tendency to privilege claims to commonality as the subject of politics. "Acting politically," she writes, "is about testing the limits of every claim to commonality."[95] Politics for her is about discovering "the extent and nature of what we have in common."[96] At these moments, Zerilli seems to embrace a vision of politics that is still captivated by the objective picture of sharing: the goal of political activity is still to answer the question of what we have in common, even if the answer can only be contingent and partial.

While I believe it is important to view claims to commonality as political, unless we also shift to adopting an intersubjective picture of sharing, we risk reproducing the antidemocratic tendencies of an objective orientation. I will argue this point in chapter 6, but for now I ask that you accept it on faith. It is not enough that we come to see claims to commonality as political; we must also shift our focus in democratic theory and practice from commonality to political freedom.

INTERSUBJECTIVE DEMOCRACY

When we adopt an intersubjective picture of sharing, we must do more than see commonality as the political product of our human capacity to build a common world: we must presume that this capacity itself is also possessed by the plural subjects with whom we inhabit this world. Just as the intersubjective picture entails that I share the world with other subjects who also have the same six senses and the capacity for linguistic communication that I have, it entails that I share the world with other subjects who also have the capacity for world-building that I possess. Sharing, then, is the world-building activity of plural subjects. We could not share a world together—indeed, we would not need to—if we had the same thoughts, desires, judgments, and ideas. The condition of sharing a world together is that we inhabit it together with plural subjects.

World-building is therefore a *nonsovereign* capacity. While any one of us has the capacity to shape the world (and some of us may be more effective at doing so than others), no one can simply shape the world at will. Rather, my ability to shape the world is always exercised in the company of others who may or may not comply with my vision. I am constrained in the interpretations I offer and the claims I make by what I am able to make intelligible and communicable to others. I may successfully communicate a thought or an idea, but I may be unable nonetheless to win the agreement of others. Insofar as I aim to alter the world, I have to work with (and against) other people, who have their own plural wills and perspectives. As Arendt puts it, we act within and into an "already existing web of human relationships, with its innumerable, conflicting wills and intentions."[97] Or as Allen writes, "We are all always awash in each other's lives." The impact others have on my actions can be negative, neutral, or even positive: I may find my efforts frustrated by miscommunication or disagreement, or I may find my ideas transformed and improved by what I learn through interacting with others.

The world we share in common with others is the ongoing product of our activity: it must be produced and reproduced through human interaction. It does not exist independently of us; it exists only when we actively build and sustain it. Action, for Arendt, is essential to creating and preserving a world in common; without action and without the public spaces in which it could appear, the world that lies in between us fades.[98] The common world for her is fragile, vulnerable, and in regular (perhaps even constant) need of renewal.[99] This is why the world needs humans to act to preserve it—whether through acting politically, or through truth-telling and witnessing—and why it is so easily endangered in dark times. Consequently, she argues for the importance of memorializing, reifying, storytelling, preserving, building a material world, and founding public spaces.[100] Commonness—our subjective experience of sharing with others—is neither a static characteristic of objects nor a quality that once achieved can be presumed into the future. Rather, commonness is the fragile product of ongoing human activity.

Our ability to experience the world as shared in common with others does not depend upon commonality and may even be heightened by interactions that expose what we do not have in common. That is, when we disagree, when we miscommunicate, when we conflict—these are moments in interaction when we are perhaps most attuned to the fact of human plurality. When in such moments we are confronted with the differences between ourselves and others, we can have a heightened awareness that we inhabit the world with plural others—that the world is not for me, but for us—in a way that the experience of agreement and understanding can obscure. Indeed, it might be that when we fail to produce commonality, we are most open to experiencing this quality of inhabiting the world with *plural* others. Where in the objective picture of sharing, experiences of disagreement and miscommunication can threaten our sense of commonality, in the intersubjective picture, they can be the occasion for renewing openness to the other and a sense of one's own nonsovereignty. The goal for a democratic politics should therefore be to cultivate this openness to these moments of disagreement and difference in a way that enables further interaction, as opposed to encouraging withdrawal.

In the remainder of the book, I aim to flesh out how our understanding of democracy must alter when we shift from an objective to an intersubjective picture of sharing. The objective picture orients us toward commonality, to thinking about what, if anything, we have in common. It assigns to commonality the capacity to produce the identity, affect, and agency that democracy is believed to require. The intersubjective picture, by contrast, orients us toward political freedom: that is, our nonsovereign world-building capacity to shape the world that we share with plural others. This is a radically democratic capacity in that it is available in principle to all human beings, and so it is not containable within borders and institutions. Intersubjective democracy demands cultivating and enabling this capacity in all. We act into a world of plural others, and so we will disagree, conflict, and misunderstand one another as a matter of course. Moreover, we cannot guarantee the outcome of our world-building activity because we cannot control how others will respond to, take up, or transform what we put into the world. We act into the plural world without knowing what the outcomes will be. This lack of certainty about the future is both exhilarating and terrifying; Zerilli aptly refers to it as an "abyss of freedom." Yet the point of political freedom is to experience the excitement and terror of the unknown, and to act anyhow.

CHAPTER 3

Imagining the Demos

Sharing Identity in Feminist and Democratic Theory

Why do we call something a "number"? Well, perhaps because it has a—direct—relationship with several things that have hitherto been called number; and this can be said to give it an indirect relationship to other things we call the same name. And we extend our concept of number as in spinning a thread we twist fibre on fibre. And the strength of the thread does not reside in the fact that some one fibre runs through its whole length, but in the overlapping of many fibres.
—Ludwig Wittgenstein[1]

The belief that democracy requires some kind of commonality is held in place by a set of corollary assumptions, one of which is the assumption that commonality is needed to make identities coherent and meaningful. In order to shift our way of seeing democracy toward the activity of political freedom, in this chapter I critically examine this assumption. I turn to feminist theory as I do this, because feminists have long been wrestling with their own commitment to this corollary assumption. The past thirty years of feminist theory illustrate well some of the conceptual and political problems produced by an objective picture of sharing, and democratic theory can learn from its example. But feminism is not just a negative example for me. I also draw enthusiastically on the work of a feminist theorist, Linda Zerilli, in order to begin to think about democratic identity beyond commonality.

Just as many democratic theorists assume that without a people that shares something in common there can be no democracy, many feminist theorists believe "that without an ontologically grounded feminist subject there can be no [feminist] politics."[2] This belief has led to what Zerilli terms feminism's preoccupation with "the subject question," with who is or could be the subject of feminism.[3] As Iris Young characterizes the problem, "Without some sense in which 'woman' is the name of a social collective, there is nothing specific to feminist politics."[4] Captivated by an objective picture of sharing, many feminists presume that a social collective must be characterized by some kind of commonality. Consequently, feminism over the past few decades has been marked by intense and often divisive debates that aim to locate a commonality that could unite all women.[5] These debates over the category of "women" reached their height in the 1980s and early 1990s but were never fully resolved.

Feminist politics seems to depend on getting a clear understanding of what women have in common for a number of reasons. First, if feminists could accurately articulate who women are and what they have in common, they could broaden their appeal. Other women would be able to see that they share commonalities with feminists, which in turn would make them want to identify and act as feminists themselves. Without a compelling account of what women have in common, it can seem as if feminists have no way to appeal to nonfeminists. Second, defining women clearly is a means of determining the scope and agenda of the women's movement: if women share a biological makeup, then certain political actions follow; but if what they share is a set of experiences, then another course of action may be more appropriate. If feminists cannot get clear on what makes women women, then it seems they will not be able to agree on a coherent political agenda, the movement will fracture, and its efforts will be scattered and less effectual. Third, getting clear on the category of women is important from a theoretical perspective: for if women do not share anything in common, this seems to call into question the entire enterprise of analyzing the world in terms of sex and gender. If women do not have anything in common, what effect can feminist scholars legitimately attribute to something like gender or patriarchy? The coherence of feminist analysis appears to depend on women sharing something in common. Finally, the legitimacy of feminism seems to require that it be able to include all women in its analysis and agenda, and not just a subset of women. Repeated challenges from working-class women, lesbians, women of color, non-Western women, and others who have felt excluded from mainstream feminist theory and politics have therefore inspired attempts to retheorize gender in ways that are more inclusive. The subsequent search for what women share in common has led feminist theory into the twin dead ends of essentialism and antiessentialism.[6]

Different feminist theorists have asserted what they believe all women share—biology, a different voice, the experience of patriarchal oppression, a socially constructed position of inferiority and exploitability, and so on.[7] However, each assertion of commonality has been met with a corresponding denial. Not all women share the same biology—some have three chromosomes or a preponderance of testosterone. Not all women share the same experiences—there are cultural variations in the treatment of women, such that different women have different experiences of oppression. Every claim that women share something in common (the essentialist moment) has met with a counterclaim that not all women share that supposed commonality (the antiessentialist moment). The result in feminist theory has been a seemingly endless dynamic of essentialist assertions followed by antiessentialist counterassertions, followed by revised essentialist assertions, and so on.

Feminist theorists have sought to escape this essentialist/antiessentialist dynamic in ways that are reminiscent of the three strategies discussed in chapter 1 that contemporary democratic theorists employ to modify the kind of commonality they think democracy requires. For example, Jennifer Baumgardner and Amy Richards adopt a kind of minimal strategy when they claim that feminists are merely "a loose collection of individuals."[8] By sidestepping the question of what women have in common, they can offer a vision of feminism that includes as many women as possible: "You're sexy, a wallflower, you shop at Calvin Klein, you are a stay-at-home mom, a big Hollywood producer, a beautiful bride all in white, an ex-wife raising three kids, or you shave, pluck, and wax. In reality, feminism wants you to be whoever you are—but with a political consciousness."[9] Here, a political consciousness (whose content they leave undefined) is the minimal commonality they believe to be necessary to unite feminists as a collectivity, albeit a loose one.

The civic strategy of restricting commonality to the political sphere has its analogue in the turn by many feminist theorists to coalition politics.[10] A coalition is a temporary and strategic union formed in order to achieve specific, shared political goals. Feminists call for coalition as a response to debates over the category of women because coalitions do not require deep and widespread commonality. A group of feminists can act together on one set of issues without having to generate consensus on a comprehensive political agenda with all feminists, let alone with all women. Feminists do not need to agree on a larger vision, nor do they have to settle deeper disagreements about what women have in common in order to act politically; they only need to be able to find some others who can agree with them on at least one agenda item. Commonality is limited to what is absolutely necessary for feminists to take some political action, and nothing more.

Perhaps the most frequent response among feminists to the subject question most closely resembles the perspectival strategy. In reply to antiessentialist challenges that women do not have anything in common, some feminists have tried to make their claims about commonality more localized and specific. Instead of making a claim about "women," for example, feminist scholars might make claims about "Latinas" or "African American lesbians" or "middle-class white women with disabilities."[11] Feminists who adopt this approach make painstaking efforts to clarify that the claims to knowledge they make fall far short of having validity for all women. Rather, they claim validity only for those women who share in a particular perspective demarcated by a combination of other identities. While there is a tendency in this scholarship toward a kind of relativism (i.e., each of us sees something quite different from our different vantage points), there is also a strong countertendency toward a kind of objectivism—that is, toward the belief that our different perspectives are perspectives on a truth common to us all.[12]

However much they appear to give feminists a way out of the essentialist/antiessentialist dynamic, like their counterparts in democratic theory, these strategies remain committed to some version of the belief that commonality is necessary to produce identity. Inasmuch as they claim that what unites feminists is a political consciousness, a particular political agenda, or a truth seen from different perspectives, feminist theorists have not fully unseated the assumption that to form a social collectivity, they must have something in common. Indeed, when we compare the feminist and democratic theory literatures, we can see many striking similarities.[13] Both start from the presumption that politics requires "a coherent, pregiven subject."[14] Whether the subject in question is "women" or "the people," these theorists tend to recapitulate familiar essentialist and antiessentialist views of collective identity: either group identities are presumed to be grounded in a commonality shared by all members; or they are considered to be ultimately incoherent and purely contingent because we cannot discover anything that all group members have in common. In both cases, the presumption is that sharing identity requires sharing commonality. This presumption sets in motion a seemingly endless back-and-forth between two positions: first, the essentialist claim that this shared x is the commonality underlying this identity; second, the antiessentialist counterclaim that x is not, in fact, common to all and therefore cannot be the basis for a shared identity. This dynamic is often motivated by a sincere desire to include diverse people within a single identity. However, each attempt at inclusion produces a new refusal from some who feel they have been excluded, which in turn inspires another go at trying to get the identity right. The result is a seemingly infinite cycle of assertions and counterassertions that essentialists find frustrating because it does not appear to get us closer to true knowledge of what we share, and antiessentialists find futile because its endlessness only confirms the incoherence of our identities.

Given the striking parallels between the two literatures, I propose to think through the question of commonality in democratic theory by reflecting on the debates about the category of women in feminism. What might we learn about democracy if we are open to the possibility that feminist theory may have some wisdom to offer about how we think about commonality? Inspired by the similar patterns of thinking that appear in both literatures, I turn in this chapter to Zerilli's recent interventions in feminist theory for help thinking beyond the logic of the essentialist/antiessentialist dynamic. As Zerilli has pointed out for feminist theory, this dynamic emerges when we misconceive of collective identity as grounded in knowable, shared characteristics. Gender identity, she argues, is something that we ordinarily do without knowing what gender is.[15] Moreover, instead of being grounded in commonality, the meaning of "women" is grounded in a multiplicity of practices. This makes gender identity resilient in the face of critique: even when we have thoroughly rejected one practice of gender, many others remain, holding it stubbornly in place. Yet even as her work shows why it is so difficult for us to abandon the category of women, she also provides insight into how it might be transformed. She reveals gender to be a product of human imagination, instituted in a multitude of social practices. Gender is thus a way of seeing the world, a set of imagined meanings that help us to make sense of our experience. We may not be able to get rid of the category of women altogether, but we can develop new radical imaginaries of gender that compete with and challenge those already in place. With this analysis of gender as a kind of doing without knowing, Zerilli reveals that feminism's preoccupation with the subject question is itself bound up with assumptions about epistemology, language and meaning, and human agency and freedom. All of these, her work suggests, must be called into question if we are to attempt to dislodge the dominance of a commonality orientation within feminist theory—and by extension, I argue, in democratic theory as well.

Through an engagement with Zerilli, I draw an intentionally provocative parallel between the category of women in feminism and the identity of the people in democratic theory. I do this not in order to suggest that gender and democratic identification function in exactly the same ways—surely they do not. Rather, I do so to illuminate some features of how theorists often conceptualize identity, and to propose an alternative. Working through perhaps the most famous text to claim that peoples are not natural entities but artifacts of human imagination—Benedict Anderson's *Imagined Communities*—I argue that collective identity is created and reproduced through human activity. Humans do the work of imagining community, of building an intersubjectively shared world in which certain collective identities have resilience and meaning. Humans do the work as well of engaging in the practices that inaugurate, sustain, and challenge collective identity. This focus on identity as doing makes possible new insight into the role that conflicting imaginaries play in democracy: rather than requiring commonality, the identity of the demos may be paradoxically more resilient where there are multiple, overlapping, and not entirely contiguous practices of democratic collective identity. The human activity necessary to democracy, then, extends far beyond what is typically understood as democratic political action: it includes not just participation in electoral politics, or in deliberation and decision making—but also participation in myriad and often seemingly trivial practices that sustain our imaginaries of the demos. Thinking of identity as human doing, then, radically expands the domain of political freedom to potentially include any site in which the human imagination works to sustain or build an intersubjectively shared world.

KNOWING IDENTITY

To understand what Zerilli's critique of the subject question has to offer democratic theorists trying to think beyond commonality, we must first take a look at what it is that she is responding to in feminist theory. To put the problem of the subject question in the terms of this book, the presumption that feminist politics requires a pregiven, collective subject characterized by what its members have in common is bound up with what I described in chapter 2 as an objective picture of sharing. While Zerilli would not state the problem in exactly this way, I believe we can fruitfully make sense of her critique by thinking in these terms. Feminists tend to make three assumptions in particular that are characteristic of an objective picture of sharing.

First of all, as Zerilli suggests, underlying the essentialist/antiessentialist dynamic in feminism is a commitment to seeing identity claims as epistemological.[16] The tendency of much feminist theorizing has been to challenge various attempts to define women: this extends from projects that critique patriarchal notions of gender roles to the internal critiques of feminists who find that feminism does not hold up to its own standard of inclusion. Zerilli identifies this tendency with skepticism: "Important strands of contemporary feminism employ the skeptic's deceptively simple question, 'How do you know?' to unsettle the sedimented certainties of life, one of which is that 'there are men and women in the world.'"[17] Feminists have challenged existing conceptions of "women" by making epistemological arguments, by challenging our ability to know who is a woman and who is not. Such arguments have ranged from those contesting the biological sameness of women to those contesting the shared "woman's voice."[18] Many of these arguments defend a different kind of knowledge: one that is more attuned to the diversity among women, for example. Yet even these claims to more specialized, contextualized knowledge are open to the skeptical critique: How do you know that all Latinas share certain experiences? This generates the dynamic of essentialist inclusion countered by antiessentialist critique of exclusion: every claim to knowledge is met with a corresponding skeptical doubt.[19]

Furthermore, this approach to identity presumes that what gives identities meaning and coherence is a commonality shared among group members. In other words, collective identity is a matter of classification. Think about the language feminists often use to talk about gender identity: they are concerned with the *category* of women. Women constitute a category or a class—this language already sets us up to think about collective identities as implying some kind of commonality. One important consequence of seeing identity in this way is that it makes our identification seem passive.[20] I am a woman regardless of whether I identify myself as a woman, and regardless of whether you identify me as a woman. It is simply an objective and observable fact about me; it has nothing to do with how I or other subjects experience my identity. Because identity is grounded in commonalities, we have only to figure out what they are, and then we can reliably classify people. False classifications—such as ones that characterize women inaccurately by reference to characteristics like biology or femininity that are not shared—may be politically motivated. But the class of women has an objective, nonpoliticized, true meaning. Conversely, if we cannot locate commonality, then the meaning of "women" is incoherent and entirely contingent. For some antiessentialist feminists, the idea that there is nothing in common to ground the category of women is to be celebrated: it means we are free to make of gender whatever we want.[21] This celebration of the groundlessness of gender, ironically, is also invested in the idea that meaning is grounded by commonality: it is because commonality is absent that the meaning of "women" is underdetermined and contingent.

The final assumption that feminist theorists tend to make is that claims about identity have the status of truth claims.[22] By a truth claim, I mean a claim that commands or compels assent because it declares itself to be true. Such claims purport to being uncontestable; if you disagree with a truth claim, you are in essence denying reality. And since truth claims compel universal agreement, they are claims that aspire to settle debates once and for all. When feminists make essentialist or antiessentialist claims about the category of women, their claims tend to be empirical or descriptive: this is what women are. Such claims are meant to correspond to reality. When confronted with a reality that does not fit the claim, it is difficult for the claimant to reconcile this with what she held to be the truth about the world. It is worth noting here that at the peak of the debates about the category of women, many essentialist feminists expressed unusually strong reactions against antiessentialist theories and tendencies: it is difficult for some to accept the antiessentialist critiques of gender identity because it simply *must* be the case that women have something in common.[23] Among antiessentialists, the disjuncture between theory and reality has resulted in an odd split-personality reaction: strategic essentialism. The strategic feminist posits antiessentialist views of gender in theory (since she knows the truth—that the category of women has no coherent center), yet she advocates a strategic assertion of an essentialist identity in politics (since she nonetheless needs to keep invoking "women" as if this word has meaning in order to achieve her political goals).[24] Her ordinary use of the word "women" does not unsettle her theoretical faith that there is no such thing as "women." I suggest that we read these two reactions as symptomatic of the investment of many feminists in the truth of the claims they make about gender: when confronted with evidence or situations that challenge their views, they have a tendency to cling steadfastly to their original positions on gender identity, since they must be true.

Essentialists and antiessentialists alike can be understood in this way to share the view that identity claims are claims to true knowledge whose meaningfulness derives from an underlying commonality. This view of identity has troubling political consequences. When we conceive of identity as something that we can know and get right once and for all, then we end up with a choice between two undesirable options: either we continue searching in the vain hope that we will succeed where many others have not and discover the true essence of our identity, or we resign ourselves to the incoherence of the subject of feminist politics. Neither choice is compelling.

DOING IDENTITY

Zerilli's response to feminism's preoccupation with the subject question contains important insights for democratic theory. She develops an account of gender identity that goes beyond both essentialism and antiessentialism by jettisoning the presumption that collective identities must be grounded in knowable commonality. She turns instead to look at what we do, how we actually use the category of women. When we examine what feminists do, she finds that neither essentialism nor antiessentialism seems to accord with feminist practice. Feminists cannot agree on what "women" have in common, yet they do not and cannot abandon the category altogether. Antiessentialists can deconstruct the category of women and show that "women" lacks an essence, yet this term still has meaning and use for feminists. We cannot simply stop using the word after having acknowledged that it lacks an essence. Even after the most blistering of antiessentialist critiques, we still find it possible to talk meaningfully about women.

Consider arguments that attempt to show that there is no clear biological division between men and women, that in fact a certain percentage of the population is intersexed.[25] Even if via "logical argument, epistemic justification, or scientific verification"[26] we come to accept that the division of society into males and females is a fraud, it is not clear how our doubts about men and women would come out in practice. Our doubts would be insufficient to unseat our belief that there are men and women in the world. When we look at a room full of people, we instantaneously see them as male or female, without even thinking about it.[27] While it is not inconceivable that we could be trained to recognize five sexes or more, it is not suddenly within our easy grasp the moment we see that evidence proves sexual difference is plural. As Zerilli notes, the problem is not one of the intellect; I can be completely convinced of the scientific evidence of intersexed people and yet still not be able to see people in this way. "Rather," Zerilli writes, "the difficulty is a problem of the will: I realize that my belief (in two sexes) is groundless, but I am still captivated by a 'picture' in which the existence of two sexes constitutes my world view, the frame of reference within which I act."[28] Antiessentialism, then, fails to give us the resources to understand the persistence of our belief in gender and other categories of identity, and it fails to provide the strength of will necessary to reimagine our form of life without these beliefs. "It is entirely possible to read about the intersexed populations and still 'know how to go on' with the language-game of two sexes."[29]

By examining how we do gender, Zerilli offers a new way of conceptualizing gender identity, one that starts with markedly different assumptions from those of essentialists and antiessentialists. First, she notes that gender is something that we do without knowing what it is. Gender is not properly conceived as an object of knowledge. It is, rather, something about which we are certain.[30] We can know propositions, but we are certain about beliefs. We do not learn gender and sex difference as a series of propositions about the world, and so we cannot unlearn them through a new set of propositions.[31] Gender and sex are instead "part of a world-picture that

I inherited."[32] My belief that there are men and women in the world is thus an "utterly groundless belief,"[33] which cannot be unseated simply by learning about the biological diversity of those we call men and women. Gender identity is a part of the web of background assumptions that together form my view of the world.

This in turn means that gender's meaning is not secured by what features men or women have in common but rather by a whole series of interrelated background assumptions. As Zerilli describes it, "Piece by piece a system forms, then, in which we come to hold our beliefs in two sexes (male and female) and in two genders (man and woman), beliefs that, because they lend each other mutual support, are far more resistant to doubt than we 'gender-troublerians' seem to think: sex supports gender, gender supports sex, and both are supported by what lies around them."[34] Gender's meaning for us is held in place not by a single proposition but by many different, overlapping beliefs. Paraphrasing Wittgenstein, Zerilli writes:

> Should one of my definitions be called into question—say, a female human being has two X chromosomes—is it not the case that I have, so to speak, a whole series of props in readiness, and am ready to lean on one if another should be taken from me and vice versa? How much of what I think a female human being is must be proved false for me to give up my definitions as false? The point is that there is no fixed point at which I'd have to abandon my definitions, though I may well abandon them at some point. I use the concept "female" (like any other concept) without fixed meaning.[35]

Antiessentialist skepticism cannot get us to give up on our belief that there are men and women in the world because this belief does not rely on any one definition of what men and women are, but rather on a complex worldview that continues to hold our belief in place.[36] Gender's meaning is not secured by the commonality among men or women but rather by its place in the dynamic web of background assumptions about the world that informs what we do. In fact, as Zerilli puts it, "Male/female (sex) and man/woman (gender) belong to a system of reference in which, paradoxical as it sounds, their stability derives from their contingency and relative plasticity."[37] If sex and gender were based on fixed propositions, then it would be possible to isolate and eliminate them from the web of background assumptions. Sex and gender, however, can be stable precisely because they are plastic: we can discover new knowledge about how sex is manifested biologically, and yet this does not unseat our belief in gender because we can quickly shift or adapt our other assumptions to compensate.

To help illustrate this point, Zerilli invokes the following comparison: "Imagine discovering that you are a brain in a vat, and you will begin to appreciate what the collapse of our two-sex hinge propositions would look like."[38] What might happen if I were to discover that I were a brain in a vat? All the assumptions I make about the world that are connected to the assumption that I am embodied in a particular way would be called into question. I would no longer be able to trust my sensory perceptions, and I would not be able to trust people who interacted with me as if I inhabited a full human body. Yet still other aspects of my worldview would have to alter: it would be incoherent, for example, for me to value appearance or body image in the same way (why shave my legs if I do not have any?). It might be difficult for me to see myself as a particular kind of autonomous being, if I were dependent upon machines and other agents for my survival in the vat. Indeed, I would have to rethink the very idea of agency itself, given my inability to move or speak in the ways I once thought ordinary. The further we think about this example, the more of our assumptions about the world come crashing down, as if they were all connected to one another in a kind of web.

It is this web that Zerilli has in mind when she talks about gender. When we challenge one proposition, it does not alter our belief that there are men and women in the world, because this belief is held in place by the other, interrelated strands of the web. Gender's meaning, then, is secured not by the commonality among men or women but rather by its place in our worldview, in our background assumptions about the world that inform what we do. To adopt a Wittgensteinian turn of phrase, the meaning of gender is its use. We see that gender is meaningful because it comes out in complex, interrelated practices that reveal that it is a part of our worldview.

Claims about gender identity, therefore, cannot have the status of truth claims. Because gender is held in place not by a single proposition but by a worldview, any claims about women cannot be claims to the truth but only claims to a particular way of seeing the world. These are political claims: claims that woo assent (rather than command it), and claims that are contestable because they are partial. Zerilli writes, "To make a [political] claim is to speak for someone and to someone. It is to assert one's power to make claims and the predicative power of one's words, and say 'This is how I see the world.' I may assume or anticipate your agreement, but I expect you will tell me how you see it."[39] Political claims "are inevitably partial and thus exclusive."[40] So, we should not be surprised when claims to speak for and about women produce refusals. "Acting politically," Zerilli argues, "is about testing the limits of every claim to community; it is about positing agreement and discovering what happens when that agreement breaks down or simply fails to materialize in the first place."[41] We cannot know until after we make our claim whether others will agree.

Zerilli's account of gender identity thus counters the three assumptions of feminist theorists caught in the essentialism/antiessentialism dynamic: (1) Gender is a matter of belief, not knowledge. It is part of the web of background assumptions that inform our worldview and are manifested through our social practices. (2) Gender derives its meaning and coherence from the overlapping ways in which it is used in social practices rather than from common characteristics shared among members. (3) Therefore, claims about gender have the status of political claims: unlike truth claims, they are partial, they seek assent, and they are contestable. In what follows, I show that we can develop Zerilli's argument by taking these propositions as general claims about collective identity. In so doing, I am consciously working against her purposes. Her hope is to direct feminist politics away from its preoccupation with identity and toward freedom. For my part, I do not see the activity of making and contesting claims to identity as at odds with political freedom. While I agree with Zerilli that feminist theorists should move beyond their preoccupation with identity, this does not mean that we should avoid politicizing and claiming identities altogether. On the contrary, the lesson I take from the reconceptualization of identity in Zerilli's work is that we should understand and embrace claims to identity as one of many possible expressions of political freedom. Just as Zerilli rethinks gender to help feminism out of the subject question, I turn next to rethink the demos in order to move democratic theory beyond its preoccupation with what we share. Understanding claims about the identity of the demos as political claims is thus the first step toward a freedom-oriented democracy.

IMAGINING IDENTITY

Identity, according to Zerilli, is a kind of doing. In particular, drawing on Hannah Arendt and Cornelius Castoriadis, she suggests that identity arises from the human faculty of imagination. We could say, then, that identity is a kind of active imagining. This is why we cannot simply debunk a conception of gender identity: evidence that contradicts how we think about gender does not alter our belief in gender because it is a matter not of knowledge but of imagination—of how we make sense of the world. What, then, does it mean to think of imagining as a kind of doing?

Imagination, in the classic Kantian formulation, is the faculty by which the human mind makes something present that is absent.[42] For Immanuel

Kant, imagination can be either productive or reproductive.[43] *Reproductive imagination* involves making present in the mind an "image" of something that the imaginer has experienced before. This could be, for example, remembering a person whom one has already met. *Productive imagination*, however, involves making present in the mind an "image" of something the imaginer has never experienced. Even in this case, however, the material used by the imagination to produce a new image for the mind itself all comes from some experience. As Arendt illustrates, "It produces, for instance, the centaur out of the given: the horse and the man."[44] To these two kinds of imagination, Castoriadis adds *radical imagination*: making present in the mind something that has no relationship to what has been experienced before. Radical imagination, he argues, "gives rise creatively to the newly thinkable."[45] This is the kind of imagination that, for Zerilli, enables us to change how we see the world, to think about the world in new ways. To put it in Arendtian terms, this is the faculty that enables us to engage in world-building.

Imagination is not opposed to reality. Rather, imagination is the faculty by which we produce our sense of what is real. Our reality is composed of a web of what Castoriadis calls "social imaginary significations": "for instance: spirits, gods, God; *polis*, citizen, nation, state, party; commodity, money, capital, interest rate; taboo, virtue, sin; and so forth."[46] These are imaginary, he says, "because they do not correspond to, or are not exhausted by, references to 'rational' or 'real' elements and because it is through a *creation* that they are posited."[47] That is, humans add imagination to the world; we give meaning to what we perceive, and we create significations that do not correspond to what is simply present in the observable world. We share imaginaries intersubjectively—they are social—and this, as I argued in the previous chapter, is what constitutes reality. Imagination, far from being opposed to the real, is what makes our experience of the real possible.

Castoriadis distinguishes between the "instituting social imaginary" and the "instituted social imaginary."[48] The instituting social imaginary is an act of radical imagination, "a power of creation, a *vis formandi*, immanent to human collectivities as well as to individual human beings."[49] When we exercise the radical imagination, we create "new forms of being," such as "language, institution qua institution, music and painting; or . . . some specific form, some work of art, be it musical, pictorial, poetic or other."[50] Yet we use imagination not just when we bring something new into being but also when we are sustaining what is already. Castoriadis writes, "Once created, both imaginary social significations and institutions crystallize, or solidify, and that is what I call the *instituted social imaginary*."[51] The institution of an imaginary, then, is its manifestation in social practices. Without being expressed in practice, an imaginary cannot be sustained. We imagine and enact imaginaries again and again through social practices. The instituted social imaginary is thus the exercise of productive and reproductive imagination: here, imagination through its activity sustains significations and institutions that are already available to the mind and to society.

This approach to identity suggests that it is a doing in two ways. First, it is something that humans *do* in the sense that we do the work of imagining identity. Radical thinkers might present us with new imaginaries that make it possible for us to think differently about who we are than we have done in the past. This is one way of thinking about the Elizabeth Eckford photos discussed in chapter 2: they made it possible for Americans to create new social imaginaries.[52] Humans do the work of reimagining identity when they create new forms of "women" or "American." Yet we are also doing the work of imagining when we conform to an existing, instituted imaginary, when we reinforce it through our thinking. The second way in which identity is a doing is that identities, once instituted, require active participation in the institutions in which they are expressed. By institutions, Castoriadis means to include not only formal organizations but also "language, customs, norms, and technique."[53] Imaginaries are instituted in both formal and informal social practices. These social practices require our active participation to be sustained. In other words, imaginaries can die out from neglect. Collective identity, then, is a doing insofar as it cannot have reality for us without us doing the work of imagining it as such, and without us doing the work of engaging in the practices that keep that imaginary alive.

I turn to Anderson's work to illustrate the role human imagination plays in creating and reproducing the identity of the demos. He, of course, is concerned not specifically with democratic forms of community but with nations. The nation, he argues, is an "imagined political community."[54] "It is *imagined*," he writes, "because the members of even the smallest nation will never know most of their fellow-members, meet them, or even hear of them, yet in the minds of each lives the image of their communion."[55] That is, we have to imagine the nation because it is a form of community that we cannot ever directly experience. It is something that cannot ever be present to the mind without our imagining it. "In fact," he notes, "all communities larger than primordial villages of face-to-face contact (and perhaps even these) are imagined."[56] And so, whether or not the demos is imagined as a nation, it is usually an imagined community.

To illustrate the role imagination plays in collective identity, let me recount a particular example Anderson gives of imagined community: the example of the failed attempt to establish Indochina as a nation. Indochina was the deliberate creation of French colonial administration. It had no existence as a unit prior to 1887. It was composed of a variety of peoples, whose various histories, cultures, and languages connected them to China or to Siam—but not to each other. And yet, Anderson notes that "for one generation of relatively well educated adolescents, the curious hybrid 'Indochine' had a real, experienced, imagined meaning."[57] How was this possible? Without any preexisting commonalities, how did these "relatively well educated adolescents" come to see themselves meaningfully as Indochinese?

Anderson's answer is that the identity of "Indochine" was reflected in real experiences, or in the language I have been using here, social practices. In particular, the colonial administration set up an educational system in the early twentieth century that gave Indochina reality for those who took part in it. This system aimed to produce a native elite capable of speaking and reading French to serve in particular in the colonial bureaucracy.[58] However, because there were a limited number of upper-level schools and only one university, the students who advanced in this school system converged in the same few places. Here, they had classmates who were Vietnamese, Laotian, and Khmer; by coming together, they experienced Indochina as real. These face-to-face interactions with other Indochinese in turn facilitated the imagining of a community beyond the schools. For those "relatively well educated adolescents" trained by this educational system, then, "'Indochine' had a real, experienced, imagined meaning."

We can see in this case an example of how collective identity is expressed through practices, through activities that give the identity meaning to the participants. These practices must be sustained in order for the identity to continue to have meaning. The Indochinese identity failed to take root beyond this one generation of students because the educational system was altered significantly, disrupting the pattern of convergence at the upper levels of schooling. In order to preserve spots in the schools for French children, additional schools were added with elementary schooling in vernacular languages, which emphasized the reality of linguistic divisions among those designated collectively as Indochinese.[59] The number of high schools increased, making it possible for students to get an advanced education without traveling around Indochina and meeting others from different ethnic groups.[60] And the bureaucracy for which many of the school system's graduates were destined offered different opportunities for members of different ethnic groups. Vietnamese—favored by the French colonialists—were able to gain appointments throughout Indochina, which therefore had for them "a rather solid meaning."[61] Members of other ethnic groups, however, returned from their studies to their "home" regions and had "very limited career prospects" beyond them.[62] This encouraged identification instead with their regions and undermined the sense of a greater Indochinese community. By 1947, "A new generation was coming on the scene for whom 'Indochine' was history and 'Vietnam' now a real and foreign country."[63] These altered practices made the Indochinese identity less relevant for those who might once have identified with it, and they made new identities more relevant.

The meaningfulness of a claim to identity rests upon social practices that make such a claim intelligible. Prior to the colonial organization of the region into Indochina, and the establishment of an Indochinese educational system, claims to be Indochinese could not possibly be meaningful. Similarly, now that the practices of the French colonial government have ceased, it would be meaningless for someone living in Cambodia, say, to claim to be Indochinese. That is, we could understand the words "I am Indochinese," but it would be unclear how we should then respond to such a claim. It would be as if someone claimed to be a citizen of the Roman Empire: we would likely take them to be joking, or perhaps mentally unstable. Without corresponding somehow to live, ongoing practices, claims to identity cease to be meaningful.

Put in another way, identity is intersubjective, not voluntaristic: I cannot simply claim an identity for myself. Or I could, but this would in no way guarantee that such a claim would have meaning for others. Think again of the argument that there are five sexes. It is not enough to point to the scientific evidence and say that there are five sexes. In order for there to be five sexes in any meaningful sense, our belief in their existence must come out somehow in practice. We cannot call new identities into being simply by naming them; they must be rooted in social practices, which means they must be able to have significance not only for the person who names them but also for others. To put this in Arendtian terms, a claim to identity requires confirmation by other subjects in order to have intersubjective validity.

So the practices that sustain an identity and give it meaning must be recognizable by at least some others to have significance. In cases like that of Indochinese in which a new identity is introduced, this may mean that the identity must have some correspondence to new practices, practices that represent a distinct rupture with the past. The educational system in Indochina was designed to break political and cultural ties with China and Siam. It did so, for example, by introducing a Romanized phonetic script and abolishing Confucian examinations previously required for entry into the bureaucracy.[64] In such cases, the meaning of an identity for others will depend upon their access to these new practices. Anderson notes that

"Indochine" had meaning for those who went through the school system—but not really for any other inhabitants of Indochina. In other cases where the transformation of an existing identity is at issue—as, for example, in debates about what it means to be a woman or an American—the new practices in question often trade on their relationship to already existing practices in order to be intelligible.

Now I have said that "at least some others" must be able to recognize a claim to identity. How many others? One? Two? Thousands? Everyone? There is no formula we could give here that would settle the question, as if there were a magic number that makes an identity meaningful.[65] I will, however, make two suggestions about how we might begin to tackle such a problem. First, the target audience of the performance of identity matters. Within Indochinese schools, for example, it may be sufficient for the identity to have meaning if simply a few hundred other students recognize its performance as meaningful. However, when those same students return to their hometowns upon graduation, the recognition of their fellow students might no longer be sufficient. Am I successful in my performance of an identity? It depends on what my goals are, who my audience is, with whom I am engaged in these practices. My lifestyle choices (e.g., pursuing a career and having no children) may be recognizable as a legitimate performance of being a woman among the people with whom I regularly associate, but this in no way means that everyone would concur. Does that disagreement matter? Sometimes, but usually not. A second way of responding to the problem would be to say that social beings, if they have mastered the practices of their society, know when a claim to identity is meaningful and when it is not.[66] What it means to be socialized is to know when such a claim is meaningful.

The practices in which identity is manifest are often overlapping, inconsistent, and even contradictory. In other words, it is not necessary for all the practices that support a particular identity to be contiguous and mutually reinforcing. That may happen, but it is not a necessary characteristic of identity. This is what enables people to share an identity and yet disagree over its meaning and over who ought to be included in its claim. But this is also what gives some identities resilience—the more complex the practices are that sustain it, the harder it is to dismantle or alter—like gender. Gender may not correspond exactly to the practice of determining sex difference, but noting this disjuncture does not undermine gender, since gender is propped up by any number of other practices. This suggests that when an identity is supported only by a limited number of practices, it may be much easier to alter or dismantle altogether. We could hypothesize, for example, that the Indochinese identity could not overcome the effects of the mid-twentieth-century changes to the educational system because it had not had much time to find expression in other practices—such as intermarriage among ethnic groups, a more egalitarian bureaucratic system, and practices that would promote the identity among the masses. Once the practice of sharing schools was altered, the identity began to lose its significance because it had no other practices to rely on instead. Contrary to what an essentialist might argue, this would suggest that an identity resting on a single commonality is in fact more unstable than an identity that has no distinct core but instead relies upon multiple, overlapping practices. Indeed, the very strength of a society may lie in the multiplicity of ways that its members can identify with and participate in it. As the epigraph to this chapter suggests, "The strength of the thread does not reside in the fact that some one fibre runs through its whole length, but in the overlapping of many fibres."[67] Thus, when one practice is eliminated or altered, others may stand fast.

Finally, if identities are held in place by multiple, overlapping, and sometimes competing practices, then any one claim to a particular identity is unlikely to capture every possible aspect of that identity. This is probably more true of complex identities like gender that find expression in many different practices than of simpler identities like Indochinese that are manifest in only a few practices. For identities like "women" and "Americans" it is impossible to locate a single characteristic common to all of the social practices that sustain them. And so, any claim about the content of such identities will inevitably be partial. Because these claims are partial, they are best understood as political: they involve a normative choice that privileges one conception of identity against others where there is no objective measure of which conception is the "right" one. Accordingly, our claims to identity are contestable because we cannot prove them to be true; we can only seek to persuade others of the validity of our views. In this way, identities produced by multiple and discontinuous practices call themselves into question. They generate a potentially infinite back-and-forth between assertions and denials of identity. That is, they produce claims of inclusion and exclusion that appear to mimic the essentialist/antiessentialist dynamic yet are not locked in its epistemological framework.

DEMOCRATIC IDENTITY AND COMMONALITY

With this revised understanding of collective identity in mind, we are now in a position to revisit the assumption in democratic theory that political unity is a product of commonality. Collectivities, in this view, are united by what they share in common. And democracy is government by a particular collectivity: the people. Therefore, the logic of this assumption is that we can secure the identity of the people by locating what they do or should have in common with one another. In this way, the commonality gives meaning and coherence to the idea of rule by "the people": it tells us who the people are—those who share *x* in common.

Yet, drawing on Zerilli and working through Anderson, I have offered a very different account of collective identity. Identities are produced not by the passive fact of commonality but by the active doing of human agents. Humans imagine collectivities, and they reinforce the reality of imagined community through engaging in practices with others who seem to imagine the same community. A single commonality is at best insufficient, and at worst an unstable ground for a collective identity. It is insufficient because humans must come to see that commonality as meaningful, and express this meaning in what they do; the commonality alone cannot produce identity. It is unstable as a ground because it is the proliferation of a diversity of practices—rather than convergence on a single set of commonalities—that ensures the coherence and resilience of an identity over time. We need therefore to reconceptualize the identity of the people not as resting on a shared set of characteristics but as arising through the richness of competing, overlapping, inconsistent, contradictory, and perhaps only occasionally convergent practices that give the identity meaning and relevance to those who would claim it.

One might object that, in the case of the identity of the demos, we do in fact have a single social practice that settles the question of who "we, the people" are: the state establishes civic identity by according citizenship and its attendant rights and duties. But why should we expect the category of citizenship to exhaust the identity of the demos? The question of who has citizenship does not settle the question of who "we" are in any final way. In particular contexts (e.g., at a border crossing), citizenship may indeed answer the question "Who is an American?" But just as biological sex does not exhaust the meaning of gender (even though it may offer criteria for deciding whether newborns count as male or female), citizenship does not exhaust the meaning of democratic identity; these may be powerful markers, but they are unable to end the debate. After all, the question of who is an American arises every day in contexts in which citizenship status is well established. A Muslim woman who veils, a legal Hispanic immigrant with a thick Spanish accent, an antiwar protestor, a mixed-race president born in Hawaii, and a Republican senator who proposes cuts to Medicaid and Medicare—all can find their Americanness called into question, whatever their passport says. There is no way to institutionally settle the question of who is an American once and for all; that is, there is no way to make it entirely immune to antiessentialist doubt.

On the contrary, rather than settling the question of who "we" are through establishing who counts as a citizen and who does not, democracy itself troubles the demos. Democracy is, in Jacques Derrida's words, "unpresentable."[68] It is impossible to fully realize democracy in practice because democracy is characterized by competing demands. Any attempt to realize democracy will therefore be incomplete and will be open to critique in the name of democracy itself. Derrida explains:

> One will never actually be able to "prove" that there is more democracy in granting or in refusing the right to vote to immigrants, notably those who live and work in the national territory, nor that there is more or less democracy in a straight majority vote as opposed to proportional voting; both forms of voting are democratic, and yet both also protect their democratic character through exclusion. . . . One electoral law is thus always at the same time more and less democratic than another.[69]

Any attempt to realize democracy is itself open to critique in the name of democracy. Another way to put this is that, for Derrida, democracy is best understood not as a form of government but as a call to self-critique.[70]

In the case of the identity of the demos, democracy produces competing demands for inclusion and exclusion that cannot be conclusively resolved. A commitment to democratic principles, for example, calls state borders into question: if we believe in liberty and equality for all, then we should be concerned about the welfare not only of American citizens but of all people. Similarly, if we think that the United States has institutionalized freedom in an important way, we should want to open our borders and let others participate in our democracy. Yet this tendency toward inclusion is matched by an equally "democratic" demand for exclusion. We should not meddle in other people's affairs, since that would violate their right to self-government. We cannot open our borders because the flood of immigrants would undermine our ability to pursue freedom and equality for those who are already here. Democracy produces an infinite set of challenges to itself, perpetually calling itself into question.

In other words, democracy fuels the dynamic of political claims to inclusion and critiques of exclusion we see reflected in the essentialist/antiessentialist dynamics in feminist and democratic theory.[71] Theorists are responding to a feature of democratic politics: that we cannot settle the question of who "we" are, and yet our commitment to democracy drives us to try to come up with more justifiable (yet ultimately contestable) bases for including some and excluding others. Even in democracies that believe they have settled the matter of identity, it can always arise again—it is in the very structure of democracy to call into question the identity of the demos.

The persistence of disagreement about who "we" are, then, is not a sign that "we" lack a center and therefore do not constitute a coherent subject of political action, but rather it is an expected and unavoidable part of practicing democracy. As long as a collective identity is experienced by some people as real, we will not be able to end contestation over its meaning. But this is only a problem for those who believe that identities must be grounded in commonalities. Those concerned with "the subject question" see the contestation generated by complex identities and intensified by democracy, and misunderstand it as a debate about what "we" really share. Their hopes that we can discover the truth of identity will always be disappointed because complex collective identities like "woman" and "American" are grounded in multiple, overlapping, and discontinuous practices. We need to treat our claims to identity, therefore, as political claims—as partisan claims about how we should understand identity, as partisan claims about which practices should continue to sustain that identity, and which should be altered or discontinued altogether.

Democratic theorists and actors alike should aim, then, not at trying to identify what is or should be the core of our shared identity but rather at perpetuating the debate over what it means. This is sharing identity with others: recognizing that our claims to identity cannot be sovereign because they are contestable. The best we can do is to persuade others to agree with us; we cannot expect or demand their agreement. The crisis for democracy is not when we do not share anything in common; it is rather when we do not find it worthwhile to engage in this debate; when, like the Indochinese or the Romans, the practices that sustain our conflicting beliefs about a shared identity fall into disuse.

Instead of trying to locate commonality, we should be proliferating competing, overlapping, and not entirely contiguous claims to identity. The resilience of identity comes from the plurality of claims we can make to it. So we should also actively resist letting any one claim to the demos become hegemonic—even one that we would endorse. If I am right to read the Indochinese example as I do, then the hegemony of any one way of thinking about an identity renders it a thin and fragile locus of identification. Moreover, when we are not mindful of the plurality of ways of imagining and practicing democratic identity, that identity risks becoming naturalized. That is, we are more likely to perceive a given identity as natural, as the inevitable result of the commonality we share, when we lose sight of its partiality and contingency. This is dangerous because it reinforces the objective picture of sharing: that sharing identity is a matter of passively having something in common, and not a matter of active human imagining. And so it risks being depoliticizing: disavowing human agency and discouraging intentional participation in practices of world-building. We need to experience and encourage conflicting claims to identity in order to stay mindful that we can contest these claims and imagine the demos anew.

At this point, my argument might sound to some like an echo of Rogers Smith's argument in *Stories of Peoplehood*, and in many ways it is. In that book, Smith offers a democratic vision in which a multiplicity of stories of how we constitute a people compete with and check one another in the public sphere. He urges us to "welcome a whole range of particularistic ethically constitutive stories, advancing visions of subgroups, national communities, and transnational associations, into political debate, while also encouraging robust and honest criticism of their claims, especially when they threaten democracy and human rights."[72] In fact, it is precisely stories that are not quite contiguous with the status quo, but present alternative imaginaries, that he is most eager to include in public discourse.[73] He acknowledges that our stories of peoplehood are always partial and partisan,[74] that they are not grounded in truth,[75] and that they must be expressed not only in imagination but also in institutions.[76] In many respects, Smith and I are in agreement. Yet what I am arguing for extends beyond what he calls for, and in ways that he would likely resist.

First, I embrace and invite contestation over political identity as an end in itself, and not as a means to produce any particular outcome. Smith, by contrast, hopes by promoting "a politics of contestation among multiple constitutive stories of peoplehood"[77] to moderate extreme views and increase political stability.[78] I contend that the outcome of contesting claims to identity is unpredictable and beyond our ability to control: we cannot know in advance which views will prove to be persuasive; we cannot know in advance whether our interlocutors will even take up our challenges. Insofar as how we do identity is through making a multiplicity of not entirely contiguous claims about it, expressed in and through varied practices, I argue we should embrace this phenomenological condition. We should seek to act in a way that is consistent with how we actually do identity, instead of accepting naturalizing and depoliticizing myths about who we are.

Additionally, I include in my account of imaginaries and practices of identity a great deal more than what can be characterized as "stories of peoplehood." What concerns Smith are first-person narratives that we tell about who we are as a people. These are more or less intentional, consciously articulated stories, some even with a historical beginning and end. In my account of identity, however, I include a variety of practices that we engage in which may not be intentional or conscious, but which may not (but could) be articulated as a part of a story that we tell about ourselves. So for the Indochinese, participation in the school system was important to experiencing that identity as real, yet in order to function in this way, it need not have been part of an explicit story about Indochinese identity. The "story of the Indochinese people" propagated by the colonial state, I imagine, was not told as a narrative of elite teenagers being educated together to enter into the bureaucracy. Social practices can express and sustain an identity without being acknowledged in the narratives we tell about ourselves. We might also think here of practices of Americanness that are so ordinary we participate in them unthinkingly. These include practices that we take for granted, but which come to light when we travel abroad or host a foreign visitor: for example, our emphasis on customer service, our style of dress, or our structural dependence on cars (and big cars at that). What I am including here, then, in my understanding of identity, is a wide range of practices that constitute us as us whether or not we note them in our explicit stories of peoplehood.

Finally, I take this contestation over who "we" are to be radically democratic, in that it is open, in principle, to anyone. Here, the difference between Smith and me could not be starker. Smith conceptualizes peoplehood as something that is primarily generated in a top-down manner. He argues that "it is actual and would-be leaders who most directly articulate and seek to institutionalize conceptions of political peoplehood."[79] "Mass publics," by contrast, "rarely if ever act consciously to create a new form of political community unless they are organized to do so through mobilizing leaders."[80] Even as he notes that both "leaders and constituents generally experience themselves as having meaningful agency in the forms of peoplehood they imagine, articulate, endorse, and institutionalize," Smith treats leaders as having an asymmetric capacity to set the agenda: the masses only have the comparatively limited agency to choose among those stories that their leaders offer them as options.[81] While he acknowledges that ordinary people have a role to play in endorsing or rejecting particular stories, I am concerned that his focus on leadership leads him to underestimate this role. As I have argued, through imagination and through engaging in practices ranging from the mundane to the exceptional, people do the work of producing and reproducing identities. An identity claim that is asserted from the top down, that is not embraced as real by the people whom it is meant to include, will fail. Arguably, the failure of Indochinese identity is just this: that it was not embraced by ordinary people. Yet if, with Smith, we recognize the mundane and often unthinking work people do to reproduce identities, we must also recognize that people have the capacity to alter the practices in which they participate, to resist existing imaginaries, and even to reimagine identities and institutions. We have this capacity not as leaders but simply by virtue of being imaginative beings with the capacity to shape the world we share with one another.

And so, when I draw attention to the work people ordinarily do in imagining identity, the demos, and the world, I am claiming for humans a broad capacity for democratic political agency. As I argued in chapter 2, how we make sense of the world, how through our imaginations and our interactions we give the world meaning, is a political matter. Humans exercise this capacity to sustain and build an intersubjectively shared world through activities that range from the seemingly mundane to the explicitly political. Just as gender is held in place by the division of labor in the home, by what we wear, and by how we sit, American identity is held in place by measuring distances in miles, by speaking particular dialects of English, and by celebrating Thanksgiving in November with a generous turkey dinner. To draw attention to the human activity of imagining democratic community and to the myriad practices that hold the identity of the demos in place is to take a view of political agency that is more in line with the tradition of feminist—than democratic—theory. Second Wave feminists famously declared that "the personal is political"—and in so doing, they invited us to see many of our imaginaries and practices that had hitherto been unacknowledged or treated as natural, as instead sites of the exercise of power. They called on us to be self-conscious about the practices in which we participate, to examine which "personal" practices sustained inequality, injustice, and unfreedom for women. It is in this feminist spirit that I call attention to the role that human activity plays in generating the conditions of democracy and, in this chapter specifically, the role it plays in producing and reproducing imaginaries of the demos.

To radically expand what can be seen as political in this way is to think about political agency in much broader terms than are usually suggested by participatory or direct democrats—and even, perhaps, than are usually suggested by radical democrats. Most political theorists focus on human democratic agency in voting, in running for or holding office, in deliberation, and in voicing opinions in public. I am deliberately pushing beyond this. Contra Smith, then, ordinary people do not have a limited agency in which they must defer to their leaders to present them with options. Rather, I argue that humans already exercise agency by participating in the many seemingly mundane or personal practices that sustain the identity of the demos. If we do the work of imagining the demos, and we do the work of sustaining the practices that give it meaning, then even in the ordinariness of what we do, we have an extraordinary power: to develop an awareness that it is we who create and re-create the meaning of our world, that we do not have to imagine it as we do or participate in the practices that we do, and that we do not have to wait for a leader to imagine the world anew.

The freedom appropriate to democratic politics, then, is the freedom to shape the world in which we live. This is not an individual freedom but an intersubjective one: it is exercised in a world of plural others, and it is limited by how others respond. No one can simply remake the world as they see fit, but we can try to persuade others to see things differently. This is what with Zerilli I call *political freedom*: "the capacity to found new forms of political association."[82]

Insofar as we do the work of imagining the demos and bringing it into being, we bear ethical responsibility for how we imagine it. If the demos, like gender, is not a natural, fixed category, then we are responsible both for how we imagine it now and for how we might imagine it in the future. I turn in the following chapter to reflect on this responsibility by thinking through the problem of democratic affect—that is, the problem of how we might come to care for and feel a sense of obligation toward those with whom we share democracy.

CHAPTER 4

Politicizing the Demos

Sharing Affect as Self-Conscious World-Building

People have a sense of constituting a society or a nationality or, as it were, a nest of communities by living and working and knowing each other in numerous and complex ways, from using the same local shops to reading the same newspapers. . . . A sense of society, of effective as opposed to nominal membership in a shared public culture over and above private and communal affiliations, may be dependent on many different points of contact and on sharing different things with different people. It may be like the philosophically proverbial cord, the strength of which does not depend upon a single thread.
—Tariq Modood[1]

CAUSATION AND CONSTRUCTION

When it comes to the matter of democratic affect, many theorists are caught in a tension between the objective and intersubjective pictures of sharing. On the one hand, they adopt the second corollary assumption that undergirds the belief that democracy requires commonality: the assumption that commonality produces affective bonds. On the other hand, in the very act of positing new sources of democratic affect, they embrace a competing idea: that human beings have the capacity to reimagine their affective ties. Affect, on this view, is not the causal consequence of commonality but a kind of intersubjective, social construction. I want to draw from this literature the insight that humans produce affect, but in order to do so I need first to detach it from the belief that affect is instead the product of commonality. I start to do this by engaging with an unlikely interlocutor—Robert Putnam—whose work lays bare this tension between causation and construction.

In June 2007, Putnam published the long-awaited analysis of his Social Capital Community Benchmark Survey. Putnam, a political scientist whose earlier research focused on Italian politics, turned in this study to the United States in order to examine in more detail the impact of diversity on "social capital"—that is, "social networks and the associated norms of reciprocity and trustworthiness."[2] Social capital, he argues, is what "makes democracy work": democracies require widespread and active participation in voluntary associations in order to build and sustain horizontal bonds of solidarity essential to sharing democratic political institutions.[3] While Putnam had previously studied the effects of social capital in the comparatively homogeneous Italy of the late twentieth century, in this survey, he hoped by turning to the United States to collect extensive data about the impact of ethnic diversity on social networks and trust.

What Putnam found, however, did not sit well with his progressive political leanings. Comparing relatively diverse communities (such as neighborhoods in Los Angeles and small towns like Yakima, Washington) with relatively homogeneous communities (such as rural areas of South Dakota and towns like Lexington, Maine), he discovered that measures of diversity were negatively correlated with measures of social capital. Inferring from the correlation a causal narrative, he concluded that "immigration and ethnic diversity tend to reduce social solidarity and social capital."[4] He released the data set from this survey in 2001, but curiously he did not immediately publish an analysis of it.[5] Over the next five years, he tested a variety of alternative hypotheses, but the results stayed stubbornly the same: the greater the ethnic diversity in a community, the lower the social capital. In 2006, he finally made public his analysis when he delivered the Johan Skytte Prize Lecture. He offered the best progressive take on his data that he could: diversity negatively affects social capital *in the short term*, but in the long term he noted that "successful immigrant societies have overcome such fragmentation by creating new, cross-cutting forms of social solidarity and more encompassing identities."[6] Confining the negative effects of diversity to the nebulous "short term" allowed Putnam to report his findings without having to concede that diversity is wholly bad for democracy.

Putnam's lecture was published in the midst of a wave of scholarship and political commentary claiming that diversity is at odds with trust and solidarity among citizens in contemporary Western democracies.[7] A literature review in 2003 found "a common theme" in recent economic scholarship—that "more-homogeneous communities foster greater levels of social-capital production."[8] One of the studies surveyed noted a negative relationship between racial and ethnic divisions, and the share of resources spent on public goods in American cities.[9] It concluded "that ethnic conflict is an important determinant of local public finances."[10] Another study examined why the United

States did not have the same kind of welfare state policies as many European countries. It found that "racial fragmentation is a powerful predictor of redistribution," and since the United States has a history of intense racial conflict along the black-white divide, "within the United States, race is the single most important predictor of support for welfare."[11] Racial diversity and conflict, then, explain why the United States has significantly lower levels of popular support for welfare state policies than European countries. In Europe, the 1990s and 2000s witnessed increasing anxiety about the relationship between immigration and declining support for the welfare state. Many commentators blamed increased immigration for the decline of the welfare state. A fierce debate flared up in Britain, for example, when in 2004 David Goodhart characterized the problem as "the progressive dilemma": progressives want a strong welfare state, and yet they also call for multiculturalist policies—policies that undermine the common culture necessary to motivate support for redistribution of wealth.[12] The perception that diversity and solidarity are in tension is reinforced by the fact that the European countries whose welfare policies are the most extensive are also the least diverse: Norway, Sweden, and Denmark. A comparative study of trust in sixty countries explained the "Nordic exception" by arguing that "ethnic homogeneity and Protestant traditions seem to have a direct impact on trust, and an indirect one through their consequences for good government, wealth and income equality."[13] It seems that Putnam's findings, far from being controversial, are consistent with the claims of many other scholars and commentators.

While the authors of that last study are careful to note that "cause and effect relations are impossible to specify exactly," not all scholars are so cautious.[14] As I mentioned earlier, Putnam's research establishes a correlation between ethnic diversity and lower levels of social capital, and yet he interprets the data as if it reflects causation: the presence of diversity "seems to affect," "encourages," and "seems to trigger" certain human behaviors.[15] His study cannot offer evidence of causation, since it only provides a snapshot of communities at one particular moment in time.[16] Even so, this does not prevent Putnam from making the claim that diversity causes a decrease in social capital. His attribution of causal agency to "diversity" is echoed in other scholarship as well. For example, Dora Costa and Matthew Kahn, in their review of the literature on social capital and heterogeneity, claim that "heterogeneity lowers social capital" and "homogeneity increases civic participation."[17] These kinds of claims are like the naturalizing claims I discussed in chapter 2 that attribute agency to commonality and correspondingly deflect attention away from the agency of humans: commonality is the agent that causes us to have an identity, solidarity, and a collective will. Putnam's claim has the inverse form: it is the absence of commonality (diversity) that causes us to fail to have solidarity. As I argued earlier, treating the relationship between diversity and commonality, on the one hand, and solidarity, on the other, as if it were a causal one is depoliticizing. It suggests that a decline in social solidarity is the inevitable and unavoidable consequence of increasing diversity; this is to imply that humans themselves bear little or no responsibility for this decline, that whether we feel solidarity has nothing to do with what we do. To put it strongly: solidarity is simply the natural outcome of a demographic condition.

Putnam situates his findings in the context of long-standing debates in the social sciences about "the effects of diversity on social connections"—debates, in other words, that he understands within the frame of the causal logic I have just outlined.[18] On one side of these debates are proponents of the "contact hypothesis," who claim that contact between diverse people fosters interethnic tolerance and increased social solidarity between out-groups—what Putnam calls "bridging" social capital.[19] On the other side are proponents of "conflict theory," who hold that contact between diverse people fosters distrust between out-group members but increased solidarity with in-group members—what he calls "bonding" social capital.[20] Both of these positions, Putnam argues, are committed to the idea that there is a fixed amount of social capital, such that "if I have lots of bonding ties, I must have few bridging ties, and vice versa."[21]

What he finds in his data, however, is that there is no necessary relationship between bridging and bonding. Instead, he observes that increased diversity is correlated with a simultaneous decrease in in-group and out-group solidarity. He derives from this observation the position that he calls "constrict theory": diversity encourages people to constrict all of their social networks.[22] He explains his data thus: "Diversity seems to trigger *not* in-group/out-group division, but anomie or social isolation. In colloquial language, people living in ethnically diverse settings appear to 'hunker down'—that is, to pull in like a turtle."[23] More specifically, when they "hunker down,"

> inhabitants of diverse communities tend to withdraw from collective life, to distrust their neighbors, regardless of the colour of their skin, to withdraw even from close friends, to expect the worst from their community and its leaders, to volunteer less, give less to charity and work on community projects less often, to register to vote less, to agitate for social reform *more*, but have less faith that they can actually make a difference, and to huddle unhappily in front of the television.[24]

Tucked in the middle of that otherwise depressing list where a careless reader might miss it is a seemingly positive observation for democracy that Putnam includes but does not dwell on: that diversity is correlated with increased agitation for social reform. He notes that people in diverse neighborhoods demonstrate "more interest and knowledge about politics and more participation in protest marches and social reform groups."[25] Yet instead of reflecting on why diversity might correlate with an increase in only certain forms of political participation, he goes on to describe people who live in ethnically diverse communities as "paranoid, television-watching introverts"—a description that hardly evokes the image of a politically informed and engaged population, likely to agitate for social reform *more* than other Americans. Perhaps this statistical curiosity does not appear so curious to Putnam because it is at odds with his larger causal narrative: that diversity makes us withdraw from other people, and therefore has a tendency (at least in the short term) to undermine democracy. It is this perceived trend toward social withdrawal that preoccupies Putnam, especially because it seems to threaten his normative commitments to immigration and ethnic diversity. This threat was apparently so great that, as the *Financial Times* reported, he "delayed publishing his research until he could develop proposals to compensate for the negative effects of diversity, saying it 'would have been irresponsible to publish without that.'"[26]

Curiously, though, when Putnam turns to develop these compensatory proposals, he abandons the causal logic of constrict theory in favor of social construction. He argues that "identity itself is socially constructed and can be socially de-constructed and re-constructed."[27] Our sense of who is like us, and who is not, is not natural but instead is a matter of convention. If the boundaries of "in-groups" and "out-groups" are not fixed, but can be "de-constructed and re-constructed," then it is not necessarily a problem for democracy if diversity produces mistrust. All that we need to do is to reconfigure our identities to *redefine* those who are different from us as being like us in some relevant way, and then the tendency to mistrust can be reversed. Putnam, in other words, is offering what I call a minimal response: we need to expand our identity by making it more general and more inclusive. This new, inclusive identity can then be promoted in order to counteract the centrifugal force of diversity. And so he calls for "creating a new, more capacious sense of 'we,' a reconstruction of diversity that does not bleach out ethnic specificities, but creates overarching identities that ensure that those specificities do not trigger the allergic, 'hunker down' reaction."[28] While in the short term, then, we might expect diversity to increase distrust and turtle-like behavior, in the long term, communities can counteract this effect by reconstructing their sense of identity.

In turning to social construction, however, Putnam offers a solution that I argue is in tension with the problem as he has described it. He presents the problem in natural, causal terms: diversity—not a socially constructed diversity, but diversity as such—produces isolation and anomie. Yet his solution is to reveal that identity is always already a product of human activity, which suggests that our behavior is not fully determined by natural laws but is changeable through intentional interventions. The world is one of our making. These two positions are at odds with one another. Putnam, however, does not reflect on how this turn to social construction that helps him out of his progressive dilemma might challenge his causal interpretation of the survey data. Consider that he describes his call for the intentional reconstruction of American identity as "becoming comfortable with diversity."[29] He raises the possibility that we can become more comfortable with difference by redefining who "we" are, but he does not ask: How did Americans become uncomfortable with diversity in the first place? How did we come to see these differences—and not those—as threatening? Consequently, our discomfort with difference remains naturalized in his narrative.[30] It is as if one does not become uncomfortable with diversity, one is born uncomfortable. Yet if we are to take Putnam seriously when he claims that identities are socially constructed, then this should change what we take his study to be measuring. He would no longer be measuring the effects of diversity but the effects of particular, contingent conceptions of identity that frame certain kinds of difference as threatening.[31] If our identities are socially constructed, then it is not diversity that does the work of making us hunker down; it is our socially constructed beliefs about who "we" are that produce the sense that we cannot trust our neighbors. If we agree with Putnam that identities are social constructions, then we cannot blame diversity for our problems; we are the ones who are responsible for hunkering down like turtles.

In a sense, though, Putnam does reconcile his causal and constructivist claims, in favor of the former. The new identity he wants us to construct is one that is broader and therefore more inclusive. Because it is so capacious, it can be "a shared identity" that cuts across racial, ethnic, or religious cleavages that otherwise would be divisive.[32] We counteract diversity by appealing to a more expansive commonality. In other words, his constructivist solution leaves in place the causal logic of his political psychology: diversity causes social withdrawal; commonality produces solidarity. He invokes social construction, then, in the service of what he appears to take as an immutable principle of human psychology. The goal is not to reconstruct identity but to reconstruct identity around a broader, more inclusive commonality, since that will make us trust one another. Putnam's appeal to social construction, in other words, still operates within the logic that commonality produces affect: it is just that humans can select which commonality is operative.

This tension between a naturalized human psychology or nature, on the one hand, and socially constructed affect, on the other, brought into sharp relief in Putnam's Skytte Lecture, emerges more subtly in democratic theory. Taking inspiration from my reading of Putnam, I explore how this tension in democratic theory is related to the belief that commonality can resolve important problems of democratic affect. Democratic affect—whether it goes under the name of civic friendship, fraternity, patriotism, nationalism, or love of country—is an emotional bond between citizens that enables them to share in self-government.[33] The affective ties between citizens help to justify the boundaries of democratic rule: we want to share in government with those people to whom we are attached, and not with those to whom we have no special connection. Moreover, democratic affect is the source of trust between citizens: it enables minorities to accept being in the minority because they trust that the majority acts out of concern for their well-being. It is also the source of solidarity—the willingness to make sacrifices for the sake of the whole. Some kind of democratic affect, then, is a necessary condition for the healthy sharing of self-government. Yet as Patchen Markell has noted, "The affects under consideration are presumptively positive—love, loyalty, and pride."[34] Democratic theorists tend to presume that affect is not only positive but further that it is something that can be controlled and directed. The goal of the theorist is (like Putnam) to figure out the correct commonality that will direct this positive affect toward the support of democracy.

Through readings of democratic affect in David Miller, Jürgen Habermas, and Charles Taylor, I argue that we should reconceptualize democratic affect as grounded not in commonality but in imaginaries of community. These imaginaries are plural, overlapping, and not entirely contiguous, and so they produce bonds of trust and mistrust, of solidarity and indifference that both reinforce and undermine one another. It is this complexity of affect that democratic theorists often appeal to commonality in order to avoid. I call instead for us to embrace it, and for us to engage actively in critically assessing existing imaginaries, and offering new ones—not with the goal of securing democratic affect but with the goal instead of taking responsibility for our part in generating relationships of trust and solidarity. Affect is a doing, it is the product of human activity. It cannot be controlled or reliably directed to the democratic state. Yet it can become the subject of a politics of self-conscious democratic world-building.

The tension between causation and construction that I identified earlier in Putnam's essay reappears in the work of theorists who take the commonality orientation to democracy, although here it is perhaps more subtle. On the one hand, theorists often presume that we need commonality in democracy, since they take commonality to be a necessary (if not also a sufficient) condition for producing solidarity. Correspondingly, they assume that too much diversity in a democracy will undermine affective ties. In adopting this deterministic position, they seem to disavow human agency in generating and sustaining bonds of trust. On the other hand, these same theorists do not act as if they believe that affective ties are fully determined by the presence or absence of commonality. Instead, they present their arguments as interventions capable of shaping with whom and how we feel trust and solidarity. In so doing, they performatively acknowledge that they believe humans have some role in producing affective ties.

As for Putnam, in democratic theory these two positions—causation and construction—are seemingly reconciled. If commonality produces affective ties, the logic seems to be, then theorists can contribute to democracy by identifying which commonality will produce the right kind of bonds. The causal relationship between commonality and affect, far from being called into question by a theory of social construction, appears to be reinforced by it. Assuming that it is commonality that produces affective ties, theorists restrict human agency to deciding which commonality to emphasize—or, in Putnam's terms, how broad the "we" should be. Consequently, the belief that democracy requires some kind of commonality, despite its potentially troubling encounter with constructivism, remains held in place by a corollary assumption about political psychology: like attracts like. Identities and solidarities may be socially constructed, but however we construct them, they are always governed by this simple, psychological logic: people are likely to care more about those whom they perceive to be like them in important ways; they are likely to care less about those whom they perceive to be different. Accordingly, democratic theorists try to allow room for diversity—but not too much, lest we be pulled apart by it—and they focus their efforts on identifying sites of commonality that will produce the right kinds of affective bonds between the right people.

Let me briefly walk through a few examples to illustrate how some prominent democratic theorists make these moves.[35] First, I consider Miller's call for a socialist nationality.[36] He argues that the kind of solidarity necessary to support a socialist welfare state requires a citizenry that has a common identity—a view echoed in Goodhart's worry about the "progressive dilemma." Support for redistributive policies, he argues, is strongest when citizens perceive social welfare as the fulfillment of obligations of justice. People are more likely to see redistribution as a matter of justice when they view the beneficiaries of welfare as bound to them by a common identity: "The stronger the ties, the more egalitarian the distribution can be."[37] Drawing on John Stuart Mill, Miller claims that this shared identity is also a necessary precondition for self-government. In order to make decisions together, citizens must be able to "respect one another's good faith in searching for grounds of agreement."[38] "Sharing a national identity," he argues, makes this respect possible because it (somewhat tautologically) means "being committed to finding terms under which fellow-nationals can agree to live together."[39]

Miller can argue that a common national identity will produce bonds of trust and support for a welfare state because he is committed to the causal logic I described earlier: commonality produces solidarity.[40] As he puts it, "A shared identity carries with it a shared loyalty."[41] While he admits that a shared national identity may not be sufficient to produce solidarity, he does claim that it is a necessary precondition.[42] Conversely, diversity poses a threat to socialist democracy. When he considers whether ethnic diversity can be tolerated, he notes:

> Subcultures threaten to undermine the overarching sense of identity that socialists are looking for. They are liable to do so in two ways: they give participants a narrower focus of loyalty that may pre-empt commitment to the wider community; and by way of reaction people outside a particular sub culture [sic] may find it difficult to identify with those who are seen as in some way separated off.[43]

If we allow people to identify strongly with subgroups, then we risk siphoning away in-group and out-group support for the national community. His solution, then, is to reinforce the nation as "the object of attachment," an attachment that is stronger than other identities.[44]

The kind of common identity Miller calls for is what he terms "nationality"—as distinct from nationalism. Nationality is grounded in shared beliefs, nationalism in shared characteristics. Because it is a matter of belief and not descent, immigrants and members of diverse ethnic or racial groups can share in a national identity; in this way, Miller recuperates a concept of the nation that aims to avoid the ethically troubling ethnic majoritarianism often associated with nationalism. The commonality that unites a people for Miller is not exactly the same for each individual; rather, he urges us to "think of national culture not as implying complete uniformity but as a set of overlapping cultural characteristics—beliefs, practices, sensibilities—which different members exhibit in different combinations and to different degrees."[45] Miller's nationality, therefore, can comprehend significantly more ethnic and individual diversity than the outdated concept of national-ism. However, there are limits to how much diversity Miller's national com-munity can tolerate. Ethnic and other identities can be tolerated only insofar as they do not produce loyalties that would compete with loyalty to one's fellow nationals.

National identity can be deployed in this way to counteract the pull of competing loyalties because Miller sees identity as, at least in part, a mat-ter of social construction. He acknowledges that identities are inherited, but that does not mean that they are natural. On the contrary, he notes that we alter our inherited identities all the time:

> For instance, we scrutinize our institutions and practices to see whether the meanings they convey (so far as these are determinate) are meanings we still want to endorse (to take a relatively trivial case, we may decide to abolish one public holiday and institute another); we decide which cultural activities are worthy of public support; more generally, our legislation may involve an attempt to influence future understanding of the meaning of membership in this society (consider the case of race-relations legislation).[46]

In particular, Miller encourages critical reflection on elements of national-ity that cannot be shared by all members of the community—such as religion—in order to reshape identity to be more inclusive.[47] This is how he seems to understand his own project: he rehabilitates the concept of nationality so that it can better match the actual boundaries of political community. Yet his willingness to reshape national identity—and even to allow for a great deal of diversity in how that identity is experienced by nationals—does not lead him to question whether the underlying causal logic that commonality produces solidarity is itself a contingent social con-struction that could also be reshaped.

Like Miller's nationality, Habermas's concept of "constitutional patriot-ism" is developed in contrast with ethnicity-based nationalism.[48] Ethnic nationalism emerged historically when European states were in transition from monarchical to democratic rule. It served the function of transforming subjects into citizens capable of sharing in self-government. Habermas explains, "Only a national consciousness, crystallized around the notion of a common ancestry, language, and history, only the consciousness of belonging to 'the same' people, makes subjects into citizens of a single polit-ical community—into members who can feel responsible *for one another*."[49]

In other words, the commonality of nationality produces the affective ties between citizens that democracy requires.[50] Today, however, we cannot rely on ethnic concepts of the nation to motivate us to care for one another because we know that they exclude many citizens and can lead to ethically objectionable policies. Nonetheless, the democratic state does require affective attachment from its people, for "A nation of citizens can sustain the institutions of freedom only by developing a certain measure of loyalty to their own state."[51] The question for Habermas is: How to produce loyalty to the state and solidarity with one's fellow citizens without appealing to an exclusionary, ethnic conception of the people?

His aim is to discover an idea of community that is at once free of ethnicity and capable of generating genuine attachment. He settles on the idea of a shared political culture: one that is defined in part by abstract universalist principles, and in part by the history of the expression of those principles in the constitution of a particular political community. The common political culture, therefore, "is rooted in an interpretation of constitutional principles from the perspective of the nation's historical experience," which in turn "give[s] rise to public debates about the citizens' political self-understanding." These "debates are always about the best interpretation of the same constitutional rights and principles." In this way, the particular history of constitutional interpretation of a given political community is "the fixed point of reference" and the "motivational anchoring" for a constitutional patriotism.[52] Unlike ethnicity, constitutional history is a self-conscious, critical inheritance; it is the history of an intentional project of self-government. A patriotism anchored to the constitution thus offers Habermas "a functional equivalent for the fusion of the nation of citizens with the ethnic nation" that does not reproduce the negative effects of a nationalism grounded in the myth of an authentic, prepolitical people.[53] Citizens share a political culture grounded in a constitution, but they can be expected to share no more than that.[54] Beyond the sphere of politics, they may be as diverse as they like (within the limits of the law). That is to say, Habermas adopts what I called in chapter 1 a "civic strategy" in locating a new source of commonality solely in the political realm, while allowing for as much diversity as he can outside of politics.

For Habermas, it is not only the case that identities are (at least in part) socially constructed; it is crucial for democracy that the identity of the people be self-consciously and critically reconstructed by the people themselves. As Markell notes, "For Habermas, constitutional patriotism seems to be a uniquely safe form of affect for liberal democracies because it is directed toward a distinctive kind of object":[55] an object that is the product of public deliberation rather than an uncritical inheritance. Habermas, in other words, does not assume a privileged role for himself in determining what the content of constitutional patriotism should be (although he does posit its form); that is a matter for the people themselves to decide. "Which of our traditions we want to carry on and which we do not, is decided in the public process of transmitting a culture."[56] He understands his theoretical interventions as contributions to this public process, and in particular to debates about German and European identity. Yet this process takes place within the logic of commonality: the people must consciously construct and reconstruct itself, but its identity is always defined by the shared and fixed reference point of the constitution, whose centrality cannot itself be called into question.

Like Habermas, Taylor wants citizens to focus their affective bonds on a single referent, yet unlike Habermas, he allows for them to have a variety of perspectives on that common thing.[57] As we saw in chapter 1, Taylor believes commonality to be important to democracy because it is the basis for trust and a commitment to one's fellow citizens, which are necessary preconditions for sustainable collective decision making. Without them, he fears "the whole process of common decision will be poisoned by division and mutual suspicion."[58] Unlike Miller and Habermas, Taylor does not look to shared political institutions for a source of solidarity because, with the Canadian experience in mind, he is aware that citizens do not always share or feel attachment toward the same laws. While the Charter of Rights and Freedoms plays the role of a "common reference point of identity" for English Canada, it appears to many Quebecois to be at odds with preserving the Quebec nation.[59] Canadians can share neither Miller's nationality nor Habermas's constitutional patriotism. Instead, Taylor looks to a shared sense of belonging as a potential common source of Canadian solidarity. He defends what he terms "deep diversity": a vision of political community in which different citizens have different ways of imagining how they belong to the community. The story a Cree might tell of being Canadian would be quite different from that a Quebecois might tell, which would be different still from that of a third-generation Chinese immigrant in Vancouver, or that of a white anglophone living in Montreal. What matters is not whether they can all tell the same story of their belonging but that they can all tell some story of belonging to Canada. Diverse cultures, beliefs, institutions, and histories can all be accommodated by this vision of commonality—so long as ultimately all citizens feel some kind of affective attachment to the same community. Horizontal bonds of trust and solidarity are generated, in turn, by the recognition of each citizen from her own perspective that her fellows all have some sense of belonging, and are therefore committed (albeit in different ways) to the project of Canada.[60] The political community, then, serves as the focal point for Taylor's patriotism.

These three theorists all express the idea that commonality is the source of democratic affect. Moreover, they present this idea as if it were an empirically verifiable truth claim: it is a claim that describes the world, and as such it can be evaluated in terms of its truth or falsehood. Miller's view that nationality can serve as the basis for democratic affect is "proved" by reference to the cases of Belgium, Canada, and Switzerland, among others.[61] The United States, however, is an important counterexample of a society with a strong national identity that lacks the expected evidence of solidarity (i.e., a strong commitment to welfare state policies).[62] Miller has to defend his theory from empirical counterexamples because he takes the claim that national identity produces affect to be a true statement about the world.[63] And so he adds a quick qualification: while the United States does have a strong national identity, it is one grounded in individualism, which counteracts the production of solidarity. Similarly, Habermas often invokes the United States as an example of the empirical realizability of constitutional patriotism.[64] In one essay he writes, "The United States does demonstrate that the nation-state can assume and maintain a republican form even without the support of . . . a culturally homogeneous population" by substituting "a civil religion rooted in the majority culture" for nationalism.[65] And as I discussed in chapter 2, Will Kymlicka, drawing on Taylor's concept of deep diversity, tries to prove that a sense of belonging is what really unites American citizens by appealing to survey data in which a significant majority of Puerto Ricans report identifying as American.[66]

Occasionally, but not always, scholars will bolster their claim that there is a causal relation between commonality and affect by appeal to human psychology or human nature. One of the most extreme and explicit versions of this claim can be found in Arthur Schlesinger Jr.'s polemical book *The Disuniting of America*, where he argues that "the hostility of one tribe for another is among the most instinctive human reactions."[67] The commonality of the tribal group must be replaced, he argues, by the commonality of a national sense of purpose.[68] Putnam appeals to literature in social psychology and sociology to support his argument.[69] Miller acknowledges that his claim that people are more likely to support redistributive policies "to the extent that they see themselves as bound to the beneficiaries of the principle by common ties"[70] is obviously "not a claim about logic but a claim about social psychology."[71] For support, he cites two studies in "empirical social psychology" from 1974 and 1975.[72]

We could agree to take these claims about commonality and affect as truth claims and argue about the extent to which they accurately describe the world. This is what Bhikhu Parekh does, for example, in his scathing critique of advocates of a common national identity. He argues that the claim that "nationalism conduces to redistributionist policies, democracy, mutual sympathy, trust, fellow-feeling and so forth . . . is too complex and vague to be tested."[73] He then turns to examples to explain his point: British national identity might be strong, but under Margaret Thatcher it certainly did not lead to solidaristic, redistributive policies; the same might be said of national identity in postindependence India.[74] Moreover, he contends that national identity might not be as commonly shared in Britain as nationality theorists presuppose.[75] Even though the theoretical claims are "too complex and vague to be tested," Parekh intends his reader to take these empirical examples as proof that they are false. And it is on the basis of a more complicated understanding of the empirical reality in Britain and India that he advocates moving away from commonality as the basis for democratic affect. Instead, having demonstrated that communities can and do generate affect in the absence of commonality, he argues for a conception of the community grounded instead in "the complex, criss-crossing and sometimes overlapping patterns of support given it by its citizens for their own different reasons."[76] Such a conception derives at least part of its validity for Parekh because it has a greater correspondence to empirical reality than conceptions grounded in commonality.

However, this kind of appeal to contradictory empirical data does not unseat the theorist's faith that some kind of commonality is the source of democratic affect. Miller has not abandoned his advocacy of nationality despite Parekh's empirical criticisms of it. The United States is at once an example of a democracy whose common identity does not produce solidarity (for Miller), and an example of a democracy whose common identity produces a constitutional patriotism that other countries would do well to emulate (for Habermas). Even the literature in social psychology offers empirical challenges to the claim that commonality is a necessary precondition for democratic affect. One recent study, for example, suggests that diversity and trust may have a different relationship in different cultures. Comparing Japanese and American subjects, researchers found support for the view that Westerners tend to trust strangers based on "categorical distinctions between ingroups and outgroups" while "East Asians may have a stronger tendency to think about groups as predominantly relationship-based."[77] This is just one study, to be sure. However, my point is to highlight that there is scholarly debate within the field that Putnam and Miller both appeal to for grounding: the empirical evidence they marshal is itself in dispute. Yet, like the belief in the existence of two sexes discussed in chapter 3, the view that commonality is the source of democratic affect is unlikely to be unseated by empirical evidence to the contrary. While theorists present it as if it were an empirically verifiable truth claim, it does not seem to function as one in their thinking.

Perhaps their commitment to the idea that commonality is a necessary (if not sufficient) condition for democratic affect is not a matter of psychological and political truth at all. What if we were to think of the proposition that commonality produces affect instead as an article of faith? I propose that, like the belief in two sexes, the belief that commonality produces affect cannot be proved or disproved because it is not at root a matter of knowledge. Instead, as I will argue in the following sections, it is alluring to political theorists despite empirical evidence to the contrary because it works to resolve two vexing problems for democratic affect: the problems of the affective deficit of the modern state and the unpredictability of plural subjects.

THE AFFECTIVE DEFICIT OF THE MODERN STATE

Democratic theorists like Miller and Habermas are concerned that the modern state does not contain the resources to generate the affect between citizens necessary for a lasting commitment to the rule of law, institutions of self-government, and democratic sacrifices. This is because modern states are "large and impersonal communities" composed of countless strangers we will never meet.[78] The state is therefore too abstract a community to reliably generate affective attachment to itself, which calls into question its ability to persist in the face of competing and stronger affective ties citizens may have to other groups that are much more vivid to their imaginations, such as those based in a shared religion, language, culture, ethnicity, or race. Theorists regularly presume that it is easier—and perhaps even more natural—to care about someone who is a fellow Southern Baptist or Unitarian, say, than to care about someone who is a fellow U.S. citizen.

Based on the presumption that the state is a weak source of affect, some theorists have argued that we should supplement political identity with other markers that they believe are more likely to generate a stronger affective bond between citizens (e.g., a shared history, culture, beliefs, ethnicity, race, religion, or origin). This move is grounded in what we might call a referential theory of affect: the assumption that affective attachment is always attachment directed toward some thing.[79] If the state as a referent for attachment is a relatively weak source of affect, then the logic seems to be that we can supplement it with additional referents that have shown themselves to be sources of stronger attachment. Yet these supposedly stronger attachments are problematic insofar as they are not coextensive with the state, and so imperfectly produce attachment to this whole political community, and only to this political community. For example, ethnic and religious groups can be in some ways smaller than and in other ways larger than the group comprehended by fellow citizens. A shared American history might include the stories of migration and reverse migration, and of money flows to immigrants' families around the globe that attach Americans economically and emotionally to people the world over. What is more, it might include the fraught stories of imperialism, slavery, and conquest that created the jurisdictions now governed by the United States, and so this history might generate affect, but with a negative valence. When we supplement the state with additional referents, we risk excluding and disaffecting some who ought to be included as citizens, and inadvertently including some who ought not. Our affective attachments might then bring us into conflict with the state, rather than reinforce a commitment to working within its institutions and with these (and only these) particular other people.

Yet relying on the shared ideas embodied in our political community to unite us is equally risky. The principles justifying the state are themselves abstract and incapable of reliably generating commitment. Habermas, for example, describes "popular sovereignty and human rights" as "dry ideas" that do not inspire political mobilization.[80] While the rare cosmopolitan citizen of the world might be genuinely motivated by abstract principle, most people cannot be. Moreover, even if they were not too abstract as referents for attachment, the principles and ideals embodied in a democratic political community on their own do not direct affect reliably to *this particular community*. A commitment to equality and liberty, for example, does not restrict a citizen's range of concerns only to her fellow citizens: it might motivate a concern for people beyond the borders of her state, or for noncitizens living within her community, or even for nonhuman creatures. These ideas on their own cannot motivate a particular attachment to just Germans or just Brazilians. Again, the source of attachment—were it to move us—refers our affect beyond the boundaries of this political community, and so undermines any special attachment to this community alone. As Miller puts it, "Without a common national identity, there is nothing to hold citizens together, no reason for extending the role just to these people and not to others."[81]

The assumption that commonality produces affect, though, points the theorist in the right direction: all we need to do is to identify some concrete commonality shared by all citizens, and only by citizens, of this particular state. We then exploit that particular commonality to attach citizens to the correct referent for their political affect. Consequently, Miller's nationality is not ethnic but is connected to a particular set of political institutions and a particular political history that resulted in the current state. Habermas's constitutional patriotism combines a commitment to abstract principles with a commitment to the particular state that makes one's enjoyment of freedom possible. Taylor's sense of belonging is a sense of belonging to a community defined by shared political institutions: Canada. The causal assumption that commonality produces affect derives its appeal, then, by giving the theorist the tools to redress the affective deficit of the modern state. If affect is generated by commonality, then the theorist simply has to identify commonalities that direct affective attachments to exactly the right political community—no more, and no less. These commonalities give concreteness to the otherwise abstract identity of the demos while reinforcing the appropriate boundaries of our political obligations. Rather than competing with attachments to our fellow citizens, nationality, constitutional patriotism, and a deeply diverse shared sense of belonging turn citizenship and the "dry ideas" of democratic principle into vivid sites of imagined community.

Conversely, if we eschew a referential theory of affect, then it is less certain that we can address the affective deficit of the modern democratic state. If we cannot direct affect to specific referents, then how do we produce the trust and solidarity that democracy seems to require? Parekh offers one solution: democracies need to nurture a multiplicity of patriotisms rather than looking to one, single source of affect. He argues that "the state rests not on a single foundation but several, each with its distinct strengths and weaknesses, each representing a different type of patriotism, and all of them in need of careful nurturing by the state."[82] This is an approach that in some ways complements the account of identity I gave in chapter 3: if identities are multiple, overlapping, and not entirely contiguous, rather than oriented toward a single, common referent, then so will their corresponding affects be. I am sympathetic to his approach, but I believe we also need to treat the project of encouraging a multiplicity of affects as neither one that is the sole responsibility of the state (and therefore not a top-down policy matter) nor one that will produce effects that will reliably support the state. What Parekh misses, but Miller and Habermas understand, is that encouraging a multiplicity of affects threatens the centrality of the state in democratic politics. If we let go of the assumption that affect is always neatly tied to a referent, we must face the possibility that there may be no way to guarantee that the demos will have enough affect—and enough of the right kinds of affect—to sustain the institutions of a democratic state.

The belief that commonality produces affect is appealing to democratic theorists not only because it promises that attachment can be directed to the right referent but also because it offers a way to forge affective bonds of trust and solidarity between strangers. Democracy seems to require us to trust and care for people we do not know. We do not have direct interactions with most of the people with whom we share political community; most of our fellow citizens will never be more than strangers to us. Consequently, we cannot know whether they are worthy of our trust and solidarity. We do not know whether they will honor and repay tomorrow the sacrifices we make on their behalf today. We do not know whether they will pay their share of taxes honestly, or whether they will try to cheat. We do not know whether they will act in ways that preserve the values we hold dear, or whether they will act in ways that irreversibly alter the character of our community. How, then, can we place our trust in these strangers? How could we feel solidarity with them? Theorists who turn to commonality respond to these concerns by saying, in effect, we can trust and make sacrifices for those who share this *x* with us. All we need to know about strangers is whether they share this commonality.

While this problem of not being able to know all of our fellow citizens could be characterized as a function of the size of modern states—that is, we lack direct knowledge of all our fellow citizens because we do not live in "face-to-face" democracies—I believe it is more fruitfully understood as just one manifestation of the unpredictability of plural subjects. Even when we do have direct interactions with people, the knowledge we accumulate about how they have acted in the past cannot give us absolute certainty about how they will act in the future. This unpredictability is a function of human plurality: that each of us is a unique subject. Even a person we have known our whole lives can surprise us and confound our expectations. To share the world with plural subjects is to live in the delightful and terrifying condition of unpredictability. Our first-person experience of ourselves and others is one of not knowing what the future will be.

As a result, trust and solidarity—whether in friendships and romances, or in relationships with one's fellow citizens—cannot be based in actual knowledge of how the other will act. In the absence of certainty about the future, we can only *imagine* what others will do. I am willing to be vulnerable with you because I *believe* that you will reciprocate, rather than because I *know* that you will. I am willing to confide in you because I *believe* you will keep my secret, rather than because I *know* you will. I am willing to make sacrifices for you because I *believe* you would make sacrifices for me, rather than because I *know* you would. I am willing to extend citizenship to you because I *believe* that you will uphold my values, and so on.

In relationships in which we do have direct interaction with another person, how we imagine she will act could be based on a history of observed words and deeds. When we can look back at that history and see a consistent pattern, we may have good reason to make inferences about whether she is trustworthy. In such instances, our beliefs about the other are supported by (but not reducible to) knowledge. We might also imagine what she will do based not on direct observation but on speculation, gossip, and prejudice. Or we may project onto her what we want to believe about her trustworthiness, regardless of what her words and behavior indicate. Our beliefs need not correspond to what we can observe: we can rationalize or ignore bad behavior to sustain a cherished image of the person we wish her to be, and we can presume the worst about her, despite ample evidence to the contrary.

When it comes to the many strangers with whom we share citizenship, we lack a history of direct observation of each individual that would allow us to check our beliefs about them against what we can know. Our affective ties to our fellow citizens, then, rely to an even greater extent on what we imagine about them. In this context, the perception that we share something in common with others can function as a kind of stand-in for direct observation of their past behavior. That is, we can infer how others will act in the future from the fact of our having something in common, and so this commonality generates bonds of trust and solidarity between us. The logic is something like this: I know how I will act in the future. You are like me. Therefore, I can infer that you will act just as I will. I can trust you, and I can feel secure in the expectation that any sacrifices I might make for you will be reciprocated in the future. Commonality, therefore, serves as a kind of conceptual device that makes it easier for us to imagine affective relationships with people we have never met. It gives us a shorthand for trust and solidarity that saves us the trouble of worrying about the fact that we cannot know how stranger-citizens will act.

Moreover, insofar as what we share in common is observable, commonality acts as a substitute for knowledge about how others will act. That is, even though we cannot know how others will act in the future, we can know whether they share objective characteristics with us today. Commonalities, therefore, can fill in for that which we cannot know. We use observable characteristics as markers for trustworthiness or untrustworthiness all the time: think of characteristics such as race, dress, or accent and language skills. While many of us might want to resist making snap judgments about other people based upon such superficial characteristics, we have all been exposed to cultural imaginaries that encourage us to interpret observable clues as signs of unobservable qualities. The belief that commonality produces affective ties, manifest in theories and policies, simply formalizes something that we already often do. It promises us that, if we observe that we share the relevant commonality with our fellow citizens, then we can infer that we can trust and care about one another.

Immigration tests offer some of the clearest instances of the substitution of objective knowledge in the present for knowledge of a person's future actions. They establish ways of observing whether newcomers are enough like us that they can be trusted with residency and citizenship. Consider a few examples. Since 2006, the Netherlands has required applicants for citizenship to take a test titled "Knowledge of Dutch Society," based on the information presented in the film *Naar Nederland*.[83] This film notoriously "featur[es] homosexuals kissing and a scene at a nude beach. The movie emphasizes the point that this is all part of normal life in the Netherlands."[84] This new policy was required, according to immigration minister Rita Verdonk, because "the Netherlands can no longer afford to welcome immigrants who will not integrate into mainstream society."[85] Applicants who pass the test, then, are presumed to be willing to accept Dutch tolerance for homosexuality and public nudity, along with other liberal values. In the same year, the French government made it mandatory for new immigrants to sign the *contrat d'acceuil et d'intégration* (CAI)—the contract of reception and integration.[86] The contract states that "you [the immigrant] give witness to your will to resolutely integrate to French society."[87] Integration amounts to acceptance of "an ensemble of non-negotiable and shared values." Immigrants who sign the CAI are therefore taken to be expressing consent and willingness to adopt these values as their own.[88] Tests, oaths of allegiance, and contracts are ways of making an external show of internal commitment and loyalty. These shows are taken as evidence that immigrants are, in fact, trustworthy: we can expect them to act in accordance with our political values, to take on the duties and obligations of being a citizen, and to become like us. Citizenship tests promise predictability: they give us reason to infer how immigrants will act in the future.

We also can read empirical data as a kind of objectified evidence of predictability and trustworthiness: Taylor does this when he cites a report on Canadians' political values as evidence of a shared commitment to liberal principles.[89] Miller's nationality can be reified and rendered observable. We can look to see whether citizens exhibit the characteristics we associate with fellow nationals: dress, accent, participation in public displays of patriotism, and so on. While not every kind of commonality that democratic theorists have advocated could be directly observed, many proposed commonalities can be. And as long as we can observe that we share the relevant commonality with our fellow citizens, then we can safely infer from that observation that we can trust and care for one another.

Nonetheless, while we may be able to observe "evidence" of commonality, this kind of evidence is actually an unstable ground for trust and solidarity. It substitutes a kind of knowledge we can have (observations about the world) for a kind of knowledge we cannot have (knowledge of other people's future actions). This is an imperfect substitution, and one that can never fully insulate itself against doubts. Even after having decided to trust someone, we can question whether they really are "like" us. Yet whether an immigrant is truly committed to integration and feels loyalty to her new country is something that cannot be an object of knowledge because it is a purely subjective experience. All we can know is what she says and does. Immigrants who have taken oaths have only said a few words; it is easy to say a few words and not mean them. We can always raise questions about whether a poll really indicates convergence on a set of political values, whether successfully passing a test is actually a sign of trustworthiness, or whether one's performance of a nationality is heartfelt. Commonality, rather than "solving" the problem of the unpredictability of plural subjects once and for all, can only stave off the doubts we have about one another for some time. Trust and solidarity must be repeatedly renewed by imagining community over and over again.

IMAGINED AFFECT AND POLITICAL RESPONSIBILITY

Our first-person experience of affective ties of trust and solidarity, I argue, reveals that these are based in *belief*, not in knowledge. We can never know in advance whether stranger-citizens can be trusted, whether our sacrifices for them would be reciprocated if our roles were reversed, whether they understand our obligations to one another as we do. We misunderstand what it is to trust or to stand with our fellows when we think we do these things because of what we know about them. We care for strangers because of how we imagine ourselves to be in relationship with them. That is to say, we humans ordinarily do the work of making assumptions about one another that substitute for knowledge of how we will act in the future. We do this in personal relationships, and we do this when we imagine relationships with strangers we will likely never meet. While these assumptions can form the basis for affective ties to others, they are not entirely stable: we can always shift from trusting to mistrusting others. One way of imagining our affective relationships with one another is to presume that they are grounded in what we have in common with others. In this case, we do the work of imagining that being alike in some way means that I can know (more or less) what you are likely to do—enough to trust you.

Now just because I am saying we do this "work" does not mean that when we make assumptions about one another, we do so consciously or intentionally. Sometimes we may, but sometimes we may not. I might unthinkingly adopt cultural prejudices against people of another race, for example, or I might make a conscious effort to not let race factor into whom I choose as friends, or for whose benefit I am willing to be taxed. My point here is that affective ties are the *product of human action*. How we imagine the world—whether we are aware of it or not—affects whom we trust and care for. Consequently, even if we cannot simply choose our affects, they are not entirely beyond our control; they are not pure products of nature or necessity (at least not to such an extent as to render human action irrelevant). And if they are the product of human action, then we can act intentionally so as to try to shape our relationships in better or worse ways—even though we cannot guarantee an outcome.

This is one way to understand what is at stake in the literature on democratic affect. Miller, Habermas, and Taylor are all interested to replace traditional sources of commonality (ethnicity, nationalism, cultural and political homogeneity) with new ones. In so doing, they—like Putnam—implicitly acknowledge that humans can exercise at least some agency over their affective relationships. If commonality is what produces affect, their work suggests, then we can decide as political agents which kinds of commonality should matter to the affective ties we have with our fellow citizens. We can decide that ethnicity should not matter; we can decide that shared political values should. These three theorists are intervening in ongoing debates about how we should imagine who we, the people, are. I join them in calling for us to make this a matter of self-conscious, public reflection.

Another way to put my claim is to say that *we humans produce commonality* (and, by extension, diversity as well). Recall my discussion in chapter 2: humans interpret certain qualities—a flat surface, legs, and solidity, perhaps—to indicate that "this" is a table. There is no such thing as a table independent of human beings to whom things with these qualities appear as such. Similarly, when we take a characteristic like skin color, religion, or a sense of belonging and make it a part of how we decide with whom to share in democracy, we are interpreting certain things in the world (whether they are observable or not) as having a certain kind of meaning for us. We have taken what might be characterized as a descriptive or demographic commonality and made it politically salient. Descriptive commonality is not intrinsically political, just as a thing's having solidity and legs is not meaningful on its own—we do the work of making it relevant to how we think about our relationships to others, to how we imagine the world we share. Diversity and commonality therefore are not objective qualities but the product of human imaginative activity that aims to make sense of the world. By assigning meaning to certain features, we render them communicable to others, salient for how we imagine community, and important to how we think about our affective relationships to strangers. Humans make meaning from certain commonalities and certain differences, rather than others. We do the work of imagining community, imagining who can be trusted, and imagining who is deserving of our care. And since these are matters of imagination, how we imagine them today is not necessary: we can imagine otherwise than we do now.

In other words, I am suggesting that we think of the claim that commonality is a necessary (if not sufficient) condition for the production of affect as a *political claim*, not a truth claim. Consider how we might evaluate an argument for a shared nationality if we understood it as a claim about how we imagine the world rather than a claim about how the world is or ought to be. Instead of asking, do we share a nationality, or are we sufficiently attached to this nationality for it to bind us as citizens, we should be asking, do we want to be a people whose relationship is imagined via a shared nationality? We could critically debate which historical events we should take as significant for our understanding of our community, and whose versions of that history we should follow. We could question whether we want to think of America as a nation of immigrants open to newcomers, or as a nation of WASPs to which any newcomers we will begrudgingly admit have to assimilate.

To see these different claims on our affections as involving political choices is to see affect itself as a political matter. Every imaginary of the demos is a political act in two senses, as I discussed in earlier chapters. It is in its first articulation an exercise of the creative, *instituting imagination*, in that it aims to bring into being a new way of seeing the world. Each claim that a different kind of commonality unites the demos is an invitation to imagine our relationships with others in one way rather than another. Putnam invites us to imagine an America united by bonds that transcend race and ethnicity. Taylor invites us to imagine a Canada open to a diversity of ways of being Canadian. Habermas invites us to imagine a Germany engaged in an enlightenment project of self-government through constitutional democracy. Second, imaginaries are an exercise of the *instituted imagination*, which reinforces this particular way of seeing and in so doing has the effect of occluding other possibilities. Putnam not only urges us toward reconfiguring American identity to be more capacious but also reinforces the belief that diversity causes isolation and anomie.

Insofar as imaginaries of democratic affect are political, then, we bear responsibility for how we imagine community. Because humans identify and give meaning to commonality and diversity, we should take responsibility for the features of our shared world that we focus on as characteristics defining the demos, defining the scope of our affective bonds and our political obligations. Political actors should be actively engaged in making and contesting political claims about who we are, why we should care about one another, what the scope of our political obligations should be. That is, rather than trying to settle the question of what commonality we share as citizens that could be the basis of affective ties of trust and solidarity, I suggest that we focus instead on cultivating a sense of responsibility for how we do and should imagine our relationships to one another. This is to shift from a need for convergence or agreement on a commonality to a practice of critical engagement with plural, competing claims to commonality.

So, while I share with Habermas the desire to make conceptions of political community a matter of self-conscious, public reflection, I diverge from him in that I believe the aim of this reflection cannot be convergence on any single "fixed point of reference." When we think of affect in this way as the product of political claims competing for our assent—rather than as the necessary result of human nature, instinct, or psychology—then we have to let go of the idea that democratic affect can be neatly directed to the referent of the state, the constitution, or the nationality. The political claims made by theorists that we should ground our political relationships in shared beliefs, constitutional histories, or senses of belonging are just political claims—they do not settle the matter once and for all, and they cannot. Claims that aim to direct our affect to the political community defined by the state—and only to that political community—will always be in competition with other claims that demand that we stand in solidarity with groups that overlap, compete with, and exceed the boundaries of the state. The goal of taking responsibility for how we imagine affective relationships is not to get affect right and make sure that it always and only reinforces the centrality of the democratic state. It is instead to see affect as a political production and to enter the fray of contesting and reimagining who we are.

That is, I resist the aspiration to solve the problem of democratic affect. Democratic theorists who aim to redirect affect seek a kind of sovereignty over something that may simply not be within human control. When I say that we produce trust and solidarity, when I say that we have responsibility for how we imagine community, I do not mean to claim that humans therefore have control over their affect. On the contrary, I acknowledge that much of our understanding of affective relationships can be unthinkingly inherited, unconscious, or simply unnoticed. What I am calling for is not for us to act as if we could be sovereign over our sense of whom we can trust and for whom we should care—we may be unable to do that as individuals, let alone as societies. Instead, I am calling for us to take responsibility for affect by making it a conscious focus of our attention—by publicly drawing awareness to the many ways people imagine community, to the effects of different imaginaries, and to the possible alternatives we might intentionally pursue. Politicizing affect in this way, then, requires renouncing an aspiration to settle the question once and for all.

Moreover, I believe we need to let go of the assumption that commonality is a necessary condition for producing democratic affect. It is possible to imagine obligations and attachments to other people without having anything in common with them. As Parekh and Taylor demonstrate, we can imagine our civic relationships as characterized not by a common understanding of that relationship but rather by a plurality of understandings of belonging. We can go further, though, and make political claims to obligation and solidarity that might be grounded in interaction and interrelationship: for example, Iris Young has argued that we have an obligation to people working in sweatshops in the third world because of our implication in the structures that exploit them—and not because we are alike or share a common set of political institutions.[90] Or we could ground affective ties in something like Arendtian plurality: our relationships with others are based in the fact of our difference—that you are not me—which produces opportunities for learning, for seeing the world differently, and the ethical growth that comes from accepting relationships of trust as acts of faith.[91] The possibilities for imagining how we might understand political relationships as relationships of trust and solidarity without insisting on commonality are potentially limitless.

There is a genuine risk here that competing affective attachments and solidarities will undermine attachment to the state. But there is also the possibility that competing, not entirely contiguous affective attachments may paradoxically strengthen and stabilize attachments to our fellow citizens. This is the possibility imagined by Tariq Modood in the epigraph to this chapter. The imaginaries that underlie our affective ties are plastic, and they can be mobilized by new political claims in unprecedented directions. My ties to my fellow American citizens may be simultaneously reinforced and undermined by other claims on my affection: my faith, for example, could reinforce my commitment to social welfare provision and my support of redistributive policies in the United States, but it might also demand of me that I work to send resources abroad to communities that are also in need. A Guatemalan immigrant might maintain loyalties to her country of origin, yet her identification with fellow migrant workers might also motivate her to become involved in justice movements focused on labor rights in the United States. What these examples suggest is the possibility that affective ties need not be directed toward the political community defined by the state in order to have the impact of sustaining democracy—that is, in order to generate expressions of political freedom and world-building. People may become engaged in political action to shape their world in ways that are not neatly defined by the state. Indeed, it may be that the democratic state benefits from the critical distance that opens up between the imagined community of citizens and our other overlapping but not entirely contiguous imagined communities.

Perhaps this is what Putnam's hunkered-down turtles are doing, after all. Rather than simply withdrawing from social networks with fellow citizens, their informed engagement in protests and social movements may indicate instead that they are actively exercising their political freedom to shape the meaning of the world that they inhabit. Putnam worries that turtles lack a positive attachment to their local communities—they are less likely to be registered to vote, and they have less faith in local government and their own ability to effect change in their communities.[92] Yet lacking attachment to one particular community is not the same thing as lacking attachment to all communities. As he points out in a footnote, while living in a diverse community is correlated with lower trust in local government, "Census tract diversity is *not* related to trust in *national* government."[93] What he sees as a threat to social capital at the local level, then, is not necessarily a failure of democratic affect altogether—only a lack of one certain kind of affect. Local governments and communities may suffer—but does democracy suffer? Perhaps not. In the same way we might ask: If citizens do not uniformly attach to one another at the national level, the state may suffer—but does that mean that democracy therefore suffers? Putnam can only maintain that hunkered-down turtles threaten democracy by taking a narrow view of democracy as a form of government, embodied in institutions. If instead we understand democracy more broadly as world-building, intersubjective activity, then the agitation of Putnam's turtles for social reform may actually be a sign of the vibrancy of democratic practice.

By calling for us to take responsibility for our many imaginaries of community, I necessarily decenter the state, since the state is not at the center of every imaginary of community. Yet it may be that the kind of affect democracy needs is not directed toward the state, nor toward local government, nor toward any particular referent at all. What I am arguing instead is that democracy needs the active *politicization of affect*—it needs the ongoing pluralization of affective ties rather than their centralization, and it needs the ongoing contestation of affective claims rather than their resolution. This is to encourage political claiming and world-building, and to take responsibility for the ways we imagine affect. This necessarily means keeping open the question of whether democratic affect should be directed toward the state and whether the appropriate demos with which we should feel solidarity is the demos defined by citizenship. Moving away from a commonality orientation to democracy means moving away from an institutionalized vision of democracy that misses or devalues much non-state-oriented political activity. In the following chapter, I aim to create some distance between democracy and the state in order to make visible possibilities of political freedom occluded by the insistence that we *must* have something in common.

CHAPTER 5

Pluralizing the Demos

Sharing Agency and the Dilemma

of Democratic Exclusion

If it were true that sovereignty and freedom are the same, then indeed no man could be free, because sovereignty, the ideal of uncompromising self-sufficiency and mastership, is contradictory to the very condition of plurality. No man can be sovereign because not one man, but men, inhabit the earth—and not, as the tradition since Plato holds, because of man's limited strength, which makes him depend upon the help of others. All the recommendations the tradition has to offer to overcome the condition of non-sovereignty and win an untouchable integrity of the human person amount to a compensation for the intrinsic "weakness" of plurality. Yet, if these recommendations were followed and this attempt to overcome the consequences of plurality were successful, the result would not be so much sovereign domination of one's self as arbitrary domination of all others, or, as in Stoicism, the exchange of the real world for an imaginary one where these others would simply not exist.

—Hannah Arendt[1]

COMMONALITY AND THE PRODUCTION OF AGENCY

Many democratic theorists presume that commonality produces collective agency. This is the third corollary assumption holding in place the belief that democracy requires sharing something in common. More specifically, and echoing the basic conceit of social contract theory, the way this assumption manifests itself in democratic theory is in the belief that the agency of "the people" is brought into being by an agreement that defines the intentions and purposes of joint action. A particular imaginary of collective agency underlies this conception of the democratic people: one in which collective agency emerges when a group of individuals agree that they want to act together to achieve a particular goal.[2] We transform ourselves from a number of individuals into a singular, collective agency in the moment when each of us commits to perform a particular action together. As in a contract, our mutual agreement is thus the commonality that produces a new agency, capable of acting as one with one will.

According to this imaginary, collective agency can only ever be exercised after individuals have agreed to act together. That is, the agreement to establish a collective agency is itself the work of individuals: "we" cannot act as a plural subject until after you and I have agreed to do so. The agreement to constitute a joint agent is analytically (if not also temporally) prior to the agency thus formed. As a consequence, the conversations and negotiations that individuals engage in to reach that agreement are themselves not the actions of a collective agency but rather those of multiple individuals. In this imaginary, collective agency is produced by common agreement, and not yet manifest in the intersubjective interactions that result in the agreement itself.

This prior agreement defines a structure for collective action that legitimates the new agency; it delimits the scope of what "we" are authorized to do together. We agree to combine forces to do *x*, but not to do *y*. The common agreement thereby facilitates individual identification with the collective: inasmuch as the agency acts in accordance with what each person agreed to, individuals can understand its actions as their own. Therefore, so long as "we" do not do anything that violates the agreement, the actions of the collective agency can claim legitimacy.

In democratic theory, this imaginary of collective agency takes the form of *sovereign democratic agency*. This agency is sovereign in that it exercises collective rule over the individuals who constitute it. It is democratic in that it is the agency—the demos—that rules in a democracy. That is, this is a conception of collective agency that arises from a view of democracy understood as a form of government. The agreement that creates a sovereign democratic agency establishes what "the people" may legitimately do as a collective: it defines the institutions and procedures that demarcate the boundaries within which the people legitimately exercises authority.

There are two broad kinds of common agreement that are taken to establish the collective agency of the people in contemporary democratic theory. The first is agreement on a shared set of rights or principles that define the purpose and limits of government. Because this agreement is what brings the people into being and establishes the framework within which this agency can act, it must itself lie beyond the scope of legitimate democratic action. Jürgen Habermas characterizes these first principles as "social-boundary conditions . . . [that] are not immediately at the disposition of the citizens' will."[3] For Charles Taylor, these include "the basic principles of republican constitutions, democracy itself, and human rights among them."[4] John Rawls is a bit more specific about what "the citizen body fixes once and for all" in a constitution, and so places beyond the reach of democratic agency: for him, the list includes "certain constitutional essentials, for example, the equal basic political rights and liberties, and freedom of speech and association, as well as those rights and liberties guaranteeing the security and independence of citizens, such as freedom of movement and choice of occupation, and the protections of the rule of law."[5] These rights and principles in turn ensure that whatever the people does, it does within the limits of the constitution. This enables citizens to identify with the agency of the people: even when they disagree with specific decisions, they can see that these decisions are made within a framework that guarantees their freedom.

The second kind of agreement that produces the sovereign collective agency of the people in democratic theory is agreement on the procedures for determining what is the will of the people. For Philip Pettit and David Schweikard, this agreement on procedures for decision making and establishing a collective will is what distinguishes a group agency from mere joint action.[6] Rawls elaborates, "It is through . . . fixed procedures that the democratic people can express, even if they do not, their reasoned democratic will, and indeed without those procedures they can have no such will."[7] And it is through following the right kinds of procedures that Habermas hopes to ensure that the outcome of will-formation processes is legitimate. In neo-Kantian strands of democratic theory, this prior procedural agreement ensures that what the people subsequently wills is something to which all citizens should be able to consent. Procedures and principles, established in advance of democratic deliberation and decision making, thereby facilitate citizens' identification of the will of the people as their own.

While theorists appeal to this imaginary of collective agency to ground the legitimacy of democratic rule, inasmuch as this legitimacy depends upon common agreement it is a very uncertain ground. Since this imaginary posits that collective agency arises from a prior agreement, any claim that calls the commonality of this agreement into question is a potential threat to the legitimacy of democratic rule. On this view, all citizens in a democracy should be parties to the agreement that produces the democratic sovereign (even if their agreement is purely hypothetical), and so they should recognize the decisions made by the people as legitimate. It is therefore a problem for democracy when any citizen or group of citizens disagrees and disidentifies with the collective agency of the people because they call into question the commonality of the agreement that authorizes the people to rule in the first place. If collective agency is produced by agreement, and yet it turns out we do not all agree on the intentions and purposes of this particular collective agency, then logically the collective agency must not exist and cannot have legitimate authority to rule. This is a consequence that is difficult to accept, as it seems to imply that the people will cease to exist if ever any citizen challenges its legitimacy. To stave off this possibility, democratic theorists try to secure the agency of the people by endlessly working to establish the terms of the "right" agreement that could be agreed to by all—whether in practice, or merely hypothetically— and so could fully and finally legitimize the agency of the people.

I believe that this effort is futile, since it is always possible for citizens to come to feel disconnected from what passes as the will of the people, no matter what efforts may be made to include them. Losses are ordinary in democracy. We cannot prevent people from feeling excluded, disappointed, and betrayed in the face of losses—whether these have happened just once or twice, or whether they are part of a persistent, structural problem. There is no agreement in advance of our acting together in democracy that can guarantee that each of us will always be able to accept the decisions of the collective. There is no way to ensure that simply because we once agreed, or because a political theorist thinks we should have agreed, we will continue to agree into the future.

Disagreement, disappointment, and disaffection are to be expected in a world that we inhabit together with plural others. We share the world with people who see matters differently, and we should expect them to surprise, confound, and annoy us from time to time. This may be especially the case when the stakes are high, as with a presidential election, a major policy proposal, congressional redistricting, redressing group discrimination, and so on. I want us to understand such moments of loss and disappointment (when the fact that we share the world with plural others is simply impossible to ignore) as themselves expressions of a kind of collective agency, rather than as necessarily threatening to it. That is, we need an imaginary of collective agency that warmly embraces disagreement as one of its many manifestations, instead of nervously viewing it as a sign of failure.

In a move that should not be surprising to you at this point, I propose that we conceive of collective agency as arising in and through intersubjective activity, what I call *democratic interagency*. We form a collective agency, on this view, when we interact with one another. Disagreeing, arguing, and losing are all forms of interaction, and so they contribute to, rather than undermine, collective agency. Indeed, agreement is neither a necessary condition for nor a necessary outcome of our interacting together. Collective agency falters not when we lack agreement about collective intentions and purposes but when our interlocutors disengage, do not respond, fail to hear us, or simply do not take us seriously. Consequently, the aim of a democratic politics emerging from this concept of interagency is to facilitate and perpetuate interaction between people, and to proliferate the opportunities for interaction.

Because democratic interagency emerges in interaction, unlike sovereign democratic agency it is not identified with institutionalized democracy; instead, it is closer to accounts of radical democracy that see the possibility for collective agency wherever multiple people come together, such as those that draw on Arendt and Sheldon Wolin. This way of thinking about democratic agency enables me to reframe democratic inclusion not as agreement and identification with the popular sovereign by all the individuals who constitute it but as exercising one's political freedom in interaction with others. Democratic inclusion therefore requires actively engaging with others who disagree in order to try to shape our world. That is, this imaginary of collective agency embraces the condition of sharing the world with plural others and calls on us to live within the tension of our disagreements instead of trying to resolve or minimize them. This is to pluralize the demos: to see it as multiple and emergent in intersubjective interactions that aim to shape the world we share, wherever and whenever these occur.

CHARLES TAYLOR AND THE DILEMMA OF DEMOCRATIC EXCLUSION

I will make the case for democratic interagency by working through Taylor's ideas about democracy, agency, and language. Taylor—like Danielle Allen and Robert Putnam—is a threshold figure for me: someone who articulates both the objective and intersubjective ways of seeing, without finally and fully embracing the latter. I turn in this chapter to his work, then, in order to read Taylor against Taylor: to develop a critique of sovereign democratic agency and to offer an alternative to it.

In his essays on democratic theory, Taylor adopts an understanding of the people consistent with what I called earlier sovereign democratic agency. His work illustrates what I have asserted: that this conception of agency generates anxieties about legitimacy and drives the corresponding attempt to correct the agreement that defines the demos. Yet in his other philosophical and political writings, Taylor treats the conception of a collective agency produced by a preexisting commonality as merely one of two ways that we moderns tend to conceptualize agency. He claims that we also think of collective agents as self-constituting, as arising dynamically through ongoing dialogical interaction. In later sections of the chapter, I will draw on his description of this second conception of agency to develop my account of democratic interagency. First, though, let me show how his belief that democracy requires commonality generates a crisis of legitimacy, or what he terms "the dilemma of democratic exclusion."

According to Taylor, democracy requires that all the people who make up the demos must be able to see themselves as belonging to it. That is, they must all be able to see themselves as a part of "an ongoing collective agency, one in which the membership realizes something very important, a kind of freedom."[8] When some of the people cannot identify with the demos, the legitimacy of its decisions becomes suspect. Taylor is particularly concerned about instances in which groups of people feel that they are not heard, that they lack influence over the agenda, and that their perspectives are not taken seriously by others. Members of such groups are likely to experience democracy as an expression not of their freedom but of their oppression. Consequently, they may see decisions made by "the will of the people" as foreign and imposed from without. As Taylor puts it, "They cannot see themselves as part of this larger sovereign people."[9] Democracy in such cases is not the legitimate rule of the whole people but the illegitimate rule of one part of the people over another. For Taylor, then, the legitimacy of democracy depends upon making it possible for all citizens to identify with the collective agency of the people.

He believes that commonality produces this identification with the collective. The demos, he insists, must have "a strong collective identity" that motivates every citizen to want to fully include the others in the processes of self-government.[10] As we already have seen in chapters 1 and 4, Taylor believes that we need such an identity in order to be able to trust one another in our decisions and deliberations. He explains, "In practice, a nation can only ensure the stability of its legitimacy if its members are strongly committed to one another by means of a common allegiance to the political community. It is the shared consciousness of this commitment which creates confidence on the part of the various subgroups that they will indeed be heard."[11] When members of subgroups trust that they will be included in decision making, they are able to accept even those decisions in which they lose out as legitimate decisions of a collective agency to which they feel they belong. A shared identity generates the horizontal bonds of trust that make it possible for citizens to imagine the will of the people as their own, that is, to understand themselves as sharing in collective agency.

Taylor notes, however, that the pursuit of a commonality that could unite all citizens is problematic: each claim about what the people has in common is in its own way exclusionary and leaves some out. This is what he calls the dilemma of democratic exclusion. He writes, "The need to form a people as a collective agent runs against the demand for inclusion of all who have a legitimate claim on citizenship."[12] That is, he is concerned that democracy's need for "a high degree of cohesion" leads to the temptation to make the identity of the demos exclusive in problematic ways.[13] Taylor has in mind here three ways that modern democracies imagine collective identity, each of which excludes some citizens who ought to be included. First, the need for social cohesion has motivated some communities to see any difference as threatening; this reaction results in policies of ethnic cleansing, forced assimilation, and the denial of citizenship.[14] Second, many self-governing societies historically have relied on ethnic homogeneity to be the glue that would hold them together; these societies are now finding it difficult to include immigrants and other outsiders in the political process.[15] Third, societies like the United States and France that ground social unity in a civic identity lack the capacity to include citizens who do not fit this mold.[16] Each of these approaches remains trapped in the same dilemma: in an attempt to provide a cohesive sense of identity to sustain democracy, they end up defining the demos in a way that excludes some who should belong. Rather than strengthening a shared commitment to democracy, these kinds of collective identity instead produce subgroups of citizens who feel excluded and alienated from the people.

While this dilemma might seem to pose an insurmountable problem for democracy, Taylor himself is optimistic that we can get out of it if we can just get the commonality right. Where other democratic theorists have argued that democracy simply cannot avoid making exclusions, Taylor refuses to attribute this dilemma to democracy itself.[17] He explains, "I do not want to claim that democracy unfailingly leads to exclusion. That would be a counsel of despair, and the situation is far from desperate."[18] He holds out hope that we could come up with an imaginary of the demos that would fully include all citizens that should be included. Democracies may always need to exclude noncitizens, but there is no necessary reason for Taylor that they should have to exclude their own. And so, he holds on to the faith that democracy does not produce these exclusions; it simply generates the *temptation* to exclude.[19] If we are aware of this temptation, then he thinks we can steer clear of it and work to get our collective identity right.

The solution that Taylor proposes is one that takes the commonality orientation to democracy to its logical political conclusion. If every claim to commonality has the potential to exclude, then the search for a fully inclusive commonality will produce an endless dynamic of claiming and counterclaiming, as we saw with the discussion of feminist theory in chapter 3.

Recognizing this, Taylor advises that we embrace and institutionalize this dynamic. That is, he advocates what he calls "sharing identity space": periodically renegotiating the commonality that undergirds democratic collective agency. Even if at one time the articulation of a particular political identity was inclusive, Taylor thinks it is highly improbable that it will forever remain so. This is because he understands collective identity to be dialogical: "The shifts in personal identity over time, through migration and moral or cultural change, can bring the established political identity out of true with the people who are supposed to live within it."[20] Because we change as individuals and as societies, Taylor thinks our conception of our shared political identity should change, too. Our sense of who we are as a people must therefore be the subject of not just one agreement but of successive and periodically revisited agreements. He explains, "Political identities have to be worked out, negotiated, and creatively compromised between peoples who have to or want to live together under the same political roof (and this coexistence is always grounded in some mixture of necessity and choice). Moreover, these solutions are never meant to last for ever [sic], but have to be discovered or invented anew by succeeding generations."[21] These repeated negotiations give us the opportunity to respond more or less dynamically when some citizens claim exclusion from the demos, and so empower us to resolve legitimacy crises as they arise.

For Taylor, this common identity that citizens articulate through their periodic negotiations enables them to establish a collective agency that is inclusive of all citizens. This inclusive identity generates the shared sense that we all belong to the collective agency of the sovereign people, that its decisions are our decisions. Moreover, Taylor indicates that there is a more or less "right" way to articulate this shared identity; there is such a thing as an identity being in or out of true with the body of citizens. It is because there is a "rightness" to identity that he believes that democracy is not necessarily exclusionary; it only excludes when we articulate our identity incorrectly. Our account of our political identity can be, he presumes, an accurate description of who we actually are, if only for a time. Thus, he treats commonality as an empirical matter: claims about who "we" are, are truth claims. Democracy can be fully inclusive because he believes there is a correct answer to the question, Who is the demos? We only need to find it out.

I contend, however, that even periodically renegotiating the terms of our collective agency will not eliminate the feelings of not belonging that concern Taylor. This is because the experiences of loss, disappointment, betrayal, and exclusion are characteristic of sharing the world together with plural others. People will have these experiences when they interact with one another despite our attempts to avoid them by clearly delineating identities, intentions, and procedures in advance. No matter how exactly or how frequently we work to identify newer and better sources of commonality, we will not rid ourselves of the possibility that some will feel excluded from the demos. To see the force of this point, I want to show you a different way of understanding collective agency. And so, I now turn to Taylor's other writings in order to put the conception of collective agency at work in his democratic theory into a broader perspective.

MONOLOGICAL AND DIALOGICAL AGENCY

The main point I want to draw from Taylor is one he makes in *Modern Social Imaginaries*, where he describes collective agency as imagined.[22] Much as I have been arguing in the previous chapters that identity and affect are products of human imagination, he claims that collective agency is as well. If we take this idea seriously, as I believe we should, then it is possible to imagine democratic agency otherwise than Taylor does. I want to work through his ideas in order to open up that possibility.

Yet in order to explain his claim that collective agency is imagined, I first want to introduce a basic distinction that Taylor draws in his philosophical writings between two kinds of agency: monological and dialogical. While it might be tempting to think of monological agency as reflecting an objective picture of sharing, and dialogical agency an intersubjective one, as we will see in the following section, it turns out that Taylor treats both kinds of agency as imagined commonalities that can be objectively shared. So I want you to pay attention to this distinction, but do not draw any inferences just yet about how it plays out in Taylor's political thinking.

The first kind of agency Taylor describes is *monological*. Agency is monological when there is only a single actor.[23] An individual person, for example, is a monological agent, a single self that has "reflection, evaluation, and will."[24] Taylor associates monologicality with the modern idea that the self has authenticity: I have some true self that only I can discover through reflection.[25] He writes, "There is a certain way of being human that is my way. I am called upon to live my life in this way, and not in imitation of anyone else's life."[26] This authentic self is expressed in the will and actions of a monological agent.

Collective agents may also be monological, insofar as the individuals who make them up can be said to constitute a single self with a singular will. Taylor, drawing upon J. G. Herder, describes peoples in this way, as having a singular, authentic identity: "Just like individuals, a *Volk* should be true to itself, that is, its own culture."[27] The identity of the collective, like that of the individual, preexists and stands outside of the agent's activity. This authentic identity gives the people a singular voice and will. When two or more people act together as a monological agent, then, they share an identity, an intention, and a will. This is the kind of collective agency Taylor seems to have in mind in his discussion of "sharing identity space": we should share an authentic identity that makes us a collective, even if it is fleeting.

The second kind of agency is *dialogical*.[28] Dialogical agency is characterized by the plurality of the persons constituting the agent, by their different situations, and their different contributions to the collective action.[29] Dialogue is the example par excellence of this kind of agency: interlocutors do different things in a conversation, but they can still be understood to be doing something together, and they can (but do not need to) come to understand themselves as a "we" doing this together. Moreover, dialogue is something that can be performed neither by one person nor by a monological collective agent: the activity itself requires a plurality of persons. Finally, in dialogical agency, the identity of the collective is brought into being by the group itself; there is no authentic self that preexists the activity of the agent. It is through acting that the dialogical agency comes to have identity and will.

Dialogical actions, unlike monological ones, are performed by an agent that is nonindividual. Some of the examples that Taylor takes as paradigmatic of dialogical action are two people sawing a log and two dancers ballroom dancing.[30] These actions—sawing and dancing—could not be performed by a single individual, acting alone. One individual could not manage a two-handled saw. One person dancing would not be doing ballroom dancing but something quite different: it takes two to tango. Furthermore, the actions of sawing and dancing are more than just the sum of the different actions performed by each individual. We can distinguish the actions performed by each individual agent. One logger pulls as the other pushes the saw. One dancer steps forward with his left foot, the other steps backward with her right. But we would be missing something important if we were to describe the sawing of the log or the dancing as simply the sum of the pushing and pulling, the left foot and the right foot. In each case, the collective action is only truly successful when the individuals involved succeed at acting together, as one.

As these examples illustrate, an action is dialogical when it involves some kind of rhythmic interaction between two or more persons.[31] It cannot simply be the chance effect of multiple individual acts taken together. While in sawing and ballroom dancing, the two participants coordinate their actions so as to act as one, this degree of complementarity is not essential to dialogical agency. Indeed, in conversation, interlocutors respond rhythmically to one another (at least when they do it well), yet their actions do not need to have the same kind of structured complementarity as in partner dancing in order to be successful.[32]

Let me work through the example of a conversation to explain how dialogical agency emerges in the rhythmic interactions between people. When I engage you in a conversation, I initiate a *common* action. I act together with you as we converse; by interacting, you and I create a "we."[33] Imagine talking with another person, even about something as trivial as the weather:

> When I open up about the weather to you over the back fence, what this does is make the weather an object for us. It is no longer just for you or for me, with perhaps the addition that I know it is for you and you know it is for me. Conversation transposes the weather into an object we are considering together. The considering is in common, in that the background understanding established is that the agency which is doing the considering is us together, rather than each of us on our own managing to dovetail our action with the other.[34]

Before you and I speak to one another, the weather can be an object for you, and it can be an object for me, but it cannot yet be an object for *us*. When we begin to speak, we make the weather an object that we are considering in common. By the same token, I could talk to myself about the weather, and you might coincidentally also talk about the weather during periods when I am silent. But this would not yet be a conversation. A conversation requires more than the chance coordination of the words each of us speaks. We must have the conversation *together*; there must be a *rapport* between the persons having the conversation. The way that my words respond to yours, the way I attend to you when you speak, the way we both follow understood rules about how to chitchat all are signs that we are doing this together. My half of the conversation would appear senseless on its own. In having a conversation, you and I have inaugurated a social relation, a shared dialogical agent, a "we." This, then, is how dialogical agency gets connected to politics for Taylor: through our interactions, we found public space, we make matters something that we can consider in common.[35] In Arendtian terms, this dialogical interaction is world-building.

MONOLOGICAL PEOPLES AND DIALOGICAL PUBLICS

The abstract notions of monological and dialogical agency show up in Taylor's *Modern Social Imaginaries* in the form of two distinctively modern concepts of collective agency: the self-ruling people and the discursive public.[36] Each of these corresponds to a different way in which moderns experience themselves as belonging to collectivities. The distinctively modern feature of collective agency is that it is shared with strangers—with people we may never meet, and whom we need not meet in order to understand ourselves as acting together.[37] As a consequence, and drawing on Benedict Anderson, Taylor asserts that we must imagine ourselves to form peoples and publics.

The peculiarly modern manifestation of monological collective agency is found in the idea of a *people* that preexists our acting together. The self-ruling people is prepolitical: that is, it is imagined as having existed prior to the founding of the political community. Taylor describes the emergence of this way of imagining community in the period of the American Revolution, culminating in the U.S. Constitution's invocation of "We, the people," a people that preexists the Constitution itself, and so is able to write and authorize it. "Here the idea is invoked that a people or, as it was also called at the time, a 'nation' can exist prior to and independently of its political constitution by its own free action in secular time."[38] This is a people with a singular personality and will, the *Volk* of the essay on recognition that must be authentic to its own culture.

Dialogical collective agency emerges in the modern world in the form of the *public*. The public comes into existence only in and through the actions that are distinctive of a public. It does not exist prior to this acting, and it disappears if the action ceases. "The public sphere," Taylor writes, "is an association that is constituted by nothing outside of the common action we carry out in it: coming to a common mind, where possible, through the exchange of ideas."[39] What is peculiar about the public is that it involves imagining ourselves to be doing something together (engaging in an exchange of ideas) without gathering in a common space to do so.[40] Because we have no immediate experience of interaction with the strangers who are a part of the public, because we may never meet them or even know for sure that they are out there engaging in an exchange of ideas with us, "a public sphere can exist only if it is imagined as such."[41]

Both peoples and publics are imagined communities for Taylor in the sense that they do not correspond to a first-person experience of community; they must be imagined because they involve conceptualizing community with strangers. As Michael Warner puts it, "The modern social imaginary does not make sense without strangers. A nation or public or market in which everyone could be known personally would be no nation or public or market at all. This constitutive and normative environment of stranger-hood is more, too, than an objectively describable *Gesellschaft*; it requires our constant imagining."[42] Yet, for Taylor, an imaginary is not in and of itself particularly modern; premodern peoples had different imaginaries of their own. Nor does he think that imaginaries always involve relationships with strangers: our personal relationships can be governed by imaginaries as well.

Taylor invokes the term "imaginary," then, both to include Anderson's understanding of modern communities as imagined and to talk about a much broader and ahistorical phenomenon: the need for human beings to make sense of their experiences of the world. I therefore take his use of "imaginary" to be compatible with the broader sense in which I have been using the word in this book. The term "social imaginary" for Taylor is meant to capture "the ways people imagine their social existence, how they fit together with others, how things go on between them and their fellows, the expectations that are normally met, and the deeper normative notions and images that underlie these expectations."[43] In other words, we moderns have to imagine collective agency in terms of peoples or publics not simply because we live in a world in which we share community with strangers, but also—and more important—because it is through imaginaries that we make sense of our world and our practices in the first place.

Imaginaries are a matter of phenomenology, not ontology. Peoples and publics do not exist as such; they only exist, as Warner puts it, through "our constant imagining." That is, these forms of collective agency have meaning for us not because they correspond to how things actually are but because they correspond to how we experience the world. There is no public without people participating in it imagining that it exists. Correspondingly, although Taylor himself never says as much, there is no people or nation without humans who imagine that it exists. Monological peoples, like dialogical publics, are equally the product of human action and meaning-making, even though they are imagined to be prior to it.

This is not to say, as Taylor himself cautions, that imaginaries are purely ideological. "Ideas always come in history wrapped up in certain practices, even if these are only discursive practices."[44] Our imaginaries have traction because they help us to make sense of what we already do; they are not independent of existing structures and discourses but symbiotic with them. For example, in describing the historical development of the public sphere, Taylor notes that while "a public sphere can exist only if it is imagined as such," ideas are an insufficient condition to produce a public. As he notes, "This doesn't mean that imagination is all-powerful. There are objective conditions: internal, for instance, that the fragmentary local discussions interrefer; and external, that is, there must be printed materials, circulating from a plurality of independent sources, for there to be bases of what can be seen as a common discussion."[45] Ideas must relate to and make sense of existing structures and practices. A social imaginary is not just ideas but practices; it is how we make sense of our world, which leads us to do things in a particular fashion. Imaginaries need not correspond to "how the world is"—they are not truth claims. Indeed, imaginaries can be ideological in the sense that they are at odds with actual practices, so long as they serve their function of helping us to make sense of the world. For example, we might subscribe to the belief that we constitute a self-governing people, at the same time as our practices of self-government—elections, representation, free exchange of ideas in a public sphere—are compromised by the corruption of government officials, the influence of corporations, and the disproportionate access by the wealthy to power.

It is in this sense that imagined collective agency is a matter of phenomenology rather than objective truth. It may correspond to a range of social practices like ballroom dancing, conversation, contracts and other mutual agreements, elections, and opinion polling. Yet in each of these instances, there is also a practice of humans interpreting these practices as performed by a collective agency. Collective agency, then, arises in social practices of meaning-making. We moderns have a particular, contingent history of conceptualizing peoples and publics as collective agents, and of associating these agencies with particular practices. Human beings do this imaginative work; collective agencies do not exist as such, but only by virtue of being imagined by human beings. Collective agency, whether conceived as monological or dialogical, on a small scale or a large one, is a matter of the first-person experience of the world and a product of human action. Peoples and publics are two kinds of imaginary—phenomenological descriptions of how humans experience their world, rather than empirical descriptions of how the world objectively is. It is this basic insight—that collective agency is the product of human imagination, rather than commonality—that I draw from Taylor's work in order to critique and move beyond it.

SHARING IMAGINARIES IN COMMON WITH OTHERS

While Taylor and I agree that collective agency is the product of human imagining, we disagree about how people share imaginaries in common. For Taylor, imaginaries of collective agency must be the same for all who share them; that is, he believes they are shared objectively. Commonality is a characteristic of all social imaginaries: if they were not actually common, they would not be *social* and could not impact large numbers of people. This is implicit in how Taylor defines the term: "The social imaginary is that common understanding that makes possible common practices and a widely shared sense of legitimacy."[46] This is why it is so threatening to him to think that some citizens might not identify with the democratic sovereign: the collective agency of the demos depends upon all of us understanding it in the same way. If we do not all have the same imaginary, then we must renegotiate how we understand ourselves as a collective agency so that we can agree about how to imagine the demos. In other words, for Taylor, the social imaginary is the agreement that brings the collective agency into being. Moreover, it is not sufficient for Taylor that we experience ourselves as having a common imaginary of democratic sovereign agency; that experience must correspond to some actual state of affairs: that we really do have that common imaginary. Social imaginaries are a matter not just of first-person experience but also of truth for Taylor. So while he does acknowledge intersubjectivity in the form of dialogicality, and the role that human activity plays in shaping the world we share, he does not fully let go of an objective picture of sharing.

I propose instead that we think of imaginaries of collective agency as intersubjectively shared. This is to think of imaginaries as political claims. Rather than reflecting an already existing understanding of who "we" are, imaginaries are expressions of the hope that others share, or could come to share, a common understanding. They are solicitations to a public, inviting them to imagine the world as we do. As Linda Zerilli explains, "Political claims have a fundamentally *anticipatory* structure: we posit the agreement of others, that is, we perform an act of closure. Whether others do agree, however, is another matter and part of the openness of democratic politics itself."[47] The limitation of Taylor's use of "imaginary," then, is that he often seems to conflate the positing of the agreement of others with the actual agreement of others. Yet we do not need to agree that we form a collective agency, nor on the scope of that agency, in order for an imaginary to exercise a powerful impact on how we interact.

I take claims about imagined collective agency to be invitations to others to imagine collective agency in that way. This is perhaps easier to see with a new imaginary: it is an attempt to create a shared understanding that does not yet exist. Yet an invocation of an already familiar imaginary is also a political claim. Even though it draws upon a history of prior invocations, this kind of claim is also anticipatory: it can hope for acceptance but cannot guarantee it. The utterer, of course, may assume that his claim will be accepted because it is so familiar, yet the utterance can still fail to meet with the desired response. Every repetition of an existing imaginary is a moment when that imaginary can be rejected, transposed, or embraced. We may believe that our audience is in agreement with how we imagine the world, yet we may find out otherwise.

Moreover, because collective agency is imagined—that is, because it is not a fact about the world but rather is how humans make sense of their world—it is a matter of meaning rather than truth. This means that different people may make sense of the same structures and practices in different ways; there is nothing to anchor a single imaginary to a single set of practices. Democratic collective agency, for example, can be simultaneously conceptualized by different people in multiple, overlapping, not entirely contiguous ways. Perhaps we moderns who share an imaginary of "the people" or "the public" share a common understanding in the same way that all English speakers share the English language: we do not need to agree on definitions, rules of grammar and usage, pronunciation, or etiquette and decorum in order to be speaking the "same" language and be able to communicate with one another.

Because collective agency is a product of human imagination, it is possible to imagine it otherwise than we do. The tendency in democratic theory to conceptualize the demos as grounded in prepolitical agreement is itself contingent. How else might we imagine peoples and publics? Taking my cues again from Taylor, in the final sections of this chapter, I turn to develop an activity-oriented alternative to sovereign democratic agency.

DEMOCRATIC INTERAGENCY

The core of the conceptual muddle for democratic theory, I believe, arises from the dominant understanding of collective agency in terms of sovereignty rather than nonsovereignty. Taylor (like many democratic theorists) conceptualizes democratic agency as the agency of a popular sovereign. To think of the demos as a sovereign is to think of it as the uncontested authority and master of its own government. The demos as sovereign is a singular self with a discrete will. As Arendt notes in the epigraph to this chapter, sovereignty is "the ideal of uncompromising self-sufficiency and mastership." The sovereign demos rules itself, with no interference from anyone else. This way of thinking about democratic agency, then, sets up a stark opposition between those who are included in the demos and those who are not. Sovereignty, that is, generates the dynamic of democratic exclusion: To be included is to rule as one; to be excluded is to have no legitimate voice in decision making.

This imaginary of the demos as sovereign reinforces the appeal of a commonality-oriented view of democracy because it promises that we can include all if we can correctly identify the commonality we share. If only the demos exercises rule, then who is included in the demos is of crucial importance: to be excluded is to be relegated to political irrelevance. Only those persons who are a part of the people have the legitimate authority to shape the will of the popular sovereign; all others are simply interlopers. I may be overstating the case here—perhaps no theorists would recognize themselves in this description—but I am doing so in order to highlight why inclusion is so very important to democratic theorists who think of agency in terms of sovereignty. They take exclusion from the democratic sovereign to be equivalent to the denial of democratic agency altogether. Consider the kind of existential terror I described in chapter 3 that grips essentialist feminists concerned about exclusions from the category of women: their fear is that, if we cannot get "women" right, then we cannot have feminism. Similarly, democratic theorists concerned about exclusion from the democratic sovereign worry that, if we cannot get "the people" right, then we cannot have democracy: those who are excluded are ruled by others and do not govern themselves; those who are included rule illegitimately. We *must* be able to get the demos right—and so Taylor assures us the problem is not with democracy but instead with our exclusionary ways of thinking.

Danielle Allen explicitly connects the problem of democratic exclusion with an understanding of sovereign democratic agency. She acknowledges that we will all lose some decisions in a democracy; however, not all citizens are prepared to accept these losses, and they experience themselves as excluded from the demos.[48] Unlike Taylor, she does attribute this problem to democracy: "Democracy puts its citizens under a strange form of psychological pressure by building them up as sovereigns and then regularly undermining each citizen's experience of sovereignty."[49] Democracy, that is, offers us the promise that we will be able to rule ourselves but fails to deliver on it. No citizen is completely sovereign, only obeying laws she would make for herself.

Allen assigns the blame here to democracy, but I contend the fault lies instead with thinking of democracy in terms of sovereignty. I believe we misunderstand democracy when we think of it as a political philosophy of sovereignty (the rule of the people by the people), when it is instead one of nonsovereignty (the intersubjective sharing of authority by plural subjects). What if sharing democracy does not look like forming a singular, sovereign agency united by a common agreement, but like sharing intersubjectively?

I draw on Taylor's account of dialogical collective agency to conceptualize democratic agency in a way that is compatible with nonsovereignty, what I call *democratic interagency*. Dialogical agency emerges in intersubjective interactions between people, like rhythmic conversation. The collective agency arises in the interaction, in the rapport, the back-and-forth between interlocutors. Ordinarily, we can interact with one another without knowing whether we share an understanding of what we are doing together, and without even needing to have such a shared understanding. In some cases, we may have an explicit agreement about what we are doing: in ballroom dance, for example, we may have a carefully choreographed sequence of moves we have decided to make together. However, prior agreement and a shared understanding of what we are doing together are neither necessary nor sufficient to produce dialogical collective action. Think of the unboundedness of an unscripted conversation, or of the unpredictability of the public response to an op-ed or a politician's speech. Our interactions with others are ordinarily characterized by us not knowing how things are going to turn out. We might believe that others are going to interact with us in particular ways, that they share with us an intention and a will, but that is just a belief. Through our interactions we may discover that we do not share an understanding of what we are doing together at all, we may discover that we do not all think of ourselves as constituting the same "we." Such a discovery would not negate the fact that we had interacted.

In the context of dialogical agency, claims about who "we" are, are attempts to make meaning out of our interactions. Just as humans select which features make "this" a table, we select which interactions with which people constitute collective agency. Recall Taylor's example of two people talking about the weather. I can describe our conversation as the interaction of two individual agents ("I am talking with you about the weather"), or I can describe it as the action of a plural agent ("we are talking about the weather"). The actions being described are exactly the same in both cases; the difference is in how they are described, what meaning I assign to them. Similarly, when we look at interactions among a much larger collection of people and describe them as "democratic will-formation" or "public deliberation," this is a matter of interpretation. We select certain kinds of dialogical interactions and attribute to them a particular kind of significance. This is to lay a claim to how we should imagine the demos as a collective agency: the demos is defined by these kinds of interactions between these persons and not those, just as the table is defined by these features and not those. "The people" is always only one particular imaginary of the people among many, an imaginary that is not to be confused either with the persons who subscribe to that particular imaginary or with the persons understood to be included in the imaginary. The demos is always plural rather than singular. To paraphrase Arendt, not one demos but demoi inhabit the world.

Democratic agency, then, lies not (as Taylor would have it) in the substance of any particular claim about the demos but in the dialogical activity of claiming itself. We exercise democratic agency together with others when we engage in making sense of the world intersubjectively, when through communication we make things like the weather matters for us to consider together, and when we make claims that go beyond our subjective experience and that seek the confirmation of others.

Democratic interagency, in other words, is the dialogical exercise of political freedom in the company of others: "the creation, and continual reinvention, of institutions that sustain a worldly in-between."[50] This agency is democratic both in the sense that it belongs equally to all humans and in the sense that it is a form of self-government. We govern ourselves by making sense of the world in that we seek to shape our world not just for ourselves but for the plural others who inhabit it with us—we seek to make meaning with others, and not merely subjectively. Yet this is a nonsovereign form of self-government: no one is sovereign over meaning. This means that no one can or should aim to control how others see the world. It also means that there is always the possibility of altering how we see the world: no matter how hegemonic a worldview may appear to be, it cannot preclude all alternatives.

The vision of democratic agency I have put forward is a radical one in the sense that it locates democracy wherever people interact with one another to create and sustain a world, rather than with specific institutions of the state and public sphere. My argument in this sense bears resemblance to Arendt (who emphasizes the spontaneous appearance of power in collective gatherings) as well as to Wolin. For Wolin, moments in which ordinary people come together to act democratically are "episodic, rare."[51] While I agree with him that democracy can emerge outside of formal institutions, I would disagree with him that such moments are rare, even if they are often episodic. Insofar as world-building relies upon both instituted and instituting imaginaries, on the repetition of established practices as well as on their critique, transformation, and rejection, it is an everyday occurrence. This is in keeping with the more expansive definition of "the political" that I take from feminism: we are engaged in world-sustaining and world-building activities in any aspect of our lives that is shared intersubjectively; potentially, everything can become the subject of political world-building.

Therefore, democratic interagency is not reducible to the agency of the popular sovereign. This is the case first in the sense that democratic interagency is not restricted to actions taking place within the formal institutions of the state and the public sphere. Yet it is also not restricted to actions taking place only among citizens of a single state. As a consequence, this understanding of democratic collective agency enables us to see those who do not engage in state-oriented politics as democratic actors. Think here of transnational political actors—environmental groups, for example, or the antisweatshop movement—who build alliances and take actions that are neither bounded by nor directed solely toward states. But think also of the kind of people that Taylor and Allen are concerned that democratic states risk excluding: those who are deeply critical of or who outright reject the legitimacy of a sovereign democratic agency that purports to include them. Taylor sees the Quebecois as simply excluded from democracy because they are repeatedly outvoted, yet we can also see the secessionist movement as an important exercise of democratic agency, insofar as it aimed to imagine a new set of political relationships for Quebec and Canada. Allen sees African Americans as distrustful of sharing democracy because of the repeated and unreciprocated sacrifices they have made for white citizens, yet we can also appreciate how claims of racial injustice and refusals to vote can be important acts contesting how white Americans make sense of the world they share. Or think of Putnam's protesting turtles, discussed in chapter 4, who do not register to vote but take part in protests and social reform movements: their opting out of institutionalized democracy need not be interpreted as opting out of democracy altogether. Finally, as I discuss further in the following chapter, think of the activism of noncitizens critical of their host state's policies; they claim the right to have a voice in decision making without claiming citizenship. These examples suggest that to adopt a dialogical view of democratic agency is to correct for a problem with sovereign democratic agency—that it at worst occludes and at best devalues forms of democratic agency that do not fall neatly within the boundaries of formal institutions. In this sense, democratic interagency ironically offers the more inclusive vision of democracy.

INCLUSION AS INTERACTION

In conclusion, let me show how this conception of interagency would address Taylor's dilemma of democratic exclusion. One might think that to acknowledge democratic agency as arising whenever and wherever people are engaged in meaning-making would mean that I could not explain that there is anything particularly unjust about exclusion from formal democratic institutions. It might seem as if democratic interagency even authorized such exclusions: as long as people can exercise agency *somewhere*, it does not matter that they cannot exercise it within institutionalized democracy. On this reading, the position I am advocating could look as if it recklessly deflects attention away from state-based injustices, as if it minimizes the very real impact of exclusion from public institutions. I do not intend my argument to make such moves. What I am doing is placing political freedom—rather than the democratic state and public sphere—at the center of our view of democratic collective agency. This does not make Taylor's democratic exclusion invisible or incomprehensible. Rather, it shifts what counts as inclusion and exclusion in the first place.

First, let me explain what inclusion looks like from the perspective of democratic interagency. People are included in democratic interagency when they can participate in the intersubjective practice of world-building. Inclusion is *acting with others* in order to make meaning of the world we share; it is the active exercise of political freedom in the company of plural subjects. Acting with others does not necessarily mean that we share the same purpose in acting, although we may. Nor does it necessarily mean that we share the same intentions in acting, although we may share those, too. Debating, disagreeing, protesting, arguing, challenging—these are all dialogical activities that we do with others, without having to share either a will or a motive. The others whom we address with our arguments and challenges do not even need to be doing the same kind of activity as us; they do not need to respond in kind with debate, argument, challenge, and so on. But in order for us to be acting with them, they do need to dialogically respond to our arguments, challenges, and protests. And they need to do so in a way that is compatible with continuing our interaction rather than bringing it to an end. Interacting thus requires establishing and reestablishing some form of rapport, some kind of acknowledgment between interlocutors—even though this may fall far short of, say, a Kantian ideal of mutual respect.

Inclusion, understood in this way, is not about achieving certain outcomes. It is not a matter of winning an argument or securing a seat at the table. It is not about reaching an agreement about who "we" are. It is not about feeling heard, being recognized, or being treated as an equal. Rather, inclusion is a matter of ongoing interaction—interaction that may itself aim at some of these goals but that need not achieve them in order to be inclusive. Inclusion is sharing in the activity of shaping the world with others, which is always going to be characterized by nonsovereignty, by loss, by not getting what one wants (at least not all of the time). We can get a response from our interlocutors that may not be the response we want, that may be rude or offensive, but that is still a response that keeps our interaction going, rather than shutting it down.

If inclusion is simply ongoing interaction, exclusion happens when the rapport and rhythm of that dialogical interaction are disrupted or refused altogether. Let me illustrate this first by way of the example of a one-on-one conversation. There are lots of ways that one could disrupt or refuse to engage in dialogical rapport with another person, such as walking away, ignoring the other's attempt at striking up a conversation, dismissing the other person as not worth talking to, or ending the conversation in such a way as to render future dialogue impossible, or at least unlikely. In larger scale interactions, this might look like a refusal to engage others who address us—as when a politician ignores a protest, a chair refuses to acknowledge a speaker, or a media outlet disregards and does not address claims that it is biased. It might also look like an inability to perceive the others who address us as legitimate interlocutors—as when claims made by underprivileged persons are dismissed as irrational, inarticulate, or lacking in the appropriate expertise. Or it might look like we simply did not notice someone trying to engage our attention, as when someone trying to intervene in a conversation is not acknowledged because those of us already engaged in it are too intent on talking to each other to take notice. Or it might look like seeking to eliminate the possibility of future dialogical interaction, as when a government forcibly or coercively shuts down protest or dissent, or when people label their opponents in a way intended to delegitimize their position—perhaps as un-American, anti-Israel, racist, or terrorist. Or it might look like ending a conversation because our business together has been concluded, as when debate on a bill is called to a close so that the legislature may vote; or like ending a conversation because we need to move on to other matters, as when a discussion is set aside for more pressing issues, or when it is simply time to go home, to end the session, to leave office. These kinds of actions signal either the failure to generate dialogical rapport, or the desire to bring interaction to an end. Some ways in which we fail to generate or prolong interaction may be healthier and more justified, and others more dysfunctional and problematic, yet they all are forms of closure and exclusion.

With this understanding of dialogical agency in mind, while democratic theorists often invoke commonality with the aim of including diverse persons, I claim that to do so is ironically to exclude. Commonality theorists aim to discover the source of commonality that does or should unite the people. In so doing, they seek to settle the question of who "we" are, thereby putting an end to dialogical exchange. Someone like Taylor might not want to end this discussion once and for all but perhaps just for as long as our negotiated identity suffices. Seeking to end (even if only temporarily) exchange about the identity of the demos is a more well-meaning form of seeking to put an end to interaction than, say, sending in the troops to quell peaceful dissent. Nonetheless, insofar as the aspiration is to settle, put an end to discussion, or at least postpone discussion for a generation or more, the impulse behind the invocation of commonality here is one that ironically functions as a form of exclusion rather than a form of inclusion. It aims to close down conversation about who "we" are, instead of opening it up. I have been arguing in this book that we should see as troubling the kinds of exclusion produced by the belief that democracy requires commonality, because they occlude and disavow our capacity for political freedom. My argument, too, is a claim that aims at exclusion: at persuading my readers to let go of one way of seeing and to adopt another. Which exclusions we should be troubled by, and which we endorse or at least can live with is a matter of interpretation and politics. I can only hope you will be persuaded to agree with me.

This shifted view of inclusion and exclusion still allows us to talk about what Taylor characterizes as "democratic exclusion" as problematic for democracy—although for slightly different reasons than he himself gives. The failure to be fully included in formal institutions of democracy is not a failure because this makes it difficult for excluded citizens to identify with the will of the popular sovereign. It is not a problem on my view if the Quebecois do not identify with the will of the Canadian people. That kind of disidentification is going to occur frequently in democracy because the demos is imagined in plural ways. An American citizen, for example, might have rejected the results of the 2000 presidential election as illegitimate because they did not reflect the will of the people as expressed by the majority of the voters, despite the fact that the will was determined by an institution assigned the task of selecting the president by a democratically ratified constitution—the Electoral College.[52] While we often designate certain procedures to approximate the will of the people (like majority rule, public opinion arising from print media, and polling data), no one of these procedures is able to settle the question of what the demos wills because collective agency is manifest in a plurality of overlapping and competing imaginaries of who "we, the people" are. As a consequence, we can expect disagreement and disaffection as by-products of institutionalized democracy. Indeed, as I said at the outset, disagreement, betrayal, loss, and disappointment are all expected features of living in a world with plural others. To take these as troubling signs of exclusion is to pathologize plurality itself.

Exclusion is a problem on my account of democratic interagency when people are in some way systematically barred from participation in shaping the world they share with others, when interaction is impossible. Let us think about this in terms of feminist demands for women to hold public office and positions of leadership in politics, business, and associational life. Women's relative absence from boardrooms and legislatures is not a problem because women are excluded from politics or pursuing certain careers. Formally, at least, women in Western democracies no longer face such forms of overt discrimination in most occupations. Nor is it a problem because "women's interests" (assuming we could even locate such a thing) are not heard or represented by male elites. There is no necessary reason why men—or even men accompanied by a handful of women—could not hear or represent women. The claim that women's relative absence is a problem is a matter of political freedom: the absence of women indicates their systematic exclusion from significant areas of involvement in shaping the world in which they live. Exclusion always involves a curtailment of political freedom, and it is on these grounds that we should evaluate the exclusions we inevitably have to make.

My discussion of democratic interagency in this chapter has been rather abstract. In the following chapter, I aim to make it a bit more concrete by working through the democratic interagency I see expressed in protests, and in particular expressed in the 2006 immigrant rights protests and co-protests with the Westboro Baptist Church and the Ku Klux Klan in the United States. Protests function for me as a model for a new imaginary of democracy, one that combines the insights of the three central chapters of this book: understanding the demos as the intersubjectively contested product of human imagination, accepting responsibility for how we imagine the demos and with whom we feel solidarity, and finally viewing democratic agency as a matter of ongoing dialogical interaction between persons engaged in trying to make sense with one another of the world we share.

CHAPTER 6

"This is What Democracy Looks Like"

Protests as Democratic Imaginary

Clearly, we do not think that to give oneself authority is an individual act. Authority is received originally from another human being who is in a position to give it, who has the authority to give it. But she cannot have it if the person who needs to receive it does not acknowledge it in her.

—The Milan Women's Bookstore Collective[1]

TWO WAYS OF SEEING DEMOCRACY

Whether we see a duck or a rabbit in the duck-rabbit depends on how we look at the drawing. The difference is in our way of seeing, not in the drawing itself, which remains unchanged. We see those lines now as a duck's bill, now as a rabbit's ears, yet they are the same lines. The duck and the rabbit represent two different ways of seeing the same phenomenon.

Similarly, I have been arguing that there are two different ways that we can look at the same phenomena of democratic politics. On the first, objective view, we see democracy in terms of commonality. We see what the people have in common, and what they do not. We see commonality as the glue that holds democracy together, that binds diverse individuals into a singular, collective agency. We see commonality as the foundation that makes it possible for us to act together, to safely disagree with and differ from one another. We see the absence of commonality as a problem for democracy that must be overcome.

On the second, intersubjective view, we see the same phenomena of democracy, but this time in terms of political freedom: the nonsovereign capacity each of us has to shape the world in which we live. We see democracy as the never-ending, ongoing process of shaping the world we inhabit together with plural others. We see commonality as the contingent and fragile product of human interaction rather than its ground. We see the occlusion of our freedom and disengagement from this world-building activity as the main threats to democracy.

While it does not matter whether we see a duck or a rabbit in the duck-rabbit, the way that we see democracy has very significant consequences for what we value, what we do, and how we relate to one another. When we focus on commonality, the result is that we take an ironically antidemocratic view of democracy. This is most clear when we treat commonality as an objective fact, entirely independent of the people who are said to share in it. Objective commonalities can be identified by elite observers, who can then report on the truth of what a democratic people does or does not share in common. On this view, the people themselves do not have an active role to play in determining what they have in common. Commonality is seen both as central to democracy and as external and prior to democratic action.

Yet it is also the case that we can take an antidemocratic view of democracy even when we treat commonality as an intersubjective artifact, the product of our political claiming and contestation, so long as we continue to view democracy in terms of what we have in common. When political theorists and actors prioritize commonality as the end of democratic politics, they devalue and occlude political freedom—even where they adopt a political conception of commonality. In order to mitigate the antidemocratic tendencies of a commonality orientation, we need to do more than just understand commonality to be the product of human action; we need to shift to an intersubjective way of seeing democracy.

I will make this argument here through a reading of a series of protest marches and rallies that took place in 2006 across the United States, protests that were more or less focused on proposed changes to US immigration law. One way that these protests can be read is as an example of commonality-oriented democratic collective action. The protesters, according to this interpretation, formed a coalition united by their common goal: opposing a bill passed by the US House of Representatives. The imaginary of the coalition—a contingent alliance formed for the moment in order to achieve a common purpose—has figured prominently in feminist and leftist attempts to rethink how democratic collective action is possible among a diverse population. It is an expression of a purely political conception of commonality: what unites the group is their present agreement on a political claim, but nothing more. Yet as these protests demonstrated, when we make the pursuit of common goals the end of democratic action, we are likely to sacrifice and occlude political freedom for its sake. When we adopt the imaginary of the coalition, we stress the *outcomes* of political action at the expense of the political *activity* itself. As I will show, protest organizers discouraged the protesters' plural voices and expressions of freedom when these threatened the achievement of their policy aims. And once the leaders' goal was achieved, the protests abruptly ended, as if collective action no longer had a purpose.

Through my reading of these protests, I argue that we should shift our way of seeing democracy to one that views the ongoing exercise of political freedom as the end of democratic activity. When we engage in politics primarily to achieve particular outcomes, we instrumentalize political action: we see our activity as valuable only insofar as it produces the results we desire. This outcome orientation to politics can undermine the motivation to act. If we achieve our goals, then it appears there is no more reason to engage in political activity. If we do not achieve our goals, then we may become demoralized and unmotivated to continue the struggle. An attachment to outcomes in politics is an unstable source of motivation because we cannot guarantee what the results of our political activity will be in a world of plural subjects. My wager is that, if we place the stress instead on the activity of political freedom itself, and acknowledge the uncertainty that we will achieve the specific outcomes we desire, we will be better able to maintain the enthusiasm and commitment to political activity that we need to weather the risks of acting in a world we share with others. This is not to say that politics should somehow be free of content, that we should abandon our goals, but that we should attenuate our attachment to those goals so as to be open to the uncertainty and the pleasure of what might come.

This vision of sharing democracy is one that requires the cultivation of *democracy sense*. Recall my discussion in chapter 2 of Hannah Arendt's understanding of "community sense": the awareness that we share the world in common with plural others, who are also themselves subjects. This, for her, is the basis for communication: it is both what makes communication necessary (that you are not the same as me) and what makes it possible (that I assume we can understand one another through the use of words and expressions that have intersubjective meaning). Democracy sense builds on this concept. It is the awareness that each of us has the capacity to make sense of our world intersubjectively, that is, to try to shape how we and others experience the world. We may not succeed at changing our world, of course. In order to do so, the claims I make about the world must be accepted by others, although I cannot guarantee that they will be (except, perhaps, by using nondemocratic means such as force and censorship of alternatives). Moreover, this way of understanding the world must find expression in practices, where its appeal is reinforced and repeated. To have democracy sense, then, is to have the awareness that we live in a world of plural subjects who each has this capacity; but it is not to have the effective ability to determine the shape of the world. We may pursue particular outcomes in politics, but we cannot guarantee them. We exercise this world-building capacity in a world we inhabit with others, and so democracy sense is also a sense of our nonsovereignty over this world that we nonetheless can play a role in shaping.

Democracy requires the cultivation of democracy sense in order to counteract the many pressures there are on us to accept our world, and our understanding of the world, as given. We might take certain aspects of our world as given for a variety of reasons: because we have inherited a particular worldview, because science or some other expert discourse declares this worldview to be a matter of truth, or perhaps because the power that holds this worldview in place seems impossible to displace. We need to be reminded that the world could be otherwise than it is, that the order of things is not inevitable, and that we can think and act differently than we do now. And we need to cultivate opportunities for people to actively engage in world-building.

Therefore, in the place of coalition, I offer protest as an imaginary of democracy that places political freedom at its center. Protests are an expression of our human capacity for political freedom: by acting together, protesters claim the radically democratic right to shape the world in which they live. I believe this is what was so inspiring about the protesters in Tahrir Square in spring 2011: the world watched as Egyptians discovered in themselves this capacity for freedom, a freedom we can all recognize as human, even if we do not actively exercise it ourselves.

Protests are also occasions that may facilitate a first-person awareness of sharing the world with plural others. In protesting, we march alongside of strangers with whom we might not otherwise interact, we confront opposition from without and disagreement from within, and we take the risk of acting into a world without knowing in advance what impact, if any, we will have. Protests are typically characterized by a cacophonous plurality of voices, by the nonsovereignty of any one actor, and by uncertainty over the outcome of our collective action. In these ways, I take protests to be exemplary of democratic action more generally. Insofar as we share the world with plural subjects, we possess the capacity for political freedom, yet can exercise it only in conditions of nonsovereignty and uncertainty. We act together with strangers, authorizing one another to act as free persons, yet without knowing how others will respond, who will turn up, whether there will be violence, in short, what the outcome will be. The point of protesting, as of all political action, is to act anyhow in the hopes that one may have some effect on shaping the world we inhabit together.

THE 2006 IMMIGRANT RIGHTS PROTESTS

To set the stage for my discussion of protesting, let me review the history of the 2006 immigrant rights protests. In December 2005, US representative Jim Sensenbrenner, a Republican from Wisconsin, introduced House Resolution 4437, The Border Protection, Anti-terrorism, and Illegal Immigration Control Act.[2] This bill, which never did become law, would have mandated increased militarization of the US borders with Mexico and Canada, made being undocumented in the United States a federal felony, and punished individuals and organizations that provided aid to undocumented persons. The bill was passed by the House of Representatives within a week and a half, with the support of most Republicans and the opposition of most Democrats. Immigrant rights groups had been lobbying politicians, organizing protests, and running voter registration campaigns long before this bill came before the House, but H.R. 4437 sparked a new round of political action that produced some of the largest protests the United States has ever witnessed. In January and February 2006, organizers from a variety of grassroots and established organizations held meetings to develop a collective strategy to oppose this bill through local, national, and transnational political actions during the course of the coming spring.[3]

Some 100,000 people participated in the first large-scale protest against the Sensenbrenner bill on March 10, 2006, in Chicago.[4] The rally at the end of the march included conventional displays of mainstream American patriotism: it began with a moment of silence in support of US troops serving in Iraq and with the recitation of the Pledge of Allegiance.[5] US representative Luis Guttierez, addressing the protesters, urged them to raise their American flags and declared both the desire and the right of immigrants to citizenship, saying, "This is our country, and this is where we will stay."[6] Yet, as many reports and photos of the protests indicate, the marchers also carried flags from a variety of other countries, including Ecuador, Guatemala, Colombia, and Mexico. While the response to the multiplicity of flags at this protest was comparatively muted, it prefigured a larger debate over protesters' tactics and motives as the protests spread across the country.[7] This debate was prompted when Lou Dobbs, the commentator on CNN who had become famous in recent years for his extreme anti-immigration stance, mentioned the flags on his show on the evening of March 10. After a correspondent gave his report on the protests, Dobbs remarked, "One of the things that I noted—I don't know if you did. I assume you did. A lot of Mexican flags in that parade. I wonder why. Just a question."[8]

The question Dobbs raised (along with his emphasis on Mexican flags in particular) became the focus of much media coverage and political criticism of the immigration rights protests in March and April. On March 25, an estimated 1.7 million people participated in protests across the country, with the largest march in Los Angeles drawing 500,000.[9] Again, protesters carried the flags of multiple nations, including that of the United States. Student walkouts followed over the next week, mostly in California.[10] In what became a key piece of evidence for anti-immigrant commentators that marchers posed a threat to America, students protesting at Montebello High School on March 27 removed the California state flag from the school's flagpole, raised a Mexican flag, and then placed the US flag upside down beneath it.[11] Criticism also came from the left, either from supporters of immigrant rights who felt the non-US flags would undermine the goals of the protesters or from critics who supported immigrant rights but saw the flags as a sign of an unacceptable refusal to assimilate.[12]

In response to these criticisms and concerns, protest organizers began to shift tactics in time for the next large wave of protests on April 10, dubbed the National Day of Action.[13] At the protest in Washington, DC, for example, organizers handed out American flags to ensure that they were plentiful for any photographs. Cardinal Roger Mahoney, the Catholic archbishop of Los Angeles who played a significant leadership role in the marches, requested of protesters in LA "that unless you have an American flag, that you roll up flags from other countries and do not use them because they do not help us get the legislation we need."[14] Not all protesters complied, of course, but the protests from April 10 onward included many fewer non-US flags. In one notable act of resistance to this shift in tactics, Jose "El Che" Elias designed a flag made up of the flags of multiple nations that was displayed at a protest in LA on April 15.[15]

The final round of protests was organized for May Day: the Great American Boycott. Inspired by the satirical film *A Day without a Mexican*, organizers encouraged undocumented workers and students to attend protests and rallies instead of going to work and attending school, so that Americans could feel the economic impact of illegal immigration. Protests took place around the country, with the largest occurring again in Chicago and Los Angeles, where many of the immigrant rights organizations involved in the original planning were located. According to Alfonso Gonzales, these protests also marked a split between the more moderate and radical immigrant groups, with moderate groups calling for immigrants to stay on the job, and radicals encouraging more confrontational tactics.[16] These marches took place in the context of a new controversy over the patriotism of the marchers. On April 28, British music producer Adam Kidron released a Spanish-language version of the US national anthem, "[feeding] into a backlash on talk radio, the Internet, cable television and Capitol Hill, with conservatives complaining that it was encouraging the very cultural balkanization that they have feared all along."[17] President George W. Bush, asked to weigh in on the matter, stated, "I think people who want to be a citizen of this country ought to learn English. . . . And they ought to learn to sing the national anthem in English."[18]

The protests on May 1 were the final round in the *Gran Marchas*. In the second half of May, the US Senate worked on and eventually passed a bill on immigration (S. 2611) that eliminated some of the more controversial aspects of the House bill. However, Congress never managed in that session to work out the differences between the House and Senate bills in a conference committee, and so the bill was never made law. Even though it was always improbable that the Sensenbrenner bill would become law,[19] some protesters took the more moderate stance of the Senate bill as a sign of their influence on policy making.[20] If the organization of the protests marked a victory for immigrant rights, however, it was one that was short-lived. Even as immigration reform remains a perennial topic in US politics, the immigrant rights movement has failed to sustain the scale of the mobilization it achieved in spring 2006, and amnesty and a path to citizenship remain hotly contested policy options.[21] The more recent protests in 2010 in response to Arizona's S.B. 1070 were nowhere near as large or as widespread as the 2006 marches.[22]

THE *GRAN MARCHAS* AS COALITION POLITICS

We can make sense of these events by focusing on commonality or by focusing on political freedom. Whichever way of seeing we adopt, different aspects of the protests will come to the fore, and others will recede into the background. I will begin here by offering an account of the protests in terms of commonality, as an example of coalition politics: the diverse protesters came together, despite their different standpoints and reasons for opposing the Sensenbrenner bill, in order to act together as one to achieve a shared strategic goal. Most if not all of the protest organizers understood what they were doing in these terms. Indeed, the organizations that put together the *Gran Marcha* in Los Angeles referred to themselves as the March 25th Coalition. Cristina Beltràn also describes the protests in this way, as an "alliance" between citizens and noncitizens, legals and illegals.[23] For Gonzales, however, the term "coalition" is inappropriate, since there was no consistent leadership behind all the different actions. Rather, he notes, leadership "was fluid with organizations coming in and out, shifting positions at different points during the spring of 2006 and beyond."[24] Nonetheless, even his account of the fluidity of what he terms the "Latino Historic Bloc" of "organic intellectuals" can be made sense of in terms of coalition politics. The coalition's members and goals may have shifted, as well as its tactics, but at any point in the spring, there was some coalition of activists organizing the protests.

On this reading, the coalition was initially formed in January by various organizations and leaders united by their opposition to H.R. 4437. However, once a more moderate bill came up for consideration in the Senate, the original coalition began to splinter: some wanted to pursue a more radical agenda, "demand[ing] an immediate and unconditional legalization for the 12 million undocumented workers in the United States, and to struggle against the forces of global capitalism that displace workers in Latin America."[25] Others simply sought an immigration reform bill that lacked the more extreme provisions of the Sensenbrenner bill, which "would have converted . . . undocumented workers into felons while criminalizing anyone who works with undocumented workers." Satisfied that "a moderate immigration reform was better than no reform,"[26] the Catholic Church, many nonprofits, and labor unions together coalesced around a new goal: working with moderate Democrats to negotiate the terms of S. 2611.[27] They no longer needed to form a coalition with more radical groups and instead worked to pursue their more specific legislative goals in a different coalition with mainstream Democrats. The shifting political coalitions throughout the spring of 2006 were shaped by shifting—but still shared—strategic goals. These strategic goals, in turn, dictated the shifting tactics for the marches. Initially, the approach was simply to get as many people as possible into the streets to oppose H.R. 4437. However, when the marches became the target of anti-immigrant criticism because protesters were carrying flags from multiple countries, organizers began to discourage foreign flags and even to distribute American ones at marches. Carrying non-US flags only became a problem, from the perspective of coalition, when it began to undermine the ability of the protesters to achieve their common goal. According to this logic, the tactic that allowed protesters to display the multiple countries of immigrant origin had to be abandoned in order for the coalition to succeed at promoting immigrant rights.

The coalition is a powerful imaginary of political collective agency for leftist politics, especially in the wake of the social identity movements of the second half of the twentieth century. Rather than being united around a single ideology or platform, the left is divided among radicals and moderates; environmentalists and neoliberals; feminists, antiracists, and gay rights activists; religious organizations, race-based organizations, and so on. In order to get anything done, it seems, groups have to form coalitions around shared interests, so they can pool their resources, their numbers, and their weight at the ballot box. This was the impetus behind Jesse Jackson's National Rainbow Coalition, formed in 1984 after his unsuccessful run for the US presidency, which aimed to unite constituencies divided by identity politics: "The white, the Hispanic, the black, the Arab, the Jew, the woman, the native American, the small farmer, the businessperson, the environmentalist, the peace activist, the young, the old, the lesbian, the gay, and the disabled."[28] Coalition, then, is a way of imagining how diverse groups can work together as a collective agency with a singular will, despite or even because of their differences.

Coalition politics has been a particularly popular, if relatively unexamined, response in US feminist theory and politics to the problem of locating some kind of commonality that could unite different people to achieve feminist goals. It promises a way of making sense of how we can form a singular, political collectivity acting as one even as we know it is characterized by diversity: we are united by our common aims. Consequently, the coalition imaginary—whether articulated in the language of coalition, solidarity, or sisterhood—frees us from the need to either locate some ontological commonality that grounds feminist politics (e.g. the category of women), or to come to complete agreement on all matters. We need only agree about our shared goals, not about our reasons for pursuing them or about any additional goals each of us may wish to pursue separately. Bell hooks articulates the aspirations of this kind of imaginary of feminist collectivity when she writes, "Women do not need to eradicate difference to feel solidarity. . . . We can be sisters united by shared interests and beliefs, united in our appreciation for diversity, united in our struggle to end sexist oppression, united in political solidarity."[29] A coalition, then, is the expression of a political conception of commonality: its unity is defined by agreement on a contingent set of political claims.

Coalition is often presented in feminist texts of the 1980s and 1990s as an alternative to the feminism of the Second Wave.[30] It emerges in the context of narratives of US feminism that assume Second Wave feminists falsely presumed the universality of women's experiences and took the subject position of white, straight, middle-class women as the model for all.[31]

Third Wave feminism, by contrast, is portrayed as smarter than and critical of earlier feminisms because it is more attentive to differences of race, class, and sexuality.[32] Yet this historical narrative of American feminism is not entirely accurate. As Janet Jakobsen has argued, questions of alliance and coalition across diversity have been central to US feminist theory and activism since at least 1970.[33] Regardless of whose characterization of the history is correct, what is important for my purposes is that feminists gravitated toward the language and imagery of coalition in the 1980s and 1990s, in part as a response to the perceived theoretical and political difficulties of generating a shared feminist movement once the diversity of women and women's experiences became undeniable.[34] Moreover, the Rainbow Coalition in the mid-1980s gave feminist activists a practical example of what a postidentity politics, leftist movement could look like.[35] The coalition became the model for feminists looking for a practical response to the problem of generating a cohesive political movement while also acknowledging the diversity of women's perspectives, experiences, and positions.

Even though there is little theoretical examination of coalition politics in feminist theory, it has been the subject of two types of criticism. The first kind of criticism is that coalition politics is not a quick fix to the difficulties of acting together with plural others but rather requires a great deal more work and struggle than feminists often expect. Bernice Johnson Reagon famously makes this point when she notes that "if you're *really* doing coalition work," then "most of the time you feel threatened to the core and if you don't, you're not really doing no coalescing." This sense of threat is so intense for her that she states, "I feel as if I'm going to keel over any minute and die."[36] What she means here, I take it, is that coalition requires working together with people who are different from you and who are therefore threatening—perhaps they won't literally kill you, but by working together with them, you might figuratively be killed in that your voice, your perspective, your position, may not survive the encounter. Coalition, then, is a complex and scary process of collaborating with others who disagree, who are different, and who in the end may not be able to work together as partners—that is, it is a matter of acting with plural subjects. In a similar vein (although less dramatically), hooks notes that feminist solidarity requires embracing conflict and struggle "on an individual and collective level" as a means "to enhance and enrich our understanding of one another, as a guide directing and shaping the parameters of our political solidarity."[37] Coalition is not a simple matter of agreeing on common goals; arriving at those common goals, and facing up to all the disagreements and differences that lie beyond them—this is where the hard work takes place. Brenda Lyshaug develops even further the idea that successful coalition-building requires cultivating appropriate ethical habits at the individual level. She argues in particular for the development of "flexibil-ity with respect to one's own self-understanding and receptivity or openness to that which may seem alien, unappealing, and even threatening in others," as well as "a tolerance for ambiguity and change."[38] Sharing political goals is not enough; coalition partners must also have the interpersonal skills to understand and be open to all that they do not share. That is, arriving at some point of commonality does not alter the intersubjective reality that we must cultivate the ability to relate to one another as plural subjects.

The second kind of criticism of coalition politics is that it emphasizes strategic interests at the expense of other goods. Lyshaug articulates this concern as well, suggesting that coalition politics establishes a "purely tacti-cal temporary bond" grounded in self-interest. This relatively superficial bond, she argues, is not enough to generate the kind of acknowledgment of difference that feminists seek when they turn to coalition as a movement model.[39] Jodi Dean is perhaps the fiercest critic of the tendency of coalition politics to emphasize strategy. She argues that "the tactical solidarity of coa-lition politics relies on the contingent meeting of disparate interests." Con-sequently, the political community formed by coalition is disposable: we have an interest in building and sustaining community only so long as our contingent interests coincide. The minute we meet our goals, or our inter-ests shift, the coalition can be tossed aside. "Solidarity is reduced to a means, subject to the calculations of success of those seeking to benefit from it."[40]

I share Lyshaug's and Dean's concerns about the emphasis in coalition politics on shared strategic goals; however, I am concerned that even the modified forms of solidarity they advocate are still to some extent locked in this logic. That is, we could understand their arguments as arguments that feminists simply need to add ethical depth to the goals they share when they act in coalition, but they are still bound together as a cohesive collective agent by virtue of (actual or ideal) commonality. Rather than simply pursu-ing policy changes or legislative action, Lyshaug and Dean argue that femi-nists in coalition also need to pursue the goals of unity and agreement. For Lyshaug, the failing of coalition politics is that it does not take unity seri-ously as a political goal: "It honors the claims of diversity among women while ignoring the importance of commonality."[41] Her aim is to encourage "the establishment of political ties that honor both the differences that sepa-rate women and the shared humanity that unites them."[42] Dean, drawing on Jürgen Habermas, argues for the communicative production of a "we," a community that is always in the process of becoming itself, that is never fin-ished, and that is always the subject of further reflection and critique.[43] Yet driving her understanding of how we produce this "we" together with diverse others is "the potential of a community of us all"—the ideal of complete inclusion in a singular, collective agency.[44] This is a regulative ideal for her, to be sure, something that we can never hope to reach; but insofar as it operates as a rule guiding feminist politics, it keeps actors focused on the goal of inclusion in a comprehensive "we"—the feminist equivalent of the sovereign democratic agency I criticized in chapter 5. To push beyond this desire for unity and inclusion, for redemption of the collective through the acknowledgment of diversity, I suggest we need to turn away from coalition.

Coalition politics gives us one account of why we might want to act together with others: to pursue shared goals, whether these are purely strategic or also ethical in character. However, as feminist theorists have pointed out, simply having some of the same goals does not make coalition partners compatible with one another, capable of acknowledging and negotiating their differences. I would go further and say that coalition partners may even discover as they interact that they do not have the same goals after all. In one sense, this is why the alliance behind the *Gran Marchas* splintered in April 2006: because it turned out that the different groups were not in agreement after all about what it meant to oppose H.R. 4437. Coalition, then, is a matter of faith: we believe that we have the same goals, that we will be able to work together, that we will agree on tactics, and that our many other differences will not affect our collaboration. But these are beliefs; we do not know, nor can we know in advance whether we share the exact same goals, whether we can work together, and so on. This lack of knowledge about the others with whom we act is not a characteristic just of coalition politics but of all politics. We ordinarily act together with plural others without knowing what they think and feel, without knowing whether they will join us, without knowing whether they share our goals, and without knowing how they will respond. And so, to think beyond a coalition politics that seeks security in the sharing of political goals is to think beyond the promised security of commonality itself, to think politics in terms of belief rather than knowledge, to think politics in terms of an intersubjectively shared world inhabited by plural subjects.

What other reasons might we have for wanting to act with others besides shared goals? Why might we consciously choose to act with people who we expect may be different from us, who we anticipate may disagree with us about strategic goals? Why would we want to act together if we think of commonality as a first-person belief that we have about our relations to others rather than as an objective truth about the world? I want to draw out two motivations for acting with others that are grounded in our first-person experience of the world rather than in the assumptions we make about others. First, we might act together out of a commitment to political freedom: the freedom of each of us to have a voice in shaping the world in which we live.[45] This motivation arises from the first-person awareness that human beings make sense of their world intersubjectively, that we are the source of the meanings we attribute to the world we experience. Acting with others is, then, an expression of my political freedom: it is an attempt to shape the world in which I live by communicating with others, by learning how they see things, by seeing whether they agree with me or whether they may be persuaded to agree.

Yet I presume that, just as other humans possess the same senses as I do, other humans also possess the capacity for political freedom. The notion I have that we share this capacity is a belief; it is not grounded in actual knowledge of others. And like my belief that others have the sense of sight or touch, it is confirmed intersubjectively when I observe others acting as if they have this capacity. This belief about other humans can generate another motivation for acting with others—and especially for acting with others who we expect will disagree with us: to sustain and promote the awareness that we humans have this capacity, that is, to promote democracy sense. In this spirit, we might act together with others as a way of keeping the rhythm and rapport of dialogical interaction going, regardless of whether we agree with those with whom we engage. We might do this out of solidarity, for example, to lend credibility to marginalized voices, or to make it safer for vulnerable people (like the undocumented workers who participated in the *Gran Marchas*) to publicly express controversial views. Or we might do it simply to pluralize the range of voices that are expressed in public, responding dialogically to others in order to prevent or disrupt hegemonic imaginaries. Whether as a more general celebration of the possibility of democratic action or as a more specific act of standing in solidarity with a particular set of people, this acting together with others in order to claim democratic power and political freedom for us all is one of the important pleasures of politics.[46] This is the pleasure of the protest march: the pleasure of occupying public space together with others, the pleasure of encountering different groups of people, with their different techniques and different messages, as one marches, the pleasure of experiencing the power of acting together with others to shape the world in which we live.

REREADING THE 2006 *GRAN MARCHAS*

I propose, therefore, that we reread the 2006 immigration protests as collective enactments of political freedom rather than as examples of coalition politics. This is to shift our way of seeing from an objective to an intersubjective orientation. Doing so, I believe, will give us a richer understanding both of what was taking place in these protests and of what was lost over the course of the spring because many organizers were focused on the strategic pursuit of their common goals, at the expense of political freedom. Rereading these protests reveals what is at stake in rejecting coalition as a democratic imaginary, while also offering a new way of conceptualizing democracy: on the model of the protest march itself.

The protesters exercised their political freedom in these marches in two different ways. First, by marching with the flags of multiple nationalities, they enacted claims about how we should imagine the demos of the United States. In so doing, they expressed their political freedom to shape the world in which they live by offering up alternatives to dominant conceptions of Americanness. Richard Pineda and Stacey Sowards have interpreted the "argument" made by the protesters' flag-waving in this spirit as a claim to "cultural citizenship"—pride in one's heritage and culture—that is compatible with a claim to legal citizenship. By juxtaposing conventional displays of American patriotism with the waving of non-US flags at rallies and marches, "flag wavers assert that they are both Mexican (or of another nationality) and American."[47] On this reading, the protesters simultaneously expressed a desire for inclusion in the sovereign people defined by US citizenship *and* a desire to hold on to affective ties to other nationalities and cultures. They challenged dominant understandings of Americanness that require exclusive allegiance to the United States and that perceive attachments to other countries or cultures as necessarily threatening to American unity and as signs of nonassimilation. Yet they asserted that this multicultural imaginary of America is compatible with at least some degree of assimilation and a sincere desire for US citizenship. This multicultural interpretation portrays the protesters as relatively conventional and nonthreatening: they just want to be good, law-abiding citizens without having to give up their culture entirely. Consequently, this interpretation downplays the threat opponents worry they pose to the status quo.[48]

We might also understand the protesters' multinational flag-waving as a more direct challenge to dominant understandings of American community, insofar as it decenters the state in favor of a visually enacted transnationalism. On this interpretation, the foreign flags waved alongside of US ones represent an American demos figured as always already multinational rather than contained neatly by well-defined political allegiances or clear borders. This imagined America exceeds political boundaries, contains multiple and conflicting loyalties, includes citizens and noncitizens alike, and therefore does not coincide with state authority as such. This is a reading that corresponds to the account of identity I developed in chapter 3: as arising through competing, overlapping, and not entirely contiguous claims to identity. The protesters, on this account, expressed the idea that American identity is not grounded in commonality, and that—despite the anxieties this lack of commonality provokes—it is vibrant and in some sense cohesive. This is the kind of imaginary that provoked anxiety in observers like Dobbs.

Whether in the form of the safer, multicultural imaginary or the form of the more threatening, transnational one, the protesters performed through their marching and flag-waving that the ways Americans tend to imagine national community are not necessary: we do not need to contain political community within state institutions; we do not need to demand cultural or linguistic uniformity and shared allegiance. In this way, the marches revealed that dominant understandings of Americanness are contingent, and that America can be imagined otherwise. That is, the protesters denaturalized and made political the question of how we imagine the American demos. They demanded of US citizens that we take responsibility not only for our immigration laws but also for how we imagine America. If we focus just on the coalition goal of defeating the Sensenbrenner bill, we miss how the protests exposed, challenged, and enacted alternative imaginaries of the American people.

The protesters also exercised their political freedom in a second way, this one a purer expression of human freedom than the first. By occupying public space together, they enacted the idea that democracy belongs to all people, regardless of whether states legitimate them as political actors. They laid claim to a democracy that does not belong exclusively to citizens, or even to legal residents—and in so doing, they challenged imaginaries of the demos that are tied to formal institutions. As Beltrán argues, the distinctive contribution of the marches is that they claimed that undocumented persons were legitimate political actors, despite their lack of US citizenship. She writes, "The demonstrations can be thought of . . . as a space in which participants publicly celebrated and legitimated the presence of the undocumented in American society."[49] Yet Beltrán reads their claim as one that is bounded by the state. It is a claim about "the presence of the undocumented *in American society*" who demonstrated a desire for inclusion in the American people by "pledging an allegiance," even though by their very presence in a public space, they were also unsettlingly "issuing a threat" to the United States.[50] While I am very sympathetic to Beltrán's work, I believe the undocumented protesters marching alongside of legal residents and citizens expressed a more radical challenge than she admits. They enacted the idea that political actors do not require prior authorization by a state in order to occupy public space and voice their views. Rather, every human being has the capacity and the right to shape the world in which she lives. Beltràn reads the undocumented protesters as "takers," taking rights already granted to others by the state *in advance* of a hoped-for naturalization.[51] I suggest instead that we understand them as acting *in defiance* of the expectation that they need to be formally included in the democratic sovereign people in order to count. From this perspective, the undocumented marchers were exercising a self-authorizing democratic power that exceeds formal institutions.[52] They were expressing political freedom as such.

However we read the protests—as conventional claims of a desire to belong and assimilate, as more challenging claims to a transnational and decentered Americanness, or as radically democratic claims to political freedom regardless of citizenship status—I suggest that the foreign flag-waving and the occupation of public space be understood as acts of world-building.[53] People took to the streets to try to shape the world in which they live by opposing H.R. 4437 but also by offering alternative ways of understanding the demos. In this sense, these protests are an example of democratic interagency: they are attempts to communicate and intersub-jectively share claims about how we should make sense of our world. By offering alternative imaginaries of the demos, the marchers suggested that we have the responsibility to reflect on how we imagine our demo-cratic communities, and they suggested that we have the capacity to imag-ine them other than how we do now. They expressed and authorized their own capacity for political freedom by acting to shape the world in which they live.

If we place the focus on political freedom rather than commonality, then the 2006 marches reveal the limits of coalition politics as an imaginary for democratic collective action. The drive to pursue the shared goal of keeping the Sensenbrenner bill from becoming law had the effect of shutting down possibilities for world-building in more transformative ways. The top-down organization of efforts to display only American flags dampened the plural cacophony of grassroots voices at the marches. It reinforced patterns of passing and assimilation among the undocumented, encouraging the per-formance of conventional forms of American patriotism rather than pro-moting critical engagement with those same conventions. The focus on portraying immigrants as fundamentally nonthreatening to American val-ues and politics was also an attempt to manage risk—to make what was a radically democratic occupation of public space and challenge to the status quo safe—safe not so much for the vulnerable undocumented persons in the marches themselves as for the already enfranchised public to whom their messages were addressed.

Furthermore, by acting together primarily for strategic reasons, the organizers undermined the educative and consciousness-raising effect of the protests. Rather than directing attention to the role of human agency in world-building, in reimagining America and democracy, they worked to portray the protests as conventional expressions of a desire to belong, consistent with how other minority groups in the United States had sought to assimilate while holding on to cultural traditions and national flags. The loss of the educative effect was first of all a loss for the marchers themselves. Instead of being encouraged to share their political views, they were urged by organizers to pledge allegiance, sing the national anthem (albeit in Spanish), and wave American flags. As an experience of political education, these protests stifled individual expressions of political agency, encouraged sacrificing political freedom for immediate policy outcomes, and reinforced the idea that undocumented immigrants had to "play by the rules"—even if this time the rules were being handed down to them from Latino/a leaders.

Yet this was also a pedagogical loss for the publics who witnessed the marches, whether in person or through media coverage. Americans who were disturbed by the early displays of foreign flags did not have to sit with their unease for very long. If they were skeptical of the sincerity of the marchers to begin with, this change in tactics only served to confirm their doubts: the protesters put away their Mexican flags in order to "pretend" that they were willing to assimilate. And for those who did take the marchers to be earnest, the increasing displays of conventional American patriotism meant that they need not feel challenged by the message of the protests. The repeated performance of the desire of the undocumented to be American served to affirm (rather than politicize) the value of Americanness, the desirability of US citizenship, and the appeal of American values.[54]

Perhaps a strategic focus on achieving shared goals is intrinsically conservative. In this case, the goals themselves were oriented toward already-existing democratic institutions: organizers wanted the Sensenbrenner bill to be defeated. They disagreed about the alternative but largely sought some form of citizenship, amnesty, or at the very least dignity (as opposed to criminalization) for the undocumented. In almost every instance, organizers sought some kind of inclusion for the undocumented within existing institutional frameworks rather than a transformation of American democracy. Yet even if the coalition had converged on a more radical set of aims, so long as the promotion and performance of political freedom were not among them, it would likely be sacrificed in the pursuit of a shared agenda. Coalition politics, even where the coalition is composed of radicals, risks being conservative, unimaginative, and complicit in the status quo insofar as it directs attention away from democracy as an expression of political freedom, away from collective action as world-building.

THE PROTEST AS DEMOCRATIC IMAGINARY

Feminists and others on the political left appeal to coalition politics as an imaginary of democracy that balances the recognition of diversity with what they presume is a need for commonality. I have argued that coalition politics' emphasis on shared goals, however, is ironically antidemocratic. It at best obscures and at worst blinds us to the differences that persist among coalition partners. As Reagon's work suggests, the expectation that we already agree with others ill prepares us for the realities of the differences between us, and may even set us up to experience disagreements and conflict as life-threatening betrayals. Moreover, the emphasis on shared goals places the stress on the outcomes of democratic action rather than on the activity of political freedom as an end in itself. In this way, coalition politics (as we saw in the case of the immigration marches) may operate counter to the promotion and expression of political freedom, by making them secondary in importance to the pursuit of an established agenda.

Democracy, if we are to move beyond an orientation to commonality, requires a new imaginary. What if, instead of coalition, we were to take the protest march as a model? While much democratic theory focuses on formal institutions, and coalition politics is oriented toward agreements negotiated among movement leaders, protests shift our attention to the potential of any one of us to engage in activism in the streets. To start with protests as an imaginary of democracy, then, is to place our focus on the radically democratic human agency expressed in world-building. Let me flesh out a bit what this might look like.

First of all, protests are *cacophonous*. While this might sound like an obvious point to make, given that demonstrators often chant slogans or sing songs, what I mean is that demonstrations usually express not a single position with a single voice but multiple positions with multiple voices. We often mistakenly think of protests on the model of coalition politics: as a temporary gathering of different people to achieve a shared goal. The immigrant rights protesters marched to oppose H.R. 4437, for example. However, while in a demonstration there is to some extent an attempt at generating a single message, commonality of vision is often elusive. A reproductive rights rally, for example, might be organized in order to put political pressure on the Food and Drug Administration to approve a new form of emergency contraception. The marchers who attend will include some who carry posters distributed by march organizers that reinforce exactly the message the leaders hope to convey. But some of the marchers will carry signs supporting abortion on demand, or opposing abstinence education, or calling for action on AIDS. Some marchers will connect the question of reproductive freedom to other government policies—for example, to health care, foreign aid, or war. And some marchers will chant slogans and carry signs that seemingly have no connection whatsoever to the purported theme of the march; they may appear to be opportunistically attaching themselves to a march just to get attention for their pet causes. While it is possible to imagine a protest organized with such discipline (or perhaps on such a small scale) that the participants stay entirely on message, ordinarily demonstrations are characterized by a plurality of voices.

The cacophony of the large protest march has made protests an easy target for pundits attempting to dismiss them. Critical coverage of the Occupy movement, for example, regularly claims that it is incoherent and politically ineffectual because protesters are neither united behind a single message nor in agreement about a single course of action.[55] The political left has made similar charges about Tea Party rallies. If we take the purpose of a protest to be to present a single, clear, and coherent position, and to seek specific policy changes, then these criticisms are legitimate. Indeed, the multivocality of a protest may seem particularly troubling to its organizers—especially, perhaps, when it results in media coverage that is directed away from the main message they want to convey.

Yet if we take the purpose of a protest to be the intersubjective expression of political freedom, then this cacophony is not a problem to be addressed with greater discipline but instead an expected characteristic of interacting together with others. The ordinary first-person experience of participating in a large protest is one of encountering plurality and disagreement. We may take pleasure in the experience of being surrounded by many different people with different points of view all showing up for the same march; we may experience safety and validation by being surrounded by diverse others who we think agree with us—yet even when we experience a protest as a kind of communion with like-minded others, this is an intersubjective experience that is grounded in the fact of our plurality. It is meaningful for me that all these people came to the same protest precisely because they are not me; I could not have that same experience of community and solidarity in a group of two, or even perhaps twenty, persons. It is our numbers, our plurality, and our diversity that generate the sense in a protest that I am a part of something much larger than myself.

The multivocality of protests enables a second characteristic I would like to highlight: that protests are *self-authorizing*. In a demonstration, people occupy public space with others for the purpose of expressing political views. This is democratic interagency: acting together with others not to do the same thing or express the same view but to authorize one another as plural actors. One of the important pleasures of protesting lies in authorizing others and being authorized by them to appear in public, to speak or shout or chant, to share one's views. It is our subjective difference from others, and not our shared viewpoints, that makes it possible for protesters to authorize one another. In describing protests as *self*-authorizing, then, I do not mean that any one protester authorizes herself to act. Rather, this is an intersubjective authorization: each of us acting in public authorizes the others, confirming and demonstrating for the others that we all have political freedom, that we all have the capacity and the right to shape the world in which we live. This is the kind of authorization that the Milan Women's Bookstore Collective describes in the chapter epigraph: "Authority is received originally from another human being who is in a position to give it, who has the authority to give it." Each of us, by protesting, shows ourselves to be in a position to give authority to the others who act with us. This authorization is a self-authorization because it comes from the demos that forms when people begin to act together rather than from any authority that stands outside the demos itself.

Consider how protests can draw in bystanders. Sally Moore, one of the organizers of the January 25, 2011, protest in Egypt that sparked the revolution there, recalls how protesters marched to Tahrir Square that day by way of one of the poorer neighborhoods in Cairo in order to spread the word: "Our group started when we were 50. When we left the neighborhood we were thousands."[56] Here, the organizers by occupying public space authorized others to join with them in expressing their political freedom. Similarly, the US citizens who marched alongside of the undocumented in 2006 authorized them as political actors. The presence of these citizens in public space calling for immigrant rights made it safer and more possible for undocumented people to occupy the streets and make political demands themselves—where they might otherwise have been hesitant to do so for legitimate fears about their security and vulnerability to deportation.[57] In the same way, marchers of different political persuasions and with different political concerns authorize each other's expression and presence by protesting side by side: from radicals claiming aboriginal rights to Aztlàn, to mainstream activists calling for a guest worker program; from the university-educated Egyptians who organized protests on Facebook, to the poorer classes of Cairo who joined with them to call for change. Protests authorize the political freedom of all, regardless of class, citizenship status, or political ideology.

The temptation here is to say: of course we authorize people to march with us when they are our allies, when they share our agenda, more or less. We can tolerate the disagreements and differences between us because they really are not so great. But we would not authorize people who radically disagree with and differ from us. A protest, in other words, even if we let go of the idea that it is an action taken by a coalition with a clear, shared agenda, is still an action taken by people who can act together because they see themselves as being on roughly the same side of an issue. Protests, in other words, do not really move us much further away from the presumption of commonality than does coalition politics in that they offer an imaginary of democratic collective action undertaken by people who basically agree with one another. This concern, I believe, arises from taking a narrow view of the phenomenon of protesting.

To clarify my position, let us look at a third element often experienced in protesting: *counterprotests*, or what I will call (drawing on one activist's self-description) *co-protests*.[58] In the form of the co-protest, protests ordinarily involve encounters between people who do radically disagree, even if the different voices are not represented equally at a given event. Sometimes co-protests are intentionally and formally organized, as when opposition groups stage events at the same time and place as a protest; and sometimes they occur more informally, as when people who come across a march heckle or challenge some of the demonstrators. Co-protests are dialogical forms of interaction that acknowledge the protesters by engaging with them. This, as I argued in chapter 5, constitutes dialogical agency: interacting with others in such a way as to continue rather than shut down or foreclose the interaction.[59] Moreover, co-protesting aims to pluralize the voices at a protest, to make the protest more cacophonous. In its most productive moments, co-protesting therefore cultivates democracy sense: the sense that protesters and co-protesters alike are engaged in the very ordinary human activity of trying to shape the world in which they live. The form of authorization present in co-protesting, then, clarifies that authorization is not at all about endorsement: co-protesters and protesters authorize one another as political agents but without agreeing or even coming close to it. Co-protesters and protesters acknowledge one another simply by interacting with each other but with this caveat: you can express yourself and try to shape our world, but you do not get to express yourself alone. That is, they express in their actions an intersubjective picture of sharing: that they inhabit the world together with plural others.

Let me offer a few examples of co-protesting to illustrate this idea. On May 26, 2007, a neo-Nazi and Ku Klux Klan (KKK) group held a rally in Knoxville, Tennessee, to which an antiracism group responded with its own simultaneous action. Dressed up as clowns, members of this group "joined" the neo-Nazi/KKK rally in chants of "White Power," except that they appeared to misunderstand what was being said. So the clowns variously chanted and waved letters spelling out "White Flour," "White Flowers," and "Tight Shower," finally ending with the female clowns gleefully shouting, "Wife Power!"[60] By co-protesting, the antiracist group forced the neo-Nazi/ KKK protesters to engage with them rather than staying on message, drew perhaps even more attention to the rally than it otherwise might have had, and refused to allow white supremacist views to be expressed and reported on without opposition. Similarly, co-protesters often join with the Westboro Baptist Church (WBC) when its members demonstrate. The WBC regularly organizes protests around the United States, most famously against gay rights and homosexuality (the organization's webpage is www.godhatesfags. com), but also against Jews and other groups. WBC members carry large, brightly colored signs declaring messages like "God hates fags," "God hates America," and "Jews killed Jesus," often including citations to biblical passages. Co-protesters have imitated WBC tactics, showing up at their pickets with signs made in the same style, with messages like "God hates signs," "I'm with stupid," "I have a sign," and "Dog hates dyslexia."[61] They alternatingly mimic, mock, and challenge the WBC. These co-protesters often position themselves physically among the protesters, so that the WBC protest cannot be taken in, filmed, or photographed by spectators or the media without their counterpresence being a part of the scene. In this way, they resist the WBC's message by deliberately pluralizing the voices at the protest. This pluralizing effect of co-protesting was vividly expressed by a recent protest in which the KKK joined leftist groups in co-protesting with the WBC.[62] Protests, far from being safe events in which we only encounter people with whom we more or less agree, are often confrontational events in which we interact with those with whom we radically disagree. As one person at Occupy Oakland reportedly warned the gathered assembly, "You're going to hear some things that you may totally disagree with."[63] Inasmuch as we are all plural subjects, it may be best to describe all protesting as co-protesting.

Finally, protests are characterized by the *nonsovereignty* of the protesters. No one person, no leader, and no preestablished agenda can determine how a given protest will go, how it will be received, and what its effects will be. When we act together with others, we cannot guarantee outcomes. This is why the emphasis on goals in coalition politics at the expense of political freedom is potentially antidemocratic: it obscures our inability to determine the outcomes of a protest and so instrumentalizes our political action. Protests, from this perspective, are valuable primarily as a means toward achieving certain goals. The participants in those protests are valuable only insofar as they help the coalition achieve those goals; otherwise, they may need to be silenced, disavowed, or handed an American flag to wave. We need instead to understand protest as an end in itself, as an expression of political freedom in comparison to which the achievement of particular goals is of secondary importance. This to accept the nonsovereignty of human interaction, the unpredictability of gathering together with others in political action, and the uncertainty of the outcomes of democratic interagency.

In a protest, we do not ordinarily know those with whom we act. We act together with strangers, whether these are fellow protesters or co-protesters. And marching alongside of whoever else shows up to a protest is very risky. There is always the danger that the "wrong" people will show up, that they will steal the headlines. Bad apples may turn to violence against property or persons, as some anarchist protesters did in the 1999 protests in Seattle during the World Trade Organization Ministerial Conference or in 2011 at Occupy Oakland. Or perhaps cowardly protesters will fail to participate in the violence once it has begun. There is a real danger—and sometimes even a hope—that confrontation will provoke the police and other state agents to use force. Protests can be dangerous, violent, and deadly; they are not always peaceful Sunday picnics on the Washington Mall. The military crackdowns on Arab Spring protests in Egypt, Libya, and Syria serve as sobering reminders of the potential for protest to provoke a disproportionate and bloody response. There is the risk that one protester will try to start something—whether a new chant or an occupation of a state building—and the other demonstrators will not follow her lead. There is no guarantee that we will be heard by those we mean to address, or that they will be persuaded to act as we should like. To act together with plural others is to open ourselves up—whether we realize it or not—to our lack of sovereignty over outcomes.

This account of protest marches is admittedly idealized—not every participant will experience a march in this way, some protests will be characterized by greater unity, and not everyone will be able to find pleasure in demonstrating, or be willing to take the risk of even showing up. Even so, there is an important *potential* ever-present in protesting: the potential to cultivate democracy sense. Democracy sense is the first-person awareness that I have the nonsovereign capacity to shape the world, and that I inhabit the world together with plural subjects who I presume also possess this capacity. Participants in a protest have the opportunity to experience their own political freedom, of course, but also to experience this as a capacity that other human beings possess as well. They may experience their freedom as something that is exercised intersubjectively, that depends upon interactions with plural others. But it is not just participants in a protest who can cultivate this democracy sense. Witnesses can experience protest as a consciousness-raising reminder of their own capacity to take part in shaping the world in which they live. Over the course of 2011, Egyptians were inspired by Tunisians to protest, Spaniards by Egyptians, and the Occupy movement by all of the preceding. There is no guarantee that protesting or witnessing a protest will have the effect of increasing any one person's democracy sense. Yet our experience again and again of being inspired (and frightened) by the courage and the power of protesters is a persistent reminder of our ordinary human capacity to make our world anew.

"THIS IS WHAT DEMOCRACY LOOKS LIKE"

If we take protesting as the paradigmatic example of democracy, as the model for a new democratic imaginary, we can radically rethink ourselves beyond a politics bound by commonality. Protesters invite us to do exactly this when they repeat the slogan "This is what democracy looks like."[64] Democracy looks like a crowd of people—some friends, some strangers—who authorize one another to occupy public space and to claim the right to shape the world they share. The democracy embodied in protest is a cacophonous democracy in which we regularly encounter difference and disagreement as constitutive of democratic action itself rather than as a problem to be overcome. This is a self-authorizing democracy that can include formal institutions but is not dependent on them to come into being. This is democracy understood as the intersubjective exercise of political freedom whenever and wherever it occurs, a freedom that can only be exercised together with others, and whose outcome cannot be guaranteed.

While I take protests as paradigmatic of democracy, I do not mean thereby to reduce democracy to the activity of protesting. This is what someone like Sheldon Wolin does when he claims that moments in which ordinary people come together to act democratically are "episodic, rare."[65] Protests themselves may be episodic and rare, and the movements that spawn them may be short-lived. My claim, however, is that in protests we see made explicit what is ordinarily the case in democratic practice: that we act into an intersubjectively shared world that is itself the ongoing and changeable product of our actions. We always have the capacity to try to shape our world, although we cannot guarantee that we will be successful. If people self-consciously exercise that capacity only rarely, I believe that is because our democracy sense has been suppressed rather than because democracy itself is extraordinary. Rather than bemoaning the rarity of democracy, or the inefficacy of protest movements, we should strive to cultivate appreciation of our freedom and our ability to imagine the world anew.

Some readers may be concerned that the vision of democracy I advocate is chaotic and dangerous. We need to have common goals, such readers might think, and we need to reach agreements. A world in which anyone can claim the authority to challenge any decision is a world that is deeply unstable. A world in which any collection of people can constitute a demos is a world in which jurisdictions are unclear, legitimacy is incoherent, and discord and conflict dominate.

I grant that if we make political freedom the end of democratic action, rather than the pursuit of common goals, the consequence may be that people will engage in politics somewhat differently. It may be more difficult to come to agreement if more people feel entitled to have a say in the world they inhabit together. It may be more difficult for decisions made through institutional channels to claim legitimacy if they are regularly challenged or thwarted from without. Yet these are risks that arise from sharing the world with plural others; they are intrinsic not to a commonality-oriented or a freedom-oriented vision of democracy but to the condition of intersubjectivity itself. Whichever way we see democracy, the human condition of plurality is a constant. Think back to the image of the duck-rabbit. Whether we see the duck or the rabbit, the lines of the drawing remain the same. The difference lies not in what appears to us but in how we see it. Whether we see the disagreement that arises from human plurality as a problem for democracy to be overcome through pursuing agreements and generating commonalities or as the manifestation of our democratic capacity for freedom, that disagreement is always a part of the picture. I believe we are better off adopting a view of democracy that acknowledges the uncertainty of acting in a world of plural others and that orients us toward accepting this uncertainty as the condition of our political freedom.

I have shown you in this book that in democratic theory and practice, we typically and uncritically assume an objective picture of sharing that places commonality at the center of democracy. Yet this is not the only way of seeing democracy: we can also think of it in terms of an intersubjective picture of sharing, which places the focus on our capacity to build a meaningful world in the company of others. I believe that this intersubjective, freedom-centered view is preferable descriptively insofar as it reflects how we share in practice, and normatively in that it is more compatible with a radical vision of democracy. While I hope to have persuaded you to shift with me to this way of seeing democracy, I will be satisfied if I have helped my readers to develop the fluency to move easily between the two. I want democratic theorists to become more self-conscious about how we see democracy, and to consider the antidemocratic costs of a focus on commonality. At the very least, being aware of the alternatives may help us to theorize and act in ways that may mitigate the negative effects of an orientation to commonality. But I hope to have persuaded at least some readers to try to see the world from an intersubjective viewpoint. This is to embrace the nonsovereignty, unpredictability, risk, and uncertainty of democratic politics—but these were characteristics that were always there, we just were looking at them in a different way.

With its leaderless and agenda-less approach to activism, the Occupy movement strikes me as offering a vision of a democracy that embraces political freedom and rejects the imperative of commonality. While the movement is in its early days yet, as I am concluding this book in spring 2012, over the past eight months Occupy groups have blossomed across the United States and around the world. It remains to be seen whether the people who have brought it into existence will be able to sustain it over time. The activists involved have wagered on political freedom itself rather than a clear, common agenda as the focal point of the movement. One observer described the aim of Occupy actions in Zuccotti Park as establishing "a long-term encampment in a public space, an improvised democratic protest village without preappointed leaders, committed to a general critique—the U.S. economy is broken, politics is corrupted by big money—but with no immediate call for specific legislative or executive action."[66] Given how quickly the 2006 immigration protests dissolved once the organizers' common goals were achieved, this may be a smart political strategy. If Occupy stated clear goals, and they were met, there would be no need for further activism. And if its goals were not met, then those intent on a particular outcome could become discouraged. By making the self-authorizing practice of democracy the end of political action, Occupy may instead encourage the cultivation of democracy sense among participants that could energize and reenergize the movement for years to come, or outlive it should it fade. Of course, we cannot yet know what the future will hold.

For Occupy, this focus on establishing communities committed to an ongoing, general critique may come at the expense of the pursuit of specific policy goals. We need not think of the pursuit of political freedom as in opposition to the pursuit of goals, however. The problem with coalition as a political imaginary is not that coalitions have specific goals but that coalitions are oriented to the pursuit of outcomes at the expense of the practice of political freedom. We can engage in freedom-centered politics without rejecting goals; we need only attenuate our attachment to particular outcomes. In other words, we need to try to shape the world in which we live without expecting or requiring success in order for our activity to be worthwhile.

Shifting to a freedom-centered view of democracy has real political costs, just as does the commonality orientation. The question for us to consider is: Which costs would we rather pay? Given the dominance of an orientation to outcomes, I would err on the side of cultivating our capacity for political freedom. There may be situations, of course, where short-term goals should be prioritized: for example, in matters of life and death, oppression, and human dignity. Yet by and large, I believe democracy would be best served if, like Occupy, we prioritize instead the active practice of sharing a life together with plural others. This is to practice living with difference, disagreement, and conflict rather than trying to overcome them in the futile search for a commonality that could finally unite us all. This is to embrace the nonsovereignty, unpredictability, risk, and uncertainty of democratic politics. The point is to see that these are the conditions in which we must exercise our political freedom, and to act anyhow.

NOTES

INTRODUCTION

1. Anthony Shadid and David D. Kirkpatrick, "Promise of Arab Uprisings Is Threatened by Divisions," *New York Times*, May 21, 2011.
2. Thomas L. Friedman, "They Did It," *New York Times*, February 12, 2011.
3. Shadid and Kirkpatrick, "Promise of Arab Uprisings."
4. Ibid.
5. Ibid.
6. Ibid.
7. Arthur Schlesinger Jr., *The Disuniting of America: Reflections on a Multicultural Society*, 2nd ed. (New York: Norton, 1998 [1992]), 23.
8. David D. Kirkpatrick, "Wired and Shrewd, Young Egyptians Guide Revolt," *New York Times*, February 9, 2011; Mona El-Naggar and Michael Slackman, "Egypt's Leader Uses Old Tricks to Defy New Demands," *New York Times*, February 9, 2011; Kareem Fahim and Mona El-Naggar, "Violent Clashes Mark Protests against Mubarak's Rule," *New York Times*, January 25, 2011.
9. Anthony Shadid, "Obama Urges Faster Shift of Power in Egypt," *New York Times*, February 1, 2011; Kareem Fahim, "Egyptian Hopes Converged in Fight for Cairo Bridge," *New York Times*, January 28, 2011; Anthony Shadid, "Discontented within Egypt Face Power of Old Elites," *New York Times*, February 4, 2011.
10. Shadid, "Obama Urges Faster Shift."
11. Anthony Shadid, "In Crowd's Euphoria, No Clear Leadership Emerges," *New York Times*, January 31, 2011; Kareem Fahim and Mona El-Naggar, "Some Fear a Street Movement's Leaderless Status May Become a Liability," *New York Times*, February 3, 2011.
12. Kirkpatrick, "Wired and Shrewd"; Anthony Shadid, "Egypt's Path after Uprising Does Not Have to Follow Iran's," *New York Times*, February 12, 2011.
13. Quoted in Shadid, "In Crowd's Euphoria."
14. Quoted in Roger Cohen, "Tehran 1979 or Berlin 1989?," *New York Times*, February 8, 2011.

CHAPTER 1

1. Ludwig Wittgenstein, *Philosophical Investigations (Reissued German-English Edition)*, trans. G. E. M. Anscombe, 2nd ed. (Malden, MA: Blackwell, 1958), I. §66.
2. Migration of non-Western-origin peoples in the West of course existed prior to the twentieth century—most notably the involuntary migration of blacks to the

New World via the African slave trade and the migration of East Asians (especially Chinese) to North America during the gold rush and to work on railroads in the nineteenth century. What have changed are the groups migrating, their reasons for migrating, their numbers, and their destinations.

3. On increasing tensions over cultural diversity in Sweden, see Suzanne Daley, "Swedes Begin to Question Liberal Migration Tenets," *New York Times*, February 27, 2011.

4. While there continue to be secessionist movements within democracies (e.g., Quebecois and Basques), democratic theorists typically note that secession cannot solve the problem of diversity but can only shift it to a different political jurisdiction. See, e.g., Avigail Eisenberg and Jeff Spinner-Halev, eds., *Minorities within Minorities* (New York: Cambridge University Press, 2005); Charles Taylor, *Reconciling the Solitudes: Essays on Canadian Federalism and Nationalism* (Montreal: McGill-Queen's University Press, 1994), esp. 184.

5. See, e.g., Joseph Carens's eloquent defense of communalism in Fiji as against the forces of liberalism and capitalism in Joseph H. Carens, *Culture, Citizenship, and Community: A Contextual Exploration of Justice as Evenhandedness* (Oxford: Oxford University Press, 2000), chap. 9.

6. "France Creates Muslim Council," http://news.bbc.co.uk/1/hi/world/europe/2593623.stm.

7. Iris Marion Young, *Justice and the Politics of Difference* (Princeton, NJ: Princeton University Press, 1990).

8. Charles Taylor, "The Politics of Recognition," in *Multiculturalism: Examining the Politics of Recognition*, ed. Amy Gutmann (Princeton, NJ: Princeton University Press, 1994), 25–73.

9. James Tully, *Strange Multiplicity: Constitutionalism in an Age of Diversity* (Cambridge: Cambridge University Press, 1995), 1.

10. E.g., Will Kymlicka, *Multicultural Citizenship: A Liberal Theory of Minority Rights* (Oxford: Clarendon Press, 1995).

11. In their eagerness to group together a variety of social and political movements, some theorists reduce the range of feminisms to those that most closely fit the model of culture. Tully, despite being aware of the multiplicity of feminisms, focuses on "cultural feminism"—which involves the demand for the recognition of women's culture. Tully, *Strange Multiplicity*, 3, 47–53. Taylor focuses on what I would call "difference feminism" in "The Politics of Recognition," 25–26.

12. E.g., Arthur Schlesinger Jr., *The Disuniting of America: Reflections on a Multicultural Society*, 2nd ed. (New York: Norton, 1998 [1992]); Samuel P. Huntington, *Who Are We? The Challenges to America's National Identity* (New York: Simon and Schuster, 2004).

13. E.g., Richard Rorty, *Achieving Our Country: Leftist Thought in Twentieth-Century America* (Cambridge, MA: Harvard University Press, 1998). For critical responses to this line of argument, see Nancy Fraser, "From Redistribution to Recognition? Dilemmas of Justice in a 'Postsocialist' Age," in *Justice Interruptus: Critical Reflections on the "Postsocialist" Condition* (New York: Routledge, 1997), 11–40; James Tully, "Struggles over Recognition and Distribution," *Constellations* 7, no. 4 (2000), 469–482.

14. E.g., John Rawls, *Political Liberalism* (New York: Columbia University Press, 1993).

15. E.g., Jürgen Habermas, *The Inclusion of the Other: Studies in Political Theory*, ed. Ciaran Cronin and Pablo De Greiff (Cambridge, MA: MIT Press, 1998); David Miller, *On Nationality* (Oxford: Oxford University Press, 1995).

16. E.g., Young, *Justice and the Politics of Difference*; Carens, *Culture, Citizenship, and Community*.
17. E.g., Michael Walzer, *What It Means to Be an American* (New York: Marsilio, 1992); Miller, *On Nationality*.
18. See the essays collected in Martha C. Nussbaum, *For Love of Country: Debating the Limits of Patriotism* (Boston: Beacon, 1996).
19. E.g., Bhikhu Parekh, "Politics of Nationhood," in *Nationalism, Ethnicity, and Cultural Identity in Europe*, ed. Keebet von Benda-Beckman and Maykel Verkuyten (Utrecht: European Research Centre on Migration and Ethnic Relations, 1995).
20. E.g., Carens, *Culture, Citizenship, and Community*; Kymlicka, *Multicultural Citizenship*.
21. E.g., Tully, *Strange Multiplicity*.
22. E.g., Iris Marion Young, *Inclusion and Democracy* (Oxford: Oxford University Press, 2000); Young, *Justice and the Politics of Difference*.
23. For an overview of the history of these negotiations and the outcome of the subsequent referenda, see Peter Russell, *Constitutional Odyssey: Can Canadians Become a Sovereign People?*, 3rd ed. (Toronto: University of Toronto Press, 2004), esp. chaps. 10 and 11. The referendum was narrowly defeated, by a vote of 49.42 percent for secession, 50.58 percent against (235).
24. Taylor, *Reconciling the Solitudes*, 200.
25. Ibid., 200.
26. Ibid., 199.
27. Ibid., 183–184.
28. Ibid., 189–190.
29. Ibid., 197.
30. Ibid.
31. Ibid.
32. Ibid., 198.
33. These two strategies are related, of course: we can understand the civic strategy as (at least in some cases) motivated by a desire to limit commonality to the political realm in order to minimize its reach. Yet not all minimal commonalities are strictly civic.
34. The belief that members of a political community should have something in common is not unique to democratic theory, of course. It is possible to argue that every form of government requires some kind of commonality, if only a common territory or common political institutions. What interests me here, though, is not the general belief that commonality is essential for politics but the peculiar way that this belief is manifest in democratic theory.
35. Commonality does not serve all three of these functions for every theorist who asserts the need for commonality in democratic societies. Rather, when commonality appears in democratic theory, it does so to meet at least one of these requirements.
36. In turning to Wittgenstein, I am indebted to and inspired by other theorists and philosophers who have recently applied his later work to questions in politics and morality. Alice Crary, *Beyond Moral Judgment* (Cambridge, MA: Harvard University Press, 2007); Aletta J. Norval, *Aversive Democracy: Inheritance and Originality in the Democratic Tradition* (Cambridge: Cambridge University Press, 2007); Christopher C. Robinson, *Wittgenstein and Political Theory: The View from Somewhere* (Edinburgh: Edinburgh University Press, 2009); James Tully, *Public*

Philosophy in a New Key, vol. 1, *Democracy and Civic Freedom* (Cambridge: Cambridge University Press, 2009); Linda M. G. Zerilli, *Feminism and the Abyss of Freedom* (Chicago: University of Chicago Press, 2005).

CHAPTER 2

1. Ludwig Wittgenstein, *Philosophical Investigations (Reissued German-English Edition)*, trans. G. E. M. Anscombe, 2nd ed. (Malden, MA: Blackwell, 1958), I.§115.
2. This history of Little Rock is drawn from these firsthand accounts: Daisy Bates, *The Long Shadow of Little Rock* (Fayetteville: University of Arkansas Press, 1986 [1962]); Will Counts, *A Life Is More Than a Moment: The Desegregation of Little Rock's Central High* (Bloomington: Indiana University Press, 2007 [1999]). The account in Counts's book is definitely rosier and more optimistic than the one given by Bates. In particular, he presents the harassment of the Little Rock Nine within the school as much less severe and widespread than Bates does.
3. Only nine students successfully enrolled. The tenth student enrolled instead in a local black-only high school. See Counts, *A Life Is More Than a Moment*, 45.
4. Bates, *The Long Shadow of Little Rock*, 61.
5. Quoted in ibid., 63.
6. Danielle Allen, *Talking to Strangers: Anxieties of Citizenship since Brown v. Board of Education* (Chicago: University of Chicago Press, 2004), xxii.
7. This photo is readily available online. It is reproduced in Allen, *Talking to Strangers*, xxii, 4. It appears on the front cover of Counts's memoir of the Battle of Little Rock, *A Life Is More Than a Moment*. A series of photos (including this one) documenting Eckford's walk are also reproduced in Counts, *A Life Is More Than a Moment*, 34–41. The pictures of the mob make it clear that Hazel Bryan was not the only person in the crowd shouting at Elizabeth.
8. Allen, *Talking to Strangers*, 5, 4, 9. She describes this in terms of truth at 30.
9. Allen uses the language of recording at ibid., 5, 13.
10. Ibid., 5.
11. Ibid., 5, 9.
12. Allen uses this language of commonality at ibid., xxi.
13. Ibid., 10.
14. Ibid., xxii.
15. Ibid.
16. Allen notes that the photos of Elizabeth have "no doubt inspired diverse epiphanies for their many viewers," yet "they still produce three that directly reveal the difficulties of democratic practice and citizenship." Ibid., 9.
17. Ibid., xxii.
18. On the controversy about this essay, see Elisabeth Young-Bruehl, *Hannah Arendt: For Love of the World* (New Haven, CT: Yale University Press, 1983), 308–318. My aim here is not to enter into the debate about this essay, although there is an ever-growing body of literature that aims to either condemn or recuperate Arendt. In addition to Allen's work, see Seyla Benhabib, *The Reluctant Modernism of Hannah Arendt* (Walnut Creek, CA: AltaMira Press, 2000), 146–155; Jean Bethke Elshtain, "Political Children," in *Feminist Interpretations of Hannah Arendt*, ed. Bonnie Honig (University Park: Pennsylvania State University Press, 1995), 263–283; Anne Norton, "Heart of Darkness: Africa and African Americans in the Writings of Hannah Arendt," in *Feminist Interpretations of Hannah Arendt*, ed. Bonnie Honig (University Park: Pennsylvania State University Press, 1995), 247–261.

19. Hannah Arendt, "Reflections on Little Rock," in *The Portable Hannah Arendt* (New York: Penguin Classics, 2003 [1959]), 236. This reprinting of her work includes both her original essay, published under the title "Reflections on Little Rock," and her "Reply to Critics" published a few months later.

20. Ibid.

21. Ellison, quoted in Robert Penn Warren, *Who Speaks for the Negro?* (New York: Vintage, 1966), 344. While much is often made in the secondary literature of Ellison's criticism of Arendt, it is extremely brief. His main criticism is contained in a single paragraph (at 343–344) from an interview reproduced in Warren's book. Ellison also makes a quick (but damning) reference to her "Reflections on Little Rock" in Ralph Ellison, "The World and the Jug," in *The Collected Essays of Ralph Ellison*, ed. John F. Callahan (New York: Modern Library, 2003), 156. Young-Bruehl discusses his criticisms as well as Arendt's personal response to him in a letter dated July 29, 1965, at *Hannah Arendt*, 315–317.

22. Allen, *Talking to Strangers*, 31. She repeats this language of accuracy again at 35.

23. Danielle Allen, "Law's Necessary Forcefulness: Ralph Ellison vs. Hannah Arendt on the Battle of Little Rock," *Oklahoma City University Law Review* 26 (Fall 2001): 887.

24. Allen, *Talking to Strangers*, 35.

25. Arendt mentions the events at Little Rock only twice: once briefly at the outset of the essay, and again in more detail in the sixth paragraph. Otherwise, her comments refer more generally to struggles over desegregating schools after *Brown*.

26. Arendt, "Reflections on Little Rock," 243.

27. Ibid., 236, described again at 243–244.

28. See Adrienne Pickett, "Images, Dialogue, and Aesthetic Education: Arendt's Response to the Little Rock Crisis," *Philosophical Studies in Education* 40 (2009): 188; Vicky Lebeau, "The Unwelcome Child: Elizabeth Eckford and Hannah Arendt," *Journal of Visual Culture* 3, no. 1 (2004): 3–4; Christine Firer Hinze, "Reconsidering Little Rock: Hannah Arendt, Martin Luther King Jr., and Catholic Social Thought on Children and Families in the Struggle for Justice," *Journal of the Society of Christian Ethics* 29, no. 1 (2009): 25. Indeed, when Jerome Kohn reproduced Arendt's essay and reply to critics in a recent collection of her work, he did so accompanied by yet another one of Counts's photographs, which he claims "had exemplary status in Arendt's judgment." Hannah Arendt, *Responsibility and Judgment*, ed. Jerome Kohn (New York: Schocken, 2003), xxxv. This photo (reproduced at ibid., 192) is neither the one that Allen takes to be iconic nor the one that appeared on the front cover of the *New York Times*. It depicts Eckford surrounded by a swarm of journalists and does not correspond at all to Arendt's description.

29. Allen, *Talking to Strangers*, 197n191.

30. See ibid., 143–145, 158.

31. Allen, "Law's Necessary Forcefulness," 873. This article contains a much more extensive discussion of Arendt's views on desegregation than *Talking to Strangers*. It also reads as more sympathetic to Arendt.

32. Allen, "Law's Necessary Forcefulness," 873ff.

33. Allen, *Talking to Strangers*, 4.

34. Allen, "Law's Necessary Forcefulness," 874–875 (emphasis added).

35. Allen, *Talking to Strangers*, xxii.

36. Hannah Arendt, *Between Past and Future: Eight Exercises in Political Thought*, enl. ed. (New York: Penguin Books, 1968), 221.

37. Wittgenstein, *Philosophical Investigations*, I.§66.

38. I focus here on the English language, but a similar object orientation is present in other languages used by my interlocutors. *Partager* in French and *teilen* in German, for example, both imply that there is a shared thing.

39. Definition 1.d of "share, v. 2," *OED Online*, March 2012, Oxford University Press, http://www.oed.com/view/Entry/177535.

40. Definition 5 of ibid.

41. Davide Panagia notes a similar complexity in the French language of *partager* (to share), which can mean to divide and allocate, or to aggregate and make common to all. See Davide Panagia, "'*Partage du sensible*': The Distribution of the Sensible," in *Jacques Rancière: Key Concepts*, ed. Jean-Philippe Deranty (Durham, UK: Acumen, 2010), 95–97.

42. See definition 5 of "share, v. 2," and definition 1 of "share, n. 3," *OED Online*, March 2012, Oxford University Press, http://www.oed.com/view/Entry/177533.

43. Definitions 1, 2 of "share, v. 2"; and (although obsolete) "† share, v. 1," *OED Online*, March 2012, Oxford University Press, http://www.oed.com/view/Entry/177534.

44. See definitions 4, 5, and 6 of "share, v. 2,"; definitions 2, 3 of "share, n. 3."

45. See definition 4 of "share, v. 2."

46. See definitions 5, 6 of "share, v. 2." On irreducibly social goods, see Charles Taylor, *Philosophical Arguments* (Cambridge, MA: Harvard University Press, 1995), 127–145, 190. I take up this aspect of his work in more detail in chapter 5.

47. Will Kymlicka, *Multicultural Citizenship: A Liberal Theory of Minority Rights* (Oxford: Clarendon Press, 1995), 190.

48. Political theorists allow for more divergence from the claimed commonality than do feminist theorists. Typically for feminists, either all women share in some same thing, or we cannot say that women have it in common at all. I discuss the parallels and divergences in how democratic and feminist theorists tend to think about commonality in chapter 3.

49. Taylor, whose argument Kymlicka references in this same section of *Multicultural Citizenship*, makes a similar claim about how scholars can observe increasing convergence in the early 1990s among Canadians around the Charter of Rights and Freedoms as "a common reference point of identity." See Charles Taylor, *Reconciling the Solitudes: Essays on Canadian Federalism and Nationalism* (Montreal: McGill-Queen's University Press, 1994), 161.

50. See, e.g., Jürgen Habermas, *The Inclusion of the Other: Studies in Political Theory*, ed. Ciaran Cronin and Pablo De Greiff (Cambridge, MA: MIT Press, 1998), chap. 4. I discuss Habermas and "constitutional patriotism" in more detail in chapter 4.

51. My discussion here is indebted to Jodi Dean's analysis of "university discourse." She elaborates, "Seemingly neutral knowledge is authoritative even as, especially as, it claims and disavows its power at the same time. . . . In Žižek's words, . . . 'the constitutive lie of the University discourse is that it disavows its performative dimension, presenting what effectively amounts to a political decision based on power as a simple sight into the factual state of things.'" Jodi Dean, *Democracy and Other Neoliberal Fantasies: Communicative Capitalism and Left Politics* (Durham, NC: Duke University Press, 2009), 88. She is quoting from Slavoj Žižek, *Iraq: The Borrowed Kettle* (New York: Verso, 2004), 139. I am also drawing

on Linda Zerilli, "Toward a Feminist Theory of Judgment," *Signs* 34, no. 2 (2009): 295–317.

52. On the question of the humanities and political theory being under threat, see, e.g., Wendy Brown, "At the Edge: The Future of Political Theory," in *Edgework: Critical Essays on Knowledge and Politics* (Princeton, NJ: Princeton University Press, 2005), 60–82; Wendy Brown, "Political Theory Is Not a Luxury: A Response to Timothy Kaufman-Osborn's 'Political Theory as a Profession,'" *Political Research Quarterly* 63 (2010): 680–685.

53. Throughout *Multicultural Citizenship*, Kymlicka repeatedly makes reference to how the United States, far from being exceptional, already operates under a model of differentiated citizenship like that available in other multicultural liberal democracies. E.g., ibid., 11–12, 22, 66.

54. This is especially apparent when we trace Kymlicka's source for the poll and see how the same data were used to suit other authors' different political claims. Kymlicka's source is not the poll itself nor an analysis of it but an opinion essay by a political scientist, Alvin Rubinstein. Rubinstein cites the poll as part of a very un-Kymlickan argument that if Puerto Rico were to be granted statehood, this would force the United States to recognize Spanish as an official language, which in turn would "destro[y] attempts to create national cohesion and the foundations of a common culture." Alvin Rubinstein, "Is Statehood for Puerto Rico in the National Interest?," *In Depth: A Journal for Values and Public Policy* 3, no. 2 (Spring 1993): 97. Like Kymlicka, Rubinstein cites not the poll itself but another opinion piece that references it, this one an op-ed that appeared a few years earlier in the *New York Times* by the then governor of Puerto Rico, Rafael Hernández Colón, who interprets the poll as indicating that Puerto Ricans "consider themselves a people with a strong national identity," who could not assimilate into American culture. For him, these data support an argument in favor of commonwealth status for Puerto Rico. Rafael Hernández Colón, "Statehood for Puerto Ricans," *New York Times*, February 26, 1990. Colón does not give a source for the poll data, and I have been unable to locate it.

55. Habermas, *The Inclusion of the Other*, 146.

56. Chantal Mouffe, *The Democratic Paradox* (New York: Verso, 2000), 55.

57. These locutions are reminiscent of a general problem in writing in the social sciences arising from a lack of theoretical clarity about who is responsible for the actions described. "Writers routinely use meaningless expressions to cover up . . . serious dilemmas of sociological theory. One problem has to do with agency: who did the things that your sentence alleges were done? Sociologists often prefer locutions that leave the answer to that question unclear, largely because many of their theorists don't tell them who is doing what. In many sociological theories, things just happen without anyone doing them. It's hard to find a subject for a sentence when 'larger social forces' or 'inexorable social processes' are at work." Howard S. Becker, *Writing for Social Scientists: How to Start and Finish Your Thesis, Book, or Article* (Chicago: University of Chicago Press, 1986), 7–8.

58. Zerilli makes a related point about our inability to be truly open to difference when we are looking to "subsume it under either a transcendent rule or a rule given by our own culture." Zerilli, "Feminist Theory of Judgment," 312.

59. Hannah Arendt, *The Life of the Mind: Thinking*, one-volume ed. (New York: Harcourt Brace Jovanovich, 1978), 50. The original concept of *sensus communis*, which is a Latin translation of κοινὴ αἰσθησις, is attributed to Aristotle. See Aristotle, *De Anima* (New York: Cosimo, 2008), bk. III, pts. 1 and 2.

60. Immanuel Kant, *Critique of Judgment*, trans. Werner S. Pluhar (Indianapolis, IN: Hackett, 1987 [1790]), §39.

61. Arendt, *Thinking*, 50. While the relation between common sense and reality is developed at length in Arendt's unfinished work, *The Life of the Mind*, it is already described in earlier works. See Hannah Arendt, *The Human Condition* (Chicago: University of Chicago Press, 1958), 208–209, 274–275; Hannah Arendt, *The Origins of Totalitarianism*, new ed. (New York: Meridian Books, 1973 [1958]), 475–476; Arendt, *Responsibility and Judgment*, 139–145; Arendt, *Between Past and Future*, 221.

62. Arendt, *Human Condition*, 199.

63. See Arendt, *Thinking*, 50.

64. See, e.g., Arendt, *Human Condition*, 50.

65. Arendt, *Thinking*, 46. For a discussion of Arendt's relationship to Merleau-Ponty, as well as a more extensive discussion of reality in her work, see Kimberley Curtis, *Our Sense of the Real: Aesthetic Experience and Arendtian Politics* (Ithaca, NY: Cornell University Press, 1999), esp. chap. 2. For the concept of "perceptual faith," see Maurice Merleau-Ponty, *The Visible and the Invisible* (Evanston, IL: Northwestern University Press, 1968 [1964]), 3–14.

66. Arendt, *Thinking*, 50.

67. Hannah Arendt, *Lectures on Kant's Political Philosophy* (Chicago: University of Chicago Press, 1982), 70. This distinction between common sense and community sense is found only in her Kant lectures. However, the idea of community sense is present in other texts as well. See Arendt, *Thinking*; Arendt, *Responsibility and Judgment*, 139; Arendt, "The Crisis in Culture," in *Between Past and Future*, 197–226. She attributes this distinction to Kant: see his *Critique of Judgment*, §20, Ak. 238; §240, Ak. 294. He distinguishes between *Gemeinsinn* (which he aligns with *sensus communis*) and *gemeinen Verstande* or *gemeinen Menschenverstande* (common understanding or common human understanding).

68. Arendt, *Human Condition*, 176, 177.

69. Ibid., 176.

70. Ibid.; Arendt, *Lectures on Kant*, 70.

71. Arendt, *Lectures on Kant*, 70–71. While she cites Kant to make this point, this is not the point Kant himself makes in the passage she quotes.

72. Immanuel Kant, *Anthropology from a Pragmatic Point of View*, trans. Robert B. Louden (New York: Cambridge University Press, 2006 [1798]), §53, p. 113 (emphasis in original).

73. Ibid., §53, p. 114.

74. Arendt, *Lectures on Kant*, 74.

75. In several of the passages where Arendt describes the "enlarged mentality" or "going visiting" (both phrases she regularly uses to describe thinking from another's standpoint), she seems to state that we actually do occupy another's position—or in some cases that we occupy every other position. In other passages, her language is more measured and implies instead that we imagine what it would be like to occupy other positions, even though we may never do so. See Arendt's discussion of imagining herself in the place of a slum dweller in *Responsibility and Judgment*, 140–141.

    There is an extensive discussion of "going visiting" and "enlarged mentality" in the place of another in the secondary literature on Arendt. See, e.g., Lisa Jane Disch, *Hannah Arendt and the Limits of Philosophy* (Ithaca, NY: Cornell University Press, 1994), chap. 5; Ronald Beiner and Jennifer Nedelsky,

Judgment, Imagination, and Politics: Themes from Kant and Arendt (Lanham, MD: Rowman and Littlefield, 2001); Benhabib, *The Reluctant Modernism of Hannah Arendt*, chap. 6.

76. Kant's account of human psychology is more complicated than this, of course. Humans are not only sociable but also unsociable—that is, they desire distance from other subjects. I discuss this feature of his work in more detail in Michaele Ferguson, "Unsocial Sociability: Perpetual Antagonism in Kant's Political Thought," in *Kant's Political Theory: Interpretations and Applications*, ed. Elisabeth Ellis (University Park: Pennsylvania State University Press, 2012), 150–169.

77. Kant, *Anthropology*, §53, p. 114.

78. Arendt, *Lectures on Kant*, 81.

79. Arendt, *Thinking*, 119.

80. Ibid., 100.

81. Ibid., 99.

82. Arendt, *Human Condition*, 204.

83. Arendt, *Between Past and Future*, 222.

84. Arendt, *Thinking*, 21.

85. Arendt, *Human Condition*, 57; Arendt, *Thinking*, 50.

86. Arendt, *Human Condition*, 52.

87. Arendt, *Lectures on Kant*, 83.

88. Ludwig Wittgenstein, *On Certainty*, ed. G. E. M. Anscombe and G. H. von Wright, trans. Denis Paul and G. E. M. Anscombe (New York: Harper Torchbooks, 1969), §160.

89. Ibid., §358.

90. While this distinction is manifest in various ways in different texts, Arendt devotes particular attention to it in "Truth and Politics," in *Between Past and Future*. I agree with Zerilli that Arendt does not mean to keep truth out of politics. Yet when Zerilli claims that there is a "truth of opinion" for Arendt, I do not think Arendt means that opinions can have the validity of truth claims. Linda Zerilli, "Truth and Politics," *Theory & Event* 9, no. 4 (2006): 54. Rather, a claim to commonality, for example, can have a kind of political truth when it turns out that the people in whose name I claim the commonality agree with me. As Zerilli puts it, a political claim has truth when "it shows us what we have in common."

91. Arendt, *Between Past and Future*, 240.

92. Sometimes Arendt's discussion of political claims seems to imply that they must be made in a particular way, as when she writes that "their validity depends upon free agreement and consent; they are arrived at by discursive, representative thinking; and they are communicated by means of persuasion and dissuasion." Arendt, *Between Past and Future*, 247. Inasmuch as this is what she means by a political claim, language and meaning are not usually political: we do not typically coin words or apply old words in new ways within discursive practices of seeking consent or explicitly aiming to persuade others. Nonetheless, the meaning of our words is intersubjective and depends upon others "agreeing"— whether expressly or not—with how we use them. In this more limited sense, then, I am suggesting here that when we use language, we are implicitly claiming the validity of the meaning we attribute to those words, and this validity is intersubjective rather than objective.

93. Linda M. G. Zerilli, *Feminism and the Abyss of Freedom* (Chicago: University of Chicago Press, 2005), 163.

94. Ibid.; Ernesto Laclau and Chantal Mouffe, *Hegemony and Socialist Strategy: Towards a Radical Democratic Politics* (London: Verso, 1985).
95. Linda M. G. Zerilli, "Doing without Knowing: Feminism's Politics of the Ordinary," *Political Theory* 26, no. 4 (1998): 454. See also Zerilli, *Feminism and the Abyss of Freedom*, 172.
96. Zerilli, *Feminism and the Abyss of Freedom*, 159.
97. Arendt, *Human Condition*, 184.
98. Ibid., 198.
99. On the fragility of factual truth, see Arendt, *Between Past and Future*, 243; and Zerilli's discussion in "Truth and Politics," 39–45.
100. Bonnie Honig's reading of Arendt stresses her concerns with founding and preservation. See Bonnie Honig, *Political Theory and the Displacement of Politics* (Ithaca, NY: Cornell University Press, 1993), chap. 4.

CHAPTER 3

1. Ludwig Wittgenstein, *Philosophical Investigations (Reissued German-English Edition)*, trans. G. E. M. Anscombe, 2nd ed. (Malden, MA: Blackwell, 1958), I.§67.
2. Judith Butler and Joan W. Scott, "Introduction," in *Feminists Theorize the Political*, ed. Judith Butler and Joan W. Scott (New York: Routledge, 1992), xiv.
3. Linda M. G. Zerilli, *Feminism and the Abyss of Freedom* (Chicago: University of Chicago Press, 2005), 36.
4. Iris Marion Young, *Intersecting Voices: Dilemmas of Gender, Political Philosophy, and Policy* (Princeton, NJ: Princeton University Press, 1997), 13.
5. Consider Zerilli's description of this phenomenon in feminist theory: "The debates over 'the category of women' have taken on the tone of a war of differences in which each attempt to theorize is subjected to accusations that more or less cluster around the problem of exclusion: every theoretical and political claim to the category brings with it a normative conception of women that excludes those who do not conform." Linda M. G. Zerilli, "Doing without Knowing: Feminism's Politics of the Ordinary," *Political Theory* 26, no. 4 (August 1998): 438. The essentialism/antiessentialism debate in feminist theory paralleled similar debates happening within various academic disciplines. See Seyla Benhabib, "Democracy and Identity: In Search of the Civic Polity," *Philosophy & Social Criticism* 24, nos. 2/3 (1998): 85–100.
6. The term "essentialism" is somewhat misleading here. Essentialism, strictly speaking, is "a belief in the real, true essence of things, the invariable and fixed properties which define the 'whatness' of a given entity." Diana Fuss, *Essentially Speaking: Feminism, Nature and Difference* (New York: Routledge, 1989), xi. Essentialist views about women, then, might include a belief in the "eternal feminine"—that is, a transcultural and ahistorical feminine character; or the position that women share a common biology, irrespective of when and where they live. Yet some feminists have laid claim to qualities they believe women share universally that are not "essences"—for example, a historically specific structural position vis-à-vis men. Indeed, essentialism is often contrasted in feminist theory with social constructivism, which "insists that essence is itself a historical construction." Ibid., 2. However, constructivists themselves are often just as committed to an objective picture of sharing as their essentialist counterparts. Much constructivist work posits universalities and commonalities among members of groups, with the difference being that these are considered

to be historically contingent rather than essential. On the essentialist-constructivist divide, see Seyla Benhabib, "Seyla Benhabib: 'Essentialism' vs. 'Constructivism' in Contemporary Theory," *Newsletter for the Institut für die Wissenschaften vom Menschen (IWM)* 55 (September–November 1996): 25–27. Advocates of both approaches, then, can be committed to the view that the category of women is held in place by commonality.

    While some feminists are careful to use "essentialism" only to indicate a belief in a common essence, the term is often deployed in a more general sense in feminist theory to include any belief that women have something in common (and thus could include at least some constructivist positions). For my purposes in this chapter, whether a given theorist believes this commonality to be an essence is unimportant, and so I follow the broader use of the term and call all views that presume that women must share something in common essentialist.

7. Feminists who argue that women share a biology include French feminist Luce Irigaray and radical feminists such as Shulamith Firestone. Those who argue that women share a set of experiences include Marxist/socialist feminists (such as Nancy Hartsock), who define women as a subordinated class that shares the experience of patriarchal oppression, and psychoanalytic feminists (such as Nancy Chodorow), who argue that women share early childhood experiences that are responsible for reproducing gender identities. See Shulamith Firestone, *The Dialectic of Sex: The Case for Feminist Revolution* (New York: Bantam, 1979 [1970]); Nancy C. M. Hartsock, "The Feminist Standpoint: Developing the Ground for a Specifically Feminist Historical Materialism," in *The Feminist Standpoint Revisited and Other Essays* (Boulder, CO: Westview Press, 1998), 105–132; Nancy Chodorow, "Family Structure and Feminine Personality," in *Feminist Philosophies*, ed. J. Kourany, J. Sterba, and R. Tong (Englewood Cliffs, NJ: Prentice Hall, 1992), 309–322; Luce Irigaray, "This Sex Which Is Not One," in *New French Feminisms*, ed. Elaine Marks and Isabelle de Courtivron (New York: Random House, 1988), 99–106.

8. Jennifer Baumgardner and Amy Richards, *Manifesta: Young Women, Feminism, and the Future* (New York: Farrar, Straus and Giroux, 2000), 54.

9. Ibid., 56–57.

10. I critically discuss coalition politics as a model for feminist and democratic theorizing in chapter 6.

11. One of the classic examples of this is the essay by Maria C. Lugones and Elizabeth V. Spelman, "Have We Got a Theory for You! Feminist Theory, Cultural Imperialism and the Demand for 'The Woman's Voice,'" *Women's Studies International Forum* 6, no. 6 (1983): 573–581. Lugones and Spelman take one particular axis of difference among women as their point of departure to expose the bias of mainstream feminism: the difference between Hispanas and white/Anglo women. Sections of the essay are self-consciously described as written "in an Hispana voice" and "in the voice of a white/Anglo woman" and "in the voice of a woman of color"—set in deliberate contrast with those sections composed "in Vicky's and Maria's voice." In other words, they have critiqued an essentialism at the heart of mainstream feminist theory and replaced it with a new essentialism: there are no "women," but there are "Hispanas" and "white/Anglo women." These latter represent new epistemologically privileged positions, which are untouched by "race, class, ethnicity, religion, sexual alliance, etc." "Have We Got a Theory for You!," 574.

12. The most influential perspectivist feminist theorist is Hartsock, whose early "standpoint theory" draws on Marxism to argue that women, as a subordinate class, have a privileged knowledge of the truth. See her essay "The Feminist Standpoint." Iris Young takes a different approach, arguing that it is through encountering a variety of perspectives that we come closer to knowledge of structural injustice. See my account of this aspect of her work in Michaele Ferguson, "Resonance and Recognition: The Role of Personal Experience in Iris Marion Young's Feminist Phenomenology," in *Dancing with Iris: Between Embodiment and the Body Politic in Iris Marion Young's Political Philosophy*, ed. Ann Ferguson and Mechthild Nagel (New York: Oxford University Press, 2009), 53–67. Young develops this position throughout her feminist and democratic theory, but its most mature articulation can be found in Iris Marion Young, *Inclusion and Democracy* (Oxford: Oxford University Press, 2000), chap. 3.

13. While neither has developed the connection between feminism and democratic theory to the extent I do here, Benhabib and Tariq Modood have also noted the parallel. See Benhabib, "'Essentialism' vs. 'Constructivism'"; Tariq Modood, "Anti-essentialism, Multiculturalism and the 'Recognition' of Religious Groups," *Journal of Political Philosophy* 6, no. 4 (1998): 378–399.

14. Zerilli, *Feminism and the Abyss of Freedom*, 36.

15. Zerilli is not the only theorist to conceptualize gender as a doing. Perhaps the most well-known theorist to do so is Judith Butler, who first introduced the idea of gender as a performative in *Gender Trouble: Feminism and the Subversion of Identity* (New York: Routledge, 1990). Zerilli is critical of Butler's approach, and she details their differences in *Feminism and the Abyss of Freedom*, chap. 1.

16. Zerilli, *Feminism and the Abyss of Freedom*, 39–40.

17. Zerilli, "Doing without Knowing," 437.

18. E.g., see Ann Fausto-Sterling, "The Five Sexes: Why Male and Female Are Not Enough," *Sciences*, March/April 1993, 20–25; Lugones and Spelman, "Have We Got a Theory for You!"

19. Zerilli describes this not in terms of essentialism and antiessentialism but in terms of temptations toward dogmatism and skepticism. See *Feminism and the Abyss of Freedom*, 37.

20. While Zerilli does not make this specific observation, she is concerned about how the subject question in feminism is connected to a means-end view of politics that treats people as passive. Ibid., 36.

21. As Zerilli notes, this celebration of gender voluntarism is a frequent reaction feminists have to reading Butler's *Gender Trouble*, even though it is a misreading of her understanding of gender as performative. See Zerilli, *Feminism and the Abyss of Freedom*, 47–48.

22. My argument here builds on the concluding paragraphs of Zerilli's essay. There, she notes that feminists misunderstand the nature of political claiming when they lament that their claims to identity inevitably exclude. She does not, however, argue that feminists often treat identity claims as if they were truth claims. See "Doing without Knowing," 454–455.

23. For one account of the emotional nature of the confrontation of feminists on these issues, see Jane Flax, "The End of Innocence," in *Feminists Theorize the Political*, ed. Judith Butler and Joan W. Scott (New York: Routledge, 1992), 445–463. Flax writes about conflict over the relationship of feminism to postmodernism, which does not map exactly onto the divisions I write about here. Nonetheless, some of the features of postmodernism that raised tensions are antiessentialist

features: "Postmodernists' deconstructions of subjectivity deny or destroy the possibility of active agency in the world. Without a unitary subject with a secure, empirical sense of history and gender, no feminist consciousness and hence no feminist politics is possible" (446). Flax is also critical of the investment of non-postmodernist feminists in making truth claims, as opposed to political claims. See Flax, "The End of Innocence," 455ff. Zerilli mentions a similar kind of reaction in *Feminism and the Abyss of Freedom*, 33.

24. The most famous proponent of strategic essentialism is Spivak, who first advocated it in the context of subaltern studies. See Gayatri Chakravorty Spivak, *In Other Worlds: Essays in Cultural Politics* (New York: Methuen, 1987), 205.

25. See Fausto-Sterliing "The Five Sexes." I take this example from Zerilli.

26. Zerilli, "Doing without Knowing," 436.

27. This is Freud's famous observation. See Sigmund Freud, "Femininity," in *Freud on Women: A Reader*, ed. Elisabeth Young-Bruehl (New York: Norton, 1990), 342–362.

28. Zerilli "Doing without Knowing," 449.

29. Ibid., 447.

30. Ibid., 451.

31. Ibid., 452.

32. Ibid.

33. Ibid., 451.

34. Ibid., 452.

35. Zerilli, *Feminism and the Abyss of Freedom*, 41–42.

36. See Ludwig Wittgenstein, *On Certainty*, ed. G. E. M. Anscombe and G. H. von Wright, trans. Denis Paul and G. E. M. Anscombe (New York: Harper Torchbooks, 1969), §225.

37. Zerilli, "Doing without Knowing," 453.

38. Ibid., 452.

39. In this passage, Zerilli uses the generic term "claim" instead of qualifying it as political. Given her earlier use of the phrase "epistemological claim," I think it is fair to say that she means to refer to only political claims in this passage. Ibid., 455. She develops the concept of political claims in *Feminism and the Abyss of Freedom*.

40. Ibid.

41. Ibid.

42. See Arendt's discussion of imagination at Hannah Arendt, *Lectures on Kant's Political Philosophy* (Chicago: University of Chicago Press, 1982), 79–85.

43. The discussion that follows is based on Immanuel Kant, *Anthropology from a Pragmatic Point of View*, trans. Robert B. Louden (New York: Cambridge University Press, 2006 [1798]), 60–62.

44. Arendt, *Lectures on Kant*, 79.

45. Cornelius Castoriadis, *World in Fragments: Writings on Politics, Society, Psychoanalysis, and the Imagination* (Stanford, CA: Stanford University Press, 1997), 269.

46. Ibid., 7.

47. Ibid., 8.

48. Cornelius Castoriadis, *Figures of the Thinkable* (Stanford, CA: Stanford University Press, 2007), 73.

49. Ibid., 72.

50. Ibid., 73.

51. Ibid.

52. Zerilli gives a reading of Monique Wittig's *Les guérillères* as an example of the radical imagination thinking gender anew. *Feminism and the Abyss of Freedom*, chap. 2.

53. Castoriadis, *Figures of the Thinkable*, 72.

54. Benedict Anderson, *Imagined Communities: Reflections on the Origin and Spread of Nationalism*, rev. ed. (London: Verso, 1991 [1983]), 6.

55. Ibid. (emphasis in original).

56. Ibid.

57. Ibid., 124.

58. Ibid., 126.

59. Ibid., 128.

60. Ibid., 129.

61. Ibid.

62. Ibid., 130.

63. Ibid., 131.

64. Ibid., 124–126.

65. "All that I can find to say is that a nation exists when a significant number of people in a community consider themselves to form a nation, or behave as if they formed one." Hugh Seton-Watson, quoted in ibid., 6n9.

66. Cf. Charles Taylor, *Human Agency and Language: Philosophical Papers I* (New York: Cambridge University Press, 1985), 260–263.

67. Wittgenstein, *Philosophical Investigations*, I.§67.

68. Jacques Derrida, *Rogues: Two Essays on Reason*, trans. Pascale-Anne Brault and Michael Naas (Stanford, CA: Stanford University Press, 2005), 74.

69. Ibid., 36.

70. Ibid., 86–87.

71. For similar arguments, see also Alan Keenan, *Democracy in Question: Democratic Openness in a Time of Political Closure* (Stanford, CA: Stanford University Press, 2003); Zerilli, *Feminism and the Abyss of Freedom*.

72. Rogers M. Smith, *Stories of Peoplehood: The Politics and Morals of Political Membership* (New York: Cambridge University Press, 2003), 156.

73. Ibid.

74. Ibid., 53.

75. Ibid., 99–100.

76. Ibid., 49.

77. Ibid., 15.

78. For discussions of stability and moderation, see ibid., 57, 133–134, 156.

79. Ibid., 32.

80. Ibid., 35–36.

81. Ibid., 36.

82. Zerilli, *Feminism and the Abyss of Freedom*, 98.

CHAPTER 4

1. Tariq Modood, "Introduction: The Politics of Multiculturalism in the New Europe," in *The Politics of Multiculturalism in the New Europe: Racism, Identity and Community*, ed. Tariq Modood and Pnina Werbner (New York: Zed Books, 1997), 18.

2. Robert D. Putnam, "*E Pluribus Unum*: Diversity and Community in the Twenty-First Century: The 2006 Johan Skytte Prize Lecture," *Scandinavian Political Studies* 30, no. 2 (2007): 137.

3. Robert D. Putnam, *Making Democracy Work: Civic Traditions in Modern Italy* (Princeton, NJ: Princeton University Press, 1994).

4. Putnam, "*E Pluribus Unum*," 137.

5. The Saguaro Seminar, "Social Capital Community Benchmark Survey" (2000), http://www.hks.harvard.edu/saguaro/communitysurvey/index.html.

6. Putnam, "*E Pluribus Unum*," 137.

7. There is also a related debate about the relationship between multiculturalist policies and social solidarity. For a brief overview of this debate as well as an intervention in it, see Keith Banting and Will Kymlicka, "Multiculturalism and Welfare," *Dissent* 50, no. 4 (2003): 59–66.

8. Dora L. Costa and Matthew E. Kahn, "Civic Engagement and Community Heterogeneity: An Economist's Perspective," *Perspectives on Politics* 1, no. 1 (2003): 103.

9. Alberto Alesina, Reza Baqir, and William Easterly, "Public Goods and Ethnic Divisions," *Quarterly Journal of Economics* 114, no. 4 (1999): 1243–1284.

10. Ibid., 1243.

11. Alberto Alesina, Edward Glaeser, and Bruce Sacerdote, "Why Doesn't the United States Have a European-Style Welfare State?," *Brookings Papers on Economic Activity* 2 (2001): 189.

12. David Goodhart, "Too Diverse?," *Prospect Magazine*, no. 95 (February 20, 2004). Alan Wolfe and Jytte Klausen argue from a philosophical perspective that support for the welfare state and support for diversity are in tension with one another, producing problems for leftist politics. Alan Wolfe and Jytte Klausen, "Identity Politics and the Welfare State," *Social Philosophy & Policy* 14, no. 2 (1997): 231–255.

13. Jan Delhey and Kenneth Newton, "Predicting Cross-National Levels of Social Trust: Global Pattern or Nordic Exceptionalism?," *European Sociological Review* 21, no. 4 (2005): 311.

14. Ibid. For criticism of the methods of "social capital" scholars more generally, see Ben Fine, *Theories of Social Capital: Researchers Behaving Badly* (London: Pluto Press, 2010).

15. Putnam, "*E Pluribus Unum*," 154, 155, 149. Putnam often uses the language of "seeming to" or "appearing to"—perhaps to avoid making the stronger causal claim that his evidence cannot support. Nonetheless, the overall implication of his analysis of the data is that diversity is causing human behavior.

16. Putnam notes that he only has data from one point in time, and yet he does not acknowledge that this limits his ability to infer causal relationships from that data. Ibid., 158.

17. Costa and Kahn, "Civic Engagement and Community Heterogeneity," 109, 108.

18. Putnam, "*E Pluribus Unum*," 141.

19. Putnam discusses the contact literature in more detail at ibid., 141–142.

20. Ibid., 142–143.

21. Ibid., 143.

22. Ibid., 144.

23. Ibid., 149 (emphasis in original).

24. Ibid., 150–151 (emphasis in original).

25. Ibid., 149.

26. John Lloyd, "Harvard Study Paints Bleak Picture of Ethnic Diversity," *Financial Times*, October 9, 2006.

27. Putnam, "*E Pluribus Unum*," 159.

28. Ibid., 163–164.

29. Ibid., 159.

30. Putnam notes American discomfort with diversity as if it were just a neutral fact
at ibid., 158.

31. Putnam hints at this possibility when he notes that the US census categories his
study was "forced" to use to measure neighborhood diversity are themselves
contingent and limited measures of difference. They include only four categories
of difference: non-Hispanic whites, Hispanics, non-Hispanic blacks, and Asians.
See ibid., 145–146, 159.

32. Ibid., 161.

33. Democratic affect is a *horizontal* affect that connects equals to one another—as
opposed to a *vertical* affect that binds unequals, or that connects citizens to
institutions that govern them. All forms of government have an interest in
generating a vertical affect that binds citizens to the government and to those
who exercise power. Democracy, however, is unique in demanding a horizontal
attachment between citizens because of its need for trust and solidarity among
equals.

34. Patchen Markell, "Making Affect Safe for Democracy? On 'Constitutional
Patriotism,'" *Political Theory* 28, no. 1 (February 2000): 54.

35. These examples are more or less representative of the range of views expressed
in the recent literature on democratic affect. Most democratic theorists try to
resuscitate some version of nationalism (David Miller, Yael Tamir), to appeal to
common institutions and principles as a source of attachment to the community
(Jürgen Habermas, John Rawls), or to find sources of affect in the diverse ways
that citizens feel attached to the community (Charles Taylor, Will Kymlicka,
Bhikhu Parekh—but also John Rawls again).

36. I develop this account of his position from David Miller, *On Nationality* (Oxford:
Oxford University Press, 1995); David Miller, "In What Sense Must Socialism Be
Communitarian?," *Social Philosophy & Policy* 6, no. 2 (1989): 51–73; David Miller,
Market, State, and Community: Theoretical Foundations of Market Socialism
(Oxford: Clarendon Press, 1989).

37. Miller, "In What Sense Must Socialism Be Communitarian?," 59. See also Miller,
On Nationality, 93; Miller, *Market, State, and Community*, 236–237, 284.

38. Miller, *On Nationality*, 98.

39. Ibid.

40. See, e.g., ibid., 90. There, he argues that "states, or more generally political
authorities, are likely to function most effectively when they embrace just a
single national community" because of "the political consequences of solidarity
and cultural homogeneity."

41. Ibid., 92.

42. Ibid.

43. Miller, *Market, State, and Community*, 279.

44. Ibid., 250, 284.

45. Miller, *On Nationality*, 85.

46. Miller, "In What Sense Must Socialism Be Communitarian?," 70.

47. Miller, *On Nationality*, 92.

48. On constitutional patriotism, see Jürgen Habermas, *The Inclusion of the Other:
Studies in Political Theory*, ed. Ciaran Cronin and Pablo De Greiff (Cambridge,
MA: MIT Press, 1998); Jürgen Habermas, "Historical Consciousness and
Post-traditional Identity: Remarks on the Federal Republic's Orientation to the

West," *Acta Sociologica* 31, no. 1 (1988): 3–13; Jürgen Habermas, "Constitutional Democracy: A Paradoxical Union of Contradictory Principles?," *Political Theory* 29, no. 6 (2001): 766–781. For secondary analysis of Habermas's work on constitutional patriotism, see Markell, "Making Affect Safe?"; Jan-Werner Müller, *Constitutional Patriotism* (Princeton, NJ: Princeton University Press, 2007).

49. Habermas, *The Inclusion of the Other*, 113 (emphasis in original).
50. Markell also takes note of this causal logic in Habermas as well as in the broader literature on nationalism. "Habermas's own account of how the nation-state originally produced 'imagined communities' of citizens, a project he hopes to continue but without the help of the 'nation,' presumes that relationships of solidarity and attachment among individuals who are themselves 'strangers' are first established by tying each individual to shared institutions at the center. On this view, the vertical identification with the central imaginary object is primary; the horizontal love for one's fellow citizens (and the resentment, hatred, or fear of those others on whom we project responsibility for the fragility of the collective imaginary) is its secondary effect." Markell, "Making Affect Safe?," 54–55.
51. Habermas, *The Inclusion of the Other*, 227.
52. Ibid., 225.
53. Habermas, *The Inclusion of the Other*, 117.
54. Ibid., 117–118.
55. Markell, "Making Affect Safe?," 43.
56. Habermas, "Historical Consciousness and Post-traditional Identity," 11.
57. Habermas explicitly does not allow for differences of perspective, which would undermine his commitment to universalist reason-giving. When they critically reflect on their constitution, "All participants must be able to recognize the project [of a voluntary association of citizens who make their own laws] as *the same* throughout history and to judge it from *the same* perspective." Habermas, "Constitutional Democracy," 775 (emphasis in original).
58. Charles Taylor, *Reconciling the Solitudes: Essays on Canadian Federalism and Nationalism* (Montreal: McGill-Queen's University Press, 1994), 197.
59. Ibid., 161–166.
60. Ibid., 182–184.
61. Miller, *On Nationality*, 94–98. He defends Mill's claims about nationalism against the charge that these three countries are empirical counterexamples at 98.
62. Ibid., 94.
63. For other examples of theorists attempting to explain the "anomaly" of the United States, see Miller, *Market, State, and Community*, 282n6; Brian Barry, *Democracy, Power, and Justice: Essays in Political Theory* (Oxford: Clarendon Press, 1989), 175ff.; Bhikhu Parekh, "Politics of Nationhood," in *Nationalism, Ethnicity, and Cultural Identity in Europe*, ed. Keebet von Benda-Beckman and Maykel Verkuyten (Utrecht: European Research Centre on Migration and Ethnic Relations, 1995), 134.
64. See also Müller, *Constitutional Patriotism*, 6–7.
65. Habermas, *The Inclusion of the Other*, 113.
66. Will Kymlicka, *Multicultural Citizenship: A Liberal Theory of Minority Rights* (Oxford: Clarendon Press, 1995), 190.
67. Arthur Schlesinger Jr., *The Disuniting of America: Reflections on a Multicultural Society*, 2nd ed. (New York: Norton, 1998 [1992]), 12.
68. Ibid., 13.

69. Putnam, *"E Pluribus Unum,"* 159.
70. Miller, *Market, State, and Community*, 237.
71. Miller, "In What Sense Must Socialism Be Communitarian?," 59.
72. Miller cites the same two studies in ibid., 59, and *Market, State, and Community*, 237.
73. Parekh, "Politics of Nationhood," 133.
74. Ibid., 134–135.
75. Ibid., 138–139.
76. Ibid., 140.
77. Masaki Yuki et al., "Cross-Cultural Differences in Relationship- and Group-Based Trust," *Personality and Social Psychology Bulletin* 31 (2005): 48.
78. Miller, *On Nationality*, 83.
79. Miller, for example, writes, "If we look at actual cases in which people identify with their community . . ., we see that they identify with it as a concrete and distinct object." Miller, *Market, State, and Community*, 231.
80. Habermas, *The Inclusion of the Other*, 113.
81. Miller, *Market, State, and Community*, 245.
82. Parekh, "Politics of Nationhood," 140.
83. The materials for applying for citizenship, including the film, are available at Naar Nederland, http://www.naarnederland.nl/en/category/homeen.
84. Jeremy Bransten, "Netherlands Leading EU Trend to More Stringent Immigration Rules," EUbusiness, http://www.eubusiness.com/europe/netherlands/immigration.2006-04-05.
85. Ibid.
86. Information about the contract is available in French at the website for the Office Français de l'Immigration et de l'Intégration, http://www.ofii.fr/.
87. I take the text and translation of the contract from Daniel Brunstetter, "The Enlightenment Strikes Back: The Dangers of France's Contrat d'Acceuil et d'Intégration" (paper presented at the annual meetings of the Western Political Science Association, San Diego, California, March 2008), 2.
88. Immigrants who fail to comply with the terms of the CAI can be denied citizenship. In one recent example, an immigrant was denied citizenship because he was found to have "ordered his wife to cover herself with a head-to-toe veil" and to have "rejected the principles of secularism and equality between men and women." "France Refuses a Citizenship over Full Islamic Veil," BBC, http://news.bbc.co.uk/2/hi/europe/8494860.stm.
89. Taylor, *Reconciling the Solitudes*, 162.
90. This is a restatement of the argument Iris Marion Young makes in the final chapter of *Global Challenges: War, Self-Determination, and Responsibility for Justice* (Cambridge: Polity Press, 2006).
91. This kind of approach to citizenship is articulated in the final chapter of Iris Marion Young, *Justice and the Politics of Difference* (Princeton, NJ: Princeton University Press, 1990).
92. Putnam, *"E Pluribus Unum,"* 149.
93. Ibid., 167n17 (emphasis in original).

CHAPTER 5

1. Hannah Arendt, *The Human Condition* (Chicago: University of Chicago Press, 1958), 234.
2. This imaginary is reflected in prominent analytic accounts of collective agency, which (while they disagree about other details) tend to assume that individuals

can only share agency when they already share an explicit, agreed-upon intention. See Philip Pettit and David Schweikard, "Joint Actions and Group Agents," *Philosophy of the Social Sciences* 36, no. 1 (2006): 23–24; Margaret Gilbert, *Sociality and Responsibility: New Essays in Plural Subject Theory* (Lanham, MD: Rowman and Littlefield, 2000).

3. Jürgen Habermas, *Between Facts and Norms: Contributions to a Discourse Theory of Law and Democracy*, trans. William Rehg (Cambridge, MA: MIT Press, 1996), 301. See also Jürgen Habermas, "Three Normative Models of Democracy," in *Democracy and Difference: Contesting the Boundaries of the Political*, ed. Seyla Benhabib (Princeton, NJ: Princeton University Press, 1996), 30.

4. Charles Taylor, "Democratic Exclusion (and Its Remedies?)," in *Citizenship, Diversity and Pluralism: Canadian and Comparative Perspectives*, ed. Alan C. Cairns et al. (Montreal: McGill-Queen's University Press, 1999), 286.

5. John Rawls, *Political Liberalism* (New York: Columbia University Press, 1993), 232.

6. Pettit and Schweikard, "Joint Actions and Group Agents," 33.

7. Rawls, *Political Liberalism*, 232.

8. Taylor, "Democratic Exclusion," 267.

9. Ibid., 266.

10. Charles Taylor, "The Dynamics of Democratic Exclusion," *Journal of Democracy* 9, no. 4 (1998): 144.

11. Ibid., 144.

12. Taylor, "Democratic Exclusion," 280. Various articulations of this dilemma can be found in many of his political works. See, e.g., Charles Taylor, *Modern Social Imaginaries* (Durham, NC: Duke University Press, 2004); Charles Taylor, *Reconciling the Solitudes: Essays on Canadian Federalism and Nationalism* (Montreal: McGill-Queen's University Press, 1994).

13. Taylor, "Democratic Exclusion," 265.

14. Ibid., 272.

15. Ibid., 273–274.

16. Ibid., 276.

17. See, e.g., Alan Keenan, *Democracy in Question: Democratic Openness in a Time of Political Closure* (Stanford, CA: Stanford University Press, 2003); Chantal Mouffe, *The Democratic Paradox* (New York: Verso, 2000); Wendy Brown, "We Are All Democrats Now . . .," *Theory & Event* 13, no. 2 (2010).

18. Taylor, "Democratic Exclusion," 274.

19. He also refers to this as a "potential" in democracy. Ibid., 280.

20. Ibid.

21. Ibid., 281.

22. As Taylor notes in the acknowledgments, *Modern Social Imaginaries* is "an expansion of a central section" of what he later published as *A Secular Age* (Cambridge, MA: Belknap, 2007), esp. 159–211. I reference the earlier publication here because its treatment of imaginaries of agency is more extensive.

23. Charles Taylor, *Philosophical Arguments* (Cambridge, MA: Harvard University Press, 1995), 171.

24. Charles Taylor, *Philosophical Papers, Vol. I: Human Agency and Language* (New York: Cambridge University Press, 1985), 23.

25. Charles Taylor, "The Politics of Recognition," in *Multiculturalism: Examining the Politics of Recognition*, ed. Amy Gutmann (Princeton, NJ: Princeton University Press, 1994), 32.

26. Ibid., 30.

27. Ibid., 31.

28. Taylor uses the terms "collective agency," "integrated agency," and "dialogical agency" interchangeably in his work.

29. This concept of dialogical collective agency is developed in some of Taylor's earlier works on agency and language. See, e.g., Taylor, *Philosophical Arguments*, 109ff., 127–145, 172ff., 189ff.; Taylor, *Philosophical Papers I*, 93ff., 234, 259ff.

30. Taylor, *Philosophical Arguments*, 171–172.

31. Ibid.

32. Ibid., 109–110, 172; Taylor, *Philosophical Papers I*, 260. He mentions other examples of dialogical action, yet he treats those (like dialogue) in which participants engage in a common rhythm as paradigmatic. Most notably for my argument, he mentions the Tiananmen Square protests as an example of dialogical action. "In a different form it can also constitute a political or religious movement, whose members may be widely scattered, but who are animated together by a sense of common purpose—such as linked the students in Tiananmen Square and their colleagues back on the campuses and, indeed, a great part of the population of Beijing." *Philosophical Arguments*, 172.

33. Taylor, *Philosophical Arguments*, 109, 171–172, 189.

34. Ibid., 109–110.

35. Taylor, *Philosophical Papers I*, 259–260.

36. Taylor, *Modern Social Imaginaries*, 76.

37. Ibid., 85, 157.

38. Ibid., 156.

39. Ibid., 94. Note how his characterization of the public is marked by a desire for unity and consensus: a common mind.

40. Ibid., 86.

41. Ibid., 85.

42. Michael Warner, *Publics and Counterpublics* (Cambridge, MA: Zone, 2005), 75–76.

43. Taylor, *Modern Social Imaginaries*, 23.

44. Ibid., 33.

45. Ibid., 85.

46. Ibid., 23.

47. Zerilli, *Feminism and the Abyss of Freedom*, 171.

48. Danielle Allen, *Talking to Strangers: Anxieties of Citizenship since Brown v. Board of Education* (Chicago: University of Chicago Press, 2004), 28.

49. Ibid., 27. See also similar formulations at 22–23, 41.

50. Zerilli, *Feminism and the Abyss of Freedom*, 125.

51. E.g., Sheldon Wolin, "Fugitive Democracy," in *Democracy and Difference: Contesting the Boundaries of the Political*, ed. Seyla Benhabib (Princeton, NJ: Princeton University Press, 1996), 31. Wolin also associates democratic politics with the experience of commonality among citizens. Despite the somewhat radical character of his account of democracy, then, I would take issue with the importance he places on objectively common concerns and interests.

52. The Supreme Court, of course, also played a significant role in the outcome of the election. It is possible to interpret its role in this case as both democratic (insofar as it is granted authority to settle constitutional disputes) and antidemocratic (insofar as its decision effectively negated the majority of the voters and arguably disenfranchised many in the state of Florida in particular).

CHAPTER 6

1. The Milan Women's Bookstore Collective, *Sexual Difference: A Theory of Social-Symbolic Practice* (Bloomington: Indiana University Press, 1990), 126.
2. The text of the bill is available at http://thomas.loc.gov. US House of Representatives, The Border Protection, Anti-terrorism, and Illegal Immigration Control Act, H.R. 4437.
3. For the history of this organizing first in the Los Angeles area and then among groups from across the United States, see Alfonso Gonzales, "The 2006 *Mega Marchas* in Greater Los Angeles: Counter-hegemonic Moment and the Future of *El Migrante* Struggle," *Latino Studies* 7, no. 1 (2009): 39–40.
4. Oscar Avila and Antonio Olivo, "A Show of Strength: Thousands March to Loop for Immigrants' Rights: Workers, Students Unite in Opposition to Toughening of Law," *Chicago Tribune*, March 11, 2006. For some reason, many accounts of these marches do not include this one in Chicago but begin instead with the marches on March 25, 2006. See Gonzales, "The 2006 *Mega Marchas* in Greater Los Angeles"; Richard D. Pineda and Stacey K. Sowards, "Flag Waving as Visual Argument: 2006 Immigration Demonstrations and Cultural Citizenship," *Argumentation and Advocacy* 43 (Winter and Spring 2007). This may be because the scale of this early protest was not as great as some of those to follow. Earlier marches also occurred in Milwaukee on March 23 and in Atlanta on March 24.
5. UPI, "100,000 Rally for Immigrants in Chicago," March 11, 2006.
6. Karen Hawkins, "100,000 March in Favor of Immigrant Rights," Associated Press, March 11, 2006.
7. The waving of non-US flags (and Mexican flags in particular) at immigration rights protests had also been an issue in the past. According to one activist, "Immigrant-rights organizers have debated the polarizing effect the Mexican flag has at large gatherings since at least 1994, when Proposition 187 was on the ballot." Hector Becerra, "World Cup Brings Mexican Flags Back to Streets of Los Angeles," *Los Angeles Times*, June 25, 2010.
8. Lou Dobbs, "Lou Dobbs Tonight," CNN, March 10, 2006.
9. Gonzales, "The 2006 *Mega Marchas* in Greater Los Angeles," 51.
10. For more details, see ibid., 44–45.
11. See, e.g., Michelle Malkin's blog post on March 29, 2006, at http://michellemalkin.com/2006/03/29/the-american-flag-comes-second/. It is also mentioned four years later as the most inflammatory flag-related incident in the spring 2006 protests in Becerra, "World Cup Brings Mexican Flags Back to Streets of Los Angeles."
12. E.g., see Ruben Navarette Jr., "End the Protesting and Start Participating," *San Diego Union-Tribune*, March 19, 2006. For an account of a range of perspectives articulated at the time about the flag-waving, see Pineda and Sowards, "Flag Waving as Visual Argument," 167–170.
13. For more details, see Gonzales, "The 2006 *Mega Marchas* in Greater Los Angeles," 45–46. Pineda and Sowards cite numerous accounts of this strategic shift at "Flag Waving as Visual Argument," 165, 171.
14. Quoted in National Public Radio, "Coordinating Flags at Immigration Marches," http://www.npr.org/templates/story/story.php?storyID=5336799.
15. A photo of this flag is available at *Life*, "Students Rally to Protest Immigrant Legislation," http://www.life.com/image/57344276. The *LA Times* reports that Mexican flags "dominated" at this rally, although other flags were still present. Elias's flag is not mentioned. Jean Merl and Richard Winton, "Somber Note to an

Upbeat Protest Rally," *Los Angeles Times*, April 16, 2006. Egyptian protesters marched with a similar flag made up of flags of Arab nations in May 2011. A photo of this flag accompanied Anthony Shadid and David D. Kirkpatrick, "Promise of Arab Uprisings Is Threatened by Divisions," *New York Times*, May 21, 2011, discussed in the introduction.

16. Gonzales, "The 2006 *Mega Marchas* in Greater Los Angeles," 46–47.
17. Jim Rutenberg, "Bush Enters Anthem Fight on Language," *New York Times*, April 29, 2006.
18. Quoted in ibid.
19. Ruth Milkman, "Critical Mass: Latino Labor and Politics in California," *North American Congress on Latin America* 40, no. 3 (2007): 31.
20. Gonzales sees the passage of S. 2611 as evidence of the success of what he terms the "counter-hegemonic moment" of the *Mega Marchas*; "The 2006 *Mega Marchas* in Greater Los Angeles," 48–50. I am less inclined to see it as such. One piece of evidence he gives is that Senator Ted Kennedy "was able to draw on the *Mega Marchas* as a way to attempt to humanize migrants and oppose SB 2611" (50). Yet far from opposing S. 2611, Kennedy was one of its six sponsors! Moreover, Kennedy was not moved to alter his own position by the protests. He was a long-standing supporter of amnesty and a path to citizenship for immigrants, and he had spoken at one of the pro-immigration rights marches in Washington, DC, that spring. While these protests may have provided him with some rhetorical power in humanizing undocumented immigrants, his position did not change as a result of the *Gran Marchas*. Arguably, his support of a somewhat less extreme immigration bill than H.R. 4437 was not a sign that the protesters had succeeded in being seen and treated as equals.
21. By 2010, it was safe to wave the Mexican flag again without the inflammatory political associations it had four years earlier. "After years of being downplayed at large political rallies that regularly punctuated the L.A. landscape, the World Cup has given the Mexican flag some of its big event presence back." Becerra, "World Cup Brings Mexican Flags Back to Streets of Los Angeles."
22. The protests in 2010 may have been smaller for a variety of reasons. First of all, undocumented workers have been subject to stepped-up immigration raids and deportation since early 2006. Gonzales even suggests this may be a response to the political mobilization of undocumented workers in the *Gran Marchas* intended to intimidate and silence them. "The 2006 *Mega Marchas* in Greater Los Angeles," 52–53. Moreover, the Arizona bill applies only to people in the state of Arizona, whereas H.R. 4437 applied to people anywhere in the United States; it may have been more difficult to mobilize protesters in states like California and Illinois, where the Arizona bill was widely unpopular but would have no direct impact. If more states pass similar bills, or if similar legislation is seriously considered at the national level, perhaps we will see a resurgence of protests.
23. Cristina Beltràn, *The Trouble with Unity: Latino Politics and the Creation of Identity* (New York: Oxford University Press, 2010), 146.
24. Gonzales, "The 2006 *Mega Marchas* in Greater Los Angeles," 42.
25. Ibid., 51.
26. Ibid.
27. See Gonzales's discussion at ibid., 50–52.
28. Jesse Jackson, "1984 Democratic National Convention Address," http://www.americanrhetoric.com/speeches/jessejackson1984dnc.htm.

29. bell hooks, "Sisterhood: Political Solidarity between Women," *Feminist Review* 23 (1986): 138.

30. One of the most frequently cited references to coalition politics is to a very brief mention of it by the very influential Judith Butler in *Gender Trouble: Feminism and the Subversion of Identity* (New York: Routledge, 1990), 14–16.

31. See, e.g., hooks, "Sisterhood," 138. She contrasts a falsely universalist and racist conception of sisterhood with a "new" vision of solidarity as involving conflict, struggle, and work around a "community of interests, shared beliefs and goals."

32. See the discussion of these generational narratives in Lori Marso, "Feminism's Quest for Common Desires," *Perspectives on Politics* 8, no. 1 (2010): 263–269.

33. Janet R. Jakobsen, *Working Alliances and the Politics of Difference: Diversity and Feminist Ethics* (Bloomington: Indiana University Press, 1998), 60–66.

34. See chapter 3 for more exploration of the theoretical debates around the category of women.

35. Iris Young, e.g., cites the Rainbow Coalition favorably in her discussion of coalition politics. Iris Marion Young, *Justice and the Politics of Difference* (Princeton, NJ: Princeton University Press, 1990), 188–189. See also the critique of Young in Chantal Mouffe, "Feminism, Citizenship, and Radical Democratic Politics," in *Feminists Theorize the Political*, ed. Judith Butler and Joan W. Scott (New York: Routledge, 1992), 380–381.

36. Bernice Johnson Reagon, "Coalition Politics: Turning the Century," in *Home Girls: A Black Feminist Anthology* (New Brunswick, NJ: Rutgers University Press, 2000 [1983]), 343 (emphasis in original).

37. hooks, "Sisterhood," 125. Mohanty makes a similar kind of critique (although she is critical of the language of sisterhood, which she associates with Robyn Morgan) and extends the idea of coalition to a global feminist movement. Chandra Talpade Mohanty, *Feminism without Borders: Decolonizing Theory, Practicing Solidarity* (Durham, NC: Duke University Press, 2003), chap. 4.

38. Brenda Lyshaug, "Solidarity without 'Sisterhood'? Feminism and the Ethics of Coalition Building," *Politics & Gender* 2 (2006): 84.

39. Ibid., 80–81.

40. Jodi Dean, *Solidarity of Strangers: Feminism after Identity Politics* (Berkeley: University of California Press, 1996), 27.

41. Lyshaug, "Solidarity without 'Sisterhood'?," 78.

42. Ibid., 79. I worry, too, that Lyshaug's emphasis on self-work as the supplement to coalition risks valuing encounters with others for what the other can do *for me*—a position that exoticizes the other and turns her into a means for my personal edification.

43. Dean, *Solidarity of Strangers*, 30–32. With its self-reflexivity and constant revision, Dean's vision of "reflective solidarity" resembles Charles Taylor's periodically renegotiated shared identity space, explored in chapter 5.

44. Ibid., 34.

45. I hesitate to say that it could be a shared goal—it is irrelevant whether all participants in a collective action share a commitment to democratic political action. It can be a reason for some to engage in collective action, even if it does not motivate them all. I have made the argument in chapter 4 that political actors need not be motivated to share in democratic institutions for the same reasons. The argument could be extended here to say that political actors need not be motivated to share in democratic interagency for the same reasons.

46. I call for celebrating the pleasures of politics as a counterpoint to the fears and
    concerns we have about acting with others who differ from and disagree with us
    in Michaele Ferguson, "Choice Feminism and the Fear of Politics," *Perspectives on
    Politics* 8, no. 1 (2010): 247–253. I hear echoes of this form of pleasure in
    Beltràn's characterization of the 2006 marches as evidencing "festive anger."
    Beltràn, *The Trouble with Unity*, 143–144.
47. Pineda and Sowards, "Flag Waving as Visual Argument," 170.
48. This, I believe, is the most sympathetic way of understanding the singing of the
    national anthem in Spanish at the May 1 protests—it was a conventional display
    of American patriotism, inflected by its translation, but still a conventional
    display that could be read as consistent with a desire for citizenship and (for the
    most part) assimilation. Butler interprets the singing of the national anthem in
    Spanish as a more radical challenge to conceptions of the nation. Judith Butler
    and Gayatri Chakravorty Spivak, *Who Sings the Nation-State?* (New York: Seagull
    Books, 2007), esp. 58–64.
49. Beltràn, *The Trouble with Unity*, 147.
50. Ibid., 144.
51. Beltràn's reference to "takers" here draws on Bonnie Honig, *Democracy and the
    Foreigner* (Princeton, NJ: Princeton University Press, 2001), 99–101.
52. Indeed, legal and illegal migrations are characterized by some degree of reverse
    migration—the return of some migrants to their state of origin. Not all migrants
    in the United States intend to or will live here forever or seek citizenship.
    Reading the protests exclusively in terms of an unequivocal desire for citizenship
    and permanent residence renders all migrants relatively safe—they all want to
    be here, and it is up to us to decide whether to let them stay. It is more chal-
    lenging to our existing conceptions of democratic community to understand
    them as demanding the right to shape the world in which they exist indepen-
    dently of whether they demand citizenship, amnesty, guest worker status, and
    so on.
53. Beltràn also suggests that the protesters were engaged in Arendtian world-
    building. However, she takes world-building to be only about natality—bringing
    something new into the world—whereas I would take it to also be about
    sustaining an already existing world. Beltràn, *The Trouble with Unity*, 148. See my
    discussion of world-building in chapter 2, and of instituting and instituted
    imaginaries in chapter 3.
54. Honig talks about a similar phenomenon with respect to the regular publication
    of photos in the *New York Times* that depict immigrants taking the oath of
    allegiance as they are naturalized. Repeatedly seeing that America is choicewor-
    thy for legal and undocumented immigrants confirms—even for those of us who
    have not chosen our nationality—the value of being American. See Honig,
    Democracy and the Foreigner, 92–95.
55. Ginia Bellafante, "Gunning for Wall Street, with Faulty Aim," *New York Times*,
    September 23, 2011; Cara Buckley and Colin Moynihan, "Occupy Wall Street
    Protest Reaches a Crossroads," *New York Times*, November 4, 2011.
56. David D. Kirkpatrick, "Wired and Shrewd, Young Egyptians Guide Revolt," *New
    York Times*, February 9, 2011.
57. Beltràn notes this as well in *The Trouble with Unity*, 145–146.
58. Aemilia Scott, "Best Church of God—Westboro Protest," http://www.yourcivic-
    doody.com/yourcivicdoody/2009/08/best-church-of-god-westboro-protest.html.

59. Acting to shut down a protest would involve trying to prevent the protesters'
    being able to express themselves. Some, but not all, co-protesting tactics (such as
    threatening or even perpetrating violence against protesters, or trying to drown
    out a chant by shouting even louder) can have the effect of preventing expres-
    sion. See, e.g., the actions taken to prevent one protest taking place reported at
    ihatethemedia.com, "Mississippi Town Figures Out Simple, Effective Way to
    Stop Westboro Baptist Church Funeral Protest," http://www.ihatethemedia.
    com/a-simple-way-to-stop-westboro-baptist-church-funeral-protesters.
60. Some descriptions of the co-protest are available at digby, "White Flour!," http://
    digbysblog.blogspot.com/2007/09/white-flour-by-digby-via-perlstein.html;
    Alex, "Clowns Kicked KKK Asses," http://www.neatorama.com/2007/09/03/
    clowns-kicked-kkk-asses/. The neo-Nazi/KKK group made a video of the event,
    available at spiritwaterblood, "Knoxville Rally, May 26, 2007," http://www.
    youtube.com/watch?v=fGOdH1js1co. A video made from the perspective of the
    co-protesters is at FreyaFire, "Racism Is Ridiculous," http://www.youtube.com/
    watch?v=zLjs08ykI8w.
61. Many photos and videos of co-protests with the Westboro Baptist Church are
    easily found online. One blog that collects images and videos of these and other
    protests is http://godhatesprotesters.wordpress.com/.
62. Laurie Ure, "Counter-protesters Confront Westboro Baptist Church at Arling-
    ton," CNN, http://www.cnn.com/2011/US/05/30/arlington.cemetery.pro-
    testers/index.html.
63. Quoted in Kurt Andersen, "The Protester," *Time*, December 14, 2011.
64. This chant is originally attributed to protesters at the 1999 anti–World Trade
    Organization protests in Seattle. It has been widely used in protests since then.
65. Sheldon Wolin, "Fugitive Democracy," in *Democracy and Difference: Contesting the
    Boundaries of the Political*, ed. Seyla Benhabib (Princeton, NJ: Princeton Univer-
    sity Press, 1996), 31.
66. Andersen, "The Protester."

BIBLIOGRAPHY

Alesina, Alberto, Reza Baqir, and William Easterly. "Public Goods and Ethnic Divisions." *Quarterly Journal of Economics* 114, no. 4 (November 1999): 1243–1284.

Alesina, Alberto, Edward Glaeser, and Bruce Sacerdote. "Why Doesn't the United States Have a European-Style Welfare State?" *Brookings Papers on Economic Activity* 2 (2001): 187–254.

Alex. "Clowns Kicked KKK Asses." http://www.neatorama.com/2007/09/03/clowns-kicked-kkk-asses/.

Allen, Danielle. "Law's Necessary Forcefulness: Ralph Ellison vs. Hannah Arendt on the Battle of Little Rock." *Oklahoma City University Law Review* 26 (Fall 2001): 857–895.

———. *Talking to Strangers: Anxieties of Citizenship since Brown v. Board of Education*. Chicago: University of Chicago Press, 2004.

Andersen, Kurt. "The Protester." *Time*, December 14, 2011.

Anderson, Benedict. *Imagined Communities: Reflections on the Origin and Spread of Nationalism*. Rev. ed. London: Verso, 1991 [1983].

Arendt, Hannah. *Between Past and Future: Eight Exercises in Political Thought*. Enl. ed. New York: Penguin Books, 1968.

———. *The Human Condition*. Chicago: University of Chicago Press, 1958.

———. *Lectures on Kant's Political Philosophy*. Chicago: University of Chicago Press, 1982.

———. *The Life of the Mind: Thinking*. One-volume ed. New York: Harcourt Brace Jovanovich, 1978.

———. *The Origins of Totalitarianism*. New ed. New York: Meridian Books, 1973 [1958].

———. "Reflections on Little Rock." In *The Portable Hannah Arendt*, 231–246. New York: Penguin Classics, 2003 [1959].

———. *Responsibility and Judgment*. Edited by Jerome Kohn. New York: Schocken, 2003.

Aristotle. *De Anima*. New York: Cosimo, 2008.

Avila, Oscar, and Antonio Olivo. "A Show of Strength: Thousands March to Loop for Immigrants' Rights: Workers, Students Unite in Opposition to Toughening of Law." *Chicago Tribune*, March 11, 2006.

Banting, Keith, and Will Kymlicka. "Multiculturalism and Welfare." *Dissent* 50, no. 4 (2003): 59–66.

Barry, Brian. *Democracy, Power, and Justice: Essays in Political Theory*. Oxford: Clarendon Press, 1989.

Bates, Daisy. *The Long Shadow of Little Rock*. Fayetteville: University of Arkansas Press, 1986 [1962].

Baumgardner, Jennifer, and Amy Richards. *Manifesta: Young Women, Feminism, and the Future*. New York: Farrar, Straus and Giroux, 2000.

Becerra, Hector. "World Cup Brings Mexican Flags Back to Streets of Los Angeles." *Los Angeles Times*, June 25, 2010.

Becker, Howard S. *Writing for Social Scientists: How to Start and Finish Your Thesis, Book, or Article*. Chicago: University of Chicago Press, 1986.

Beiner, Ronald, and Jennifer Nedelsky. *Judgment, Imagination, and Politics: Themes from Kant and Arendt*. Lanham, MD: Rowman and Littlefield, 2001.

Bellafante, Ginia. "Gunning for Wall Street, with Faulty Aim." *New York Times*, September 23, 2011.

Beltràn, Cristina. *The Trouble with Unity: Latino Politics and the Creation of Identity*. New York: Oxford University Press, 2010.

Benhabib, Seyla. "Democracy and Identity: In Search of the Civic Polity." *Philosophy & Social Criticism* 24, nos. 2/3 (April 1998): 85–100.

———. *The Reluctant Modernism of Hannah Arendt*. Walnut Creek, CA: AltaMira Press, 2000.

———. "Seyla Benhabib: 'Essentialism' vs. 'Constructivism' in Contemporary Theory." *Newsletter for the Institut für die Wissenschaften vom Menschen (IWM)* 55 (September–November 1996): 25–27.

Bransten, Jeremy. "Netherlands Leading EU Trend to More Stringent Immigration Rules." EUbusiness, http://www.eubusiness.com/europe/netherlands/immigration.2006-04-05.

Brown, Wendy. "At the Edge: The Future of Political Theory." In *Edgework: Critical Essays on Knowledge and Politics*, 60–82. Princeton, NJ: Princeton University Press, 2005.

———. "Political Theory Is Not a Luxury: A Response to Timothy Kaufman-Osborn's 'Political Theory as a Profession.'" *Political Research Quarterly* 63 (2010): 680–685.

———. "We Are All Democrats Now. . . ." *Theory & Event* 13, no. 2 (2010).

Brunstetter, Daniel. "The Enlightenment Strikes Back: The Dangers of France's Contrat D'acceuil Et D'intégration." Paper presented at the annual meetings of the Western Political Science Association. San Diego, California, March 2008.

Buckley, Cara, and Colin Moynihan. "Occupy Wall Street Protest Reaches a Crossroads." *New York Times*, November 4, 2011.

Butler, Judith. *Gender Trouble: Feminism and the Subversion of Identity*. New York: Routledge, 1990.

Butler, Judith, and Joan W. Scott. "Introduction." In *Feminists Theorize the Political*, edited by Judith Butler and Joan W. Scott, xiii–xvii. New York: Routledge, 1992.

Butler, Judith, and Gayatri Chakravorty Spivak. *Who Sings the Nation-State?* New York: Seagull Books, 2007.

Carens, Joseph H. *Culture, Citizenship, and Community: A Contextual Exploration of Justice as Evenhandedness*. Oxford: Oxford University Press, 2000.

Castoriadis, Cornelius. *Figures of the Thinkable*. Stanford, CA: Stanford University Press, 2007.

———. *World in Fragments: Writings on Politics, Society, Psychoanalysis, and the Imagination*. Stanford, CA: Stanford University Press, 1997.

Chodorow, Nancy. "Family Structure and Feminine Personality." In *Feminist Philosophies*, edited by J. Kourany, J. Sterba and R. Tong, 309–322. Englewood Cliffs, NJ: Prentice Hall, 1992.

Cohen, Roger. "Tehran 1979 or Berlin 1989?" *New York Times*, February 8, 2011.

Colón, Rafael Hernández. "Statehood for Puerto Ricans." *New York Times*, February 26, 1990.

Costa, Dora L., and Matthew E. Kahn. "Civic Engagement and Community Hetero-geneity: An Economist's Perspective." *Perspectives on Politics* 1, no. 1 (2003): 103–111.

Counts, Will. *A Life Is More Than a Moment: The Desegregation of Little Rock's Central High*. Bloomington: Indiana University Press, 2007 [1999].

Crary, Alice. *Beyond Moral Judgment*. Cambridge, MA: Harvard University Press, 2007.

Curtis, Kimberley. *Our Sense of the Real: Aesthetic Experience and Arendtian Politics*. Ithaca, NY: Cornell University Press, 1999.

Daley, Suzanne. "Swedes Begin to Question Liberal Migration Tenets." *New York Times*, February 27, 2011.

Dean, Jodi. *Democracy and Other Neoliberal Fantasies: Communicative Capitalism and Left Politics*. Durham, NC: Duke University Press, 2009.

———. *Solidarity of Strangers: Feminism after Identity Politics*. Berkeley: University of California Press, 1996.

Delhey, Jan, and Kenneth Newton. "Predicting Cross-National Levels of Social Trust: Global Pattern or Nordic Exceptionalism?" *European Sociological Review* 21, no. 4 (2005): 311–327.

Derrida, Jacques. *Rogues: Two Essays on Reason*. Translated by Pascale-Anne Brault and Michael Naas. Stanford, CA: Stanford University Press, 2005.

digby. "White Flour!" http://digbysblog.blogspot.com/2007/09/white-flour-by-digby-via-perlstein.html.

Disch, Lisa Jane. *Hannah Arendt and the Limits of Philosophy*. Ithaca, NY: Cornell University Press, 1994.

Dobbs, Lou. "Lou Dobbs Tonight." CNN, March 10, 2006.

Eisenberg, Avigail, and Jeff Spinner-Halev, eds. *Minorities within Minorities*. New York: Cambridge University Press, 2005.

El-Naggar, Mona, and Michael Slackman. "Egypt's Leader Uses Old Tricks to Defy New Demands." *New York Times*, February 9, 2011.

Ellison, Ralph. "The World and the Jug." In *The Collected Essays of Ralph Ellison*, edited by John F. Callahan, 155–188. New York: Modern Library, 2003.

Elshtain, Jean Bethke. "Political Children." In *Feminist Interpretations of Hannah Arendt*, edited by Bonnie Honig, 263–283. University Park: Pennsylvania State University Press, 1995.

Fahim, Kareem. "Egyptian Hopes Converged in Fight for Cairo Bridge." *New York Times*, January 28, 2011.

Fahim, Kareem, and Mona El-Naggar. "Some Fear a Street Movement's Leaderless Status May Become a Liability." *New York Times*, February 3, 2011.

———. "Violent Clashes Mark Protests against Mubarak's Rule." *New York Times*, January 25, 2011.

Fausto-Sterling, Ann. "The Five Sexes: Why Male and Female Are Not Enough." *Sciences*, March/April 1993, 20–25.

Ferguson, Michaele. "Choice Feminism and the Fear of Politics." *Perspectives on Politics* 8, no. 1 (2010): 247–253.

———. "Resonance and Recognition: The Role of Personal Experience in Iris Marion Young's Feminist Phenomenology." In *Dancing with Iris: Between Embodiment and the Body Politic in Iris Marion Young's Political Philosophy*, edited by Ann Ferguson and Mechthild Nagel, 53–67. New York: Oxford University Press, 2009.

———. "Unsocial Sociability: Perpetual Antagonism in Kant's Political Thought." In *Kant's Political Theory: Interpretations and Applications*, edited by Elisabeth Ellis, 150–169. University Park: Pennsylvania State University Press, 2012.

Fine, Ben. *Theories of Social Capital: Researchers Behaving Badly*. London: Pluto Press, 2010.

Firestone, Shulamith. *The Dialectic of Sex: The Case for Feminist Revolution*. New York: Bantam, 1979 [1970].

Flax, Jane. "The End of Innocence." In *Feminists Theorize the Political*, edited by Judith Butler and Joan W. Scott, 445–463. New York: Routledge, 1992.

"France Creates Muslim Council." BBC, http://news.bbc.co.uk/1/hi/world/europe/2593623.stm.

"France Refuses a Citizenship over Full Islamic Veil." BBC, http://news.bbc.co.uk/2/hi/europe/8494860.stm.

Fraser, Nancy. "From Redistribution to Recognition? Dilemmas of Justice in a 'Postsocialist' Age." In *Justice Interruptus: Critical Reflections on the "Postsocialist" Condition*, 11–40. New York: Routledge, 1997.

Freud, Sigmund. *"Femininity."* In *Freud on Women: A Reader*, edited by Elisabeth Young-Bruehl, 342–362. New York: Norton, 1990.

FreyaFire. "Racism Is Ridiculous." http://www.youtube.com/watch?v=zLjs08ykI8w.

Friedman, Thomas L. "They Did It." *New York Times*, February 12, 2011.

Fuss, Diana. *Essentially Speaking: Feminism, Nature and Difference*. New York: Routledge, 1989.

Gilbert, Margaret. *Sociality and Responsibility: New Essays in Plural Subject Theory*. Lanham, MD: Rowman and Littlefield, 2000.

Gonzales, Alfonso. "The 2006 *Mega Marchas* in Greater Los Angeles: Counter-hegemonic Moment and the Future of *El Migrante* Struggle." *Latino Studies* 7, no. 1 (2009): 30–59.

Goodhart, David. "Too Diverse?" *Prospect Magazine*, no. 95 (February 20, 2004).

Habermas, Jürgen. *Between Facts and Norms: Contributions to a Discourse Theory of Law and Democracy*. Translated by William Rehg. Cambridge, MA: MIT Press, 1996.

———. "Constitutional Democracy: A Paradoxical Union of Contradictory Principles?" *Political Theory* 29, no. 6 (2001): 766–781.

———. "Historical Consciousness and Post-traditional Identity: Remarks on the Federal Republic's Orientation to the West." *Acta Sociologica* 31, no. 1 (1988): 3–13.

———. *The Inclusion of the Other: Studies in Political Theory*. Edited by Ciaran Cronin and Pablo De Greiff. Cambridge, MA: MIT Press, 1998.

———. "Three Normative Models of Democracy." In *Democracy and Difference: Contesting the Boundaries of the Political*, edited by Seyla Benhabib, 21–30. Princeton, NJ: Princeton University Press, 1996.

Hartsock, Nancy C. M. "The Feminist Standpoint: Developing the Ground for a Specifically Feminist Historical Materialism." In *The Feminist Standpoint Revisited and Other Essays*, 105–132. Boulder, CO: Westview Press, 1998.

Hawkins, Karen. "100,000 March in Favor of Immigrant Rights." Associated Press, March 11, 2006.

Hinze, Christine Firer. "Reconsidering Little Rock: Hannah Arendt, Martin Luther King Jr., and Catholic Social Thought on Children and Families in the Struggle for Justice." *Journal of the Society of Christian Ethics* 29, no. 1 (2009): 25–50.

Honig, Bonnie. *Democracy and the Foreigner*. Princeton, NJ: Princeton University Press, 2001.

———. *Political Theory and the Displacement of Politics*. Ithaca, NY: Cornell University Press, 1993.

hooks, bell. "Sisterhood: Political Solidarity between Women." *Feminist Review* 23 (1986): 125–138.

Huntington, Samuel P. *Who Are We? The Challenges to America's National Identity*. New York: Simon and Schuster, 2004.

ihatethemedia.com. "Mississippi Town Figures Out Simple, Effective Way to Stop Westboro Baptist Church Funeral Protest." http://www.ihatethemedia.com/a-simple-way-to-stop-westboro-baptist-church-funeral-protesters.

Irigaray, Luce. "This Sex Which Is Not One." In *New French Feminisms*, edited by Elaine Marks and Isabelle de Courtivron, 99–106. New York: Random House, 1988.

Jackson, Jesse. "1984 Democratic National Convention Address." http://www.americanrhetoric.com/speeches/jessejackson1984dnc.htm.

Jakobsen, Janet R. *Working Alliances and the Politics of Difference: Diversity and Feminist Ethics*. Bloomington: Indiana University Press, 1998.

Kant, Immanuel. *Anthropology from a Pragmatic Point of View*. Translated by Robert B. Louden. New York: Cambridge University Press, 2006 [1798].

———. *Critique of Judgment*. Translated by Werner S. Pluhar. Indianapolis, IN: Hackett, 1987 [1790].

Keenan, Alan. *Democracy in Question: Democratic Openness in a Time of Political Closure*. Stanford, CA: Stanford University Press, 2003.

Kirkpatrick, David D. "Wired and Shrewd, Young Egyptians Guide Revolt." *New York Times*, February 9, 2011.

Kymlicka, Will. *Multicultural Citizenship: A Liberal Theory of Minority Rights*. Oxford: Clarendon Press, 1995.

Laclau, Ernesto, and Chantal Mouffe. *Hegemony and Socialist Strategy: Towards a Radical Democratic Politics*. London: Verso, 1985.

Lebeau, Vicky. "The Unwelcome Child: Elizabeth Eckford and Hannah Arendt." *Journal of Visual Culture* 3, no. 1 (2004): 1–12.

Life. "Students Rally to Protest Immigrant Legislation." http://www.life.com/image/57344276.

Lloyd, John. "Harvard Study Paints Bleak Picture of Ethnic Diversity." *Financial Times*, October 9, 2006.

Lugones, Maria C., and Elizabeth V. Spelman. "Have We Got a Theory for You! Feminist Theory, Cultural Imperialism and the Demand for 'the Woman's Voice.'" *Women's Studies International Forum* 6, no. 6 (1983): 573–581.

Lyshaug, Brenda. "Solidarity without 'Sisterhood'? Feminism and the Ethics of Coalition Building." *Politics & Gender* 2 (2006): 77–100.

Markell, Patchen. "Making Affect Safe for Democracy? On 'Constitutional Patriotism.'" *Political Theory* 28, no. 1 (February 2000): 38–63.

Marso, Lori. "Feminism's Quest for Common Desires." *Perspectives on Politics* 8, no. 1 (2010): 263–269.

Merl, Jean, and Richard Winton. "Somber Note to an Upbeat Protest Rally." *Los Angeles Times*, April 16, 2006.

Merleau-Ponty, Maurice. *The Visible and the Invisible*. Evanston, IL: Northwestern University Press, 1968 [1964].

The Milan Women's Bookstore Collective. *Sexual Difference: A Theory of Social-Symbolic Practice*. Bloomington: Indiana University Press, 1990.

Milkman, Ruth. "Critical Mass: Latino Labor and Politics in California." *North American Congress on Latin America* 40, no. 3 (2007): 30–36, 42.

Miller, David. "In What Sense Must Socialism Be Communitarian?" *Social Philosophy & Policy* 6, no. 2 (1989): 51–73.

———. *Market, State, and Community: Theoretical Foundations of Market Socialism*. Oxford: Clarendon Press, 1989.

———. *On Nationality*. Oxford: Oxford University Press, 1995.

Modood, Tariq. "Anti-essentialism, Multiculturalism and the 'Recognition' of Religious Groups." *Journal of Political Philosophy* 6, no. 4 (1998): 378–399.

———. "Introduction: The Politics of Multiculturalism in the New Europe." In *The Politics of Multiculturalism in the New Europe: Racism, Identity and Community*, edited by Tariq Modood and Pnina Werbner, 1–26. New York: Zed Books, 1997.

Mohanty, Chandra Talpade. *Feminism without Borders: Decolonizing Theory, Practicing Solidarity*. Durham, NC: Duke University Press, 2003.

Mouffe, Chantal. *The Democratic Paradox*. New York: Verso, 2000.

———. "Feminism, Citizenship, and Radical Democratic Politics." In *Feminists Theorize the Political*, edited by Judith Butler and Joan W. Scott, 369–384. New York: Routledge, 1992.

Müller, Jan-Werner. *Constitutional Patriotism*. Princeton, NJ: Princeton University Press, 2007.

Naar Nederland. http://www.naarnederland.nl/en/category/homeen.

National Public Radio. "Coordinating Flags at Immigration Marches." http://www.npr.org/templates/story/story.php?storyID=5336799.

Navarette, Ruben, Jr. "End the Protesting and Start Participating." *San Diego Union-Tribune*, March 19, 2006.

Norton, Anne. "Heart of Darkness: Africa and African Americans in the Writings of Hannah Arendt." In *Feminist Interpretations of Hannah Arendt*, edited by Bonnie Honig, 247–261. University Park: Pennsylvania State University Press, 1995.

Norval, Aletta J. *Aversive Democracy: Inheritance and Originality in the Democratic Tradition*. Cambridge: Cambridge University Press, 2007.

Nussbaum, Martha C. *For Love of Country: Debating the Limits of Patriotism*. Boston: Beacon, 1996.

Office Français de l'immigration et de l'intégration. http://www.ofii.fr/.

Panagia, Davide. "'Partage Du Sensible': The Distribution of the Sensible." In *Jacques Rancière: Key Concepts*, edited by Jean-Philippe Deranty. Durham, UK: Acumen, 2010.

Parekh, Bhikhu. "Politics of Nationhood." In *Nationalism, Ethnicity, and Cultural Identity in Europe*, edited by Keebet von Benda-Beckman and Maykel Verkuyten, 122–143. Utrecht: European Research Centre on Migration and Ethnic Relations, 1995.

Pettit, Philip, and David Schweikard. "Joint Actions and Group Agents." *Philosophy of the Social Sciences* 36, no. 1 (2006): 18–39.

Pickett, Adrienne. "Images, Dialogue, and Aesthetic Education: Arendt's Response to the Little Rock Crisis." *Philosophical Studies in Education* 40 (2009): 188–199.

Pineda, Richard D., and Stacey K. Sowards. "Flag Waving as Visual Argument: 2006 Immigration Demonstrations and Cultural Citizenship." *Argumentation and Advocacy* 43 (Winter and Spring 2007): 164–174.

Putnam, Robert D. "*E Pluribus Unum*: Diversity and Community in the Twenty-First Century: The 2006 Johan Skytte Prize Lecture." *Scandinavian Political Studies* 30, no. 2 (2007): 137–174.

———. *Making Democracy Work: Civic Traditions in Modern Italy*. Princeton, NJ: Princeton University Press, 1994.

Rawls, John. *Political Liberalism*. New York: Columbia University Press, 1993.

Reagon, Bernice Johnson. "Coalition Politics: Turning the Century." In *Home Girls: A Black Feminist Anthology*, 343–355. New Brunswick, NJ: Rutgers University Press, 2000 [1983].

Robinson, Christopher C. *Wittgenstein and Political Theory: The View from Somewhere.* Edinburgh: Edinburgh University Press, 2009.

Rorty, Richard. *Achieving Our Country: Leftist Thought in Twentieth-Century America.* Cambridge, MA: Harvard University Press, 1998.

Rubinstein, Alvin. "Is Statehood for Puerto Rico in the National Interest?" *In Depth: A Journal for Values and Public Policy* 3, no. 2 (Spring 1993): 87–99.

Russell, Peter. *Constitutional Odyssey: Can Canadians Become a Sovereign People?* 3rd ed. Toronto: University of Toronto Press, 2004.

Rutenberg, Jim. "Bush Enters Anthem Fight on Language." *New York Times*, April 29, 2006.

The Saguaro Seminar. "Social Capital Community Benchmark Survey." 2000. http://www.hks.harvard.edu/saguaro/communitysurvey/index.html.

Schlesinger, Arthur, Jr. *The Disuniting of America: Reflections on a Multicultural Society.* 2nd ed. New York: Norton, 1998 [1992].

Scott, Aemilia. "Best Church of God—Westboro Protest." http://www.yourcivicdoody.com/yourcivicdoody/2009/08/best-church-of-god-westboro-protest.html.

Shadid, Anthony. "Discontented within Egypt Face Power of Old Elites." *New York Times*, February 4, 2011.

———. "Egypt's Path after Uprising Does Not Have to Follow Iran's." *New York Times*, February 12, 2011.

———. "In Crowd's Euphoria, No Clear Leadership Emerges." *New York Times*, January 31, 2011.

———. "Obama Urges Faster Shift of Power in Egypt." *New York Times*, February 1, 2011.

Shadid, Anthony, and David D. Kirkpatrick. "Promise of Arab Uprisings Is Threatened by Divisions." *New York Times*, May 21, 2011.

Smith, Rogers M. *Stories of Peoplehood: The Politics and Morals of Political Membership.* New York: Cambridge University Press, 2003.

spiritwaterblood. "Knoxville Rally, May 26, 2007." http://www.youtube.com/watch?v=fGOdH1js1co.

Spivak, Gayatri Chakravorty. *In Other Worlds: Essays in Cultural Politics.* New York: Methuen, 1987.

Taylor, Charles. "Democratic Exclusion (and Its Remedies?)." In *Citizenship, Diversity and Pluralism: Canadian and Comparative Perspectives*, edited by Alan C. Cairns et al., 265–287. Montreal: McGill-Queen's University Press, 1999.

———. "The Dynamics of Democratic Exclusion." *Journal of Democracy* 9, no. 4 (1998): 143–156.

———. *Philosophical Papers, Vol. I: Human Agency and Language.* New York: Cambridge University Press, 1985.

———. *Modern Social Imaginaries.* Durham, NC: Duke University Press, 2004.

———. *Philosophical Arguments.* Cambridge, MA: Harvard University Press, 1995.

———. "The Politics of Recognition." In *Multiculturalism: Examining the Politics of Recognition*, edited by Amy Gutmann, 25–73. Princeton, NJ: Princeton University Press, 1994.

———. *Reconciling the Solitudes: Essays on Canadian Federalism and Nationalism.* Montreal: McGill-Queen's University Press, 1994.

———. *A Secular Age.* Cambridge, MA: Belknap, 2007.

Tully, James. *Public Philosophy in a New Key.* Vol. 1, *Democracy and Civic Freedom.* Cambridge: Cambridge University Press, 2009.

———. *Strange Multiplicity: Constitutionalism in an Age of Diversity.* Cambridge: Cambridge University Press, 1995.

———. "Struggles over Recognition and Distribution." *Constellations* 7, no. 4 (2000): 469–482.

UPI. "100,000 Rally for Immigrants in Chicago." March 11, 2006.

Ure, Laurie. "Counter-protesters Confront Westboro Baptist Church at Arlington." CNN, http://www.cnn.com/2011/US/05/30/arlington.cemetery.protesters/index.html.

US House of Representatives. The Border Protection, Anti-terrorism, and Illegal Immigration Control Act. H.R. 4437.

Walzer, Michael. *What It Means to Be an American*. New York: Marsilio, 1992.

Warner, Michael. *Publics and Counterpublics*. Cambridge, MA: Zone, 2005.

Warren, Robert Penn. *Who Speaks for the Negro?* New York: Vintage, 1966.

Wittgenstein, Ludwig. *On Certainty*. Translated by Denis Paul and G. E. M. Anscombe. edited by G. E. M. Anscombe and G. H. von Wright. New York: Harper Torchbooks, 1969.

———. *Philosophical Investigations (Reissued German-English Edition)*. Translated by G. E. M. Anscombe. 2nd ed. Malden, MA: Blackwell, 1958.

Wolfe, Alan, and Jytte Klausen. "Identity Politics and the Welfare State." *Social Philosophy & Policy* 14, no. 2 (1997): 231–255.

Wolin, Sheldon. "Fugitive Democracy." In *Democracy and Difference: Contesting the Boundaries of the Political*, edited by Seyla Benhabib, 31–45. Princeton, NJ: Princeton University Press, 1996.

Young, Iris Marion. *Global Challenges: War, Self-Determination, and Responsibility for Justice*. Cambridge: Polity Press, 2006.

———. *Inclusion and Democracy*. Oxford: Oxford University Press, 2000.

———. *Intersecting Voices: Dilemmas of Gender, Political Philosophy, and Policy*. Princeton, NJ: Princeton University Press, 1997.

———. *Justice and the Politics of Difference*. Princeton, NJ: Princeton University Press, 1990.

Young-Bruehl, Elisabeth. *Hannah Arendt: For Love of the World*. New Haven, CT: Yale University Press, 1983.

Yuki, Masaki, William W. Maddux, Marilynn B. Brewer, and Kosuke Takemura. "Cross-Cultural Differences in Relationship- and Group-Based Trust." *Personality and Social Psychology Bulletin* 31 (2005): 48–62.

Zerilli, Linda M. G. "Doing without Knowing: Feminism's Politics of the Ordinary." *Political Theory* 26, no. 4 (August 1998): 435–458.

———. *Feminism and the Abyss of Freedom*. Chicago: University of Chicago Press, 2005.

———. "Toward a Feminist Theory of Judgment." *Signs* 34, no. 2 (2009): 295–317.

———. "Truth and Politics." *Theory & Event* 9, no. 4 (2006).

Žižek, Slavoj. *Iraq: The Borrowed Kettle*. New York: Verso, 2004.

INDEX

demoi, 130
demos (the people), 23–24, 72, 80,
        84–85, 95, 96, 97, 108, 112, 113,
        114, 115–116, 117, 118, 124, 129,
        150, 156, 161
Derrida, Jacques, 80
desegregation, 33, 169n25, 169n31
dialogical agency, 11, 121–123, 124, 125,
        126, 129, 130, 134, 157,
        184nn28–29, 184n32
dialogicality, 120, 127, 130, 131, 132,
        133–134, 149
dialogue, 122–123, 184n32 (*see also*
        conversation)
difference, 19, 46, 146, 148, 154, 155,
        156, 157, 180n31 (*see also* diversity)
    accommodation of, 14, 16, 17, 18, 23
    expectedness of, 160, 163
    threat to democracy posed by, 25, 119
dilemma of democratic exclusion, 118–121,
        128–129, 132–136, 183n12
disagreement, 35, 36, 37, 38, 53, 59, 63,
        133, 140, 146, 148, 149, 154, 155,
        157, 161
    expectedness of, 39, 47, 81, 116, 135,
        160, 161, 163
    as manifestation of collective agency,
        116–117
    radical, 157, 158
disappointment, 116, 120, 135
disavowal. *See* agency, disavowal of;
        freedom, disavowal of; responsibility,
        disavowal of
distrust, 5, 10, 32, 89, 97, 106, 132
diversity, 10, 14, 15, 16, 41, 64, 67, 79,
        87, 90, 95, 96, 99, 145, 146, 147,
        154, 155, 180n30
    acceptance of, 17, 18, 21
    agency attributed to, 88
    anomie caused by, 89–91, 109, 179n15
    centrifugal force of, 4, 10, 47, 90, 93,
        94, 111
    deep. (*See* deep diversity)
    as produced by human activity, 107,
        108
    relation to social capital of, 87, 88, 89,
        111
    welfare state threatened by, 179n12
Dobbs, Lou, 141–142, 151
doubt, 67, 69, 80, 106, 153

duck-rabbit, 12, 13, 28–29, 31, 137, 138,
        161

Eckford, Elizabeth, 30–32, 34–35, 36, 37,
        38, 54, 74, 168n7, 168n16, 169n28
Egypt, 3, 6–8, 140, 156, 159, 160,
        185–186n15
Elias, Jose "El Che", 185–186n15
elites, 28, 37, 46, 75, 83, 136, 138
        (*see also* leaders; observation)
Ellison, Ralph, 33–36, 169n21
empirical claim, 42, 43, 68, 98, 100, 120
empirical truth, 5, 99, 126
epistemology, 26, 40, 43, 64, 65, 66–67,
        78, 177n39
essentialism, 62–63, 68–69, 78, 129,
        174–175n6, 175n11
essentialism/antiessentialism dynamic,
        63–65, 66–69, 78, 80, 119–120,
        174n5, 176n13, 176n19
ethnicity, 4, 8, 12, 15, 17, 21, 43, 75, 78,
        87–90, 91, 94–96, 100, 101, 102,
        107, 108, 119, 175n11
exclusion, 10, 16, 67, 71, 78, 80–81,
        116, 118–121, 128–129, 132–136,
        174n5, 176n22 (*see also* dilemma of
        democratic exclusion)
experience, 22, 39, 47, 48, 59, 63, 67, 73,
        74, 82, 83, 125, 127, 129, 145, 146,
        149, 153, 155, 159, 160, 175n7
        (*see also* first-person experience)

facts, 26, 34, 35–36, 37, 44, 46, 54, 55,
        67, 79, 104, 105, 110, 116, 128, 130,
        135, 138, 155, 170–171n51, 174n99
Faubus, Orval, 31
feminism, 62, 131, 135–136, 138,
        145–146, 148, 166n11, 187n37
feminist theory, 9, 11, 28, 61–65, 66–72,
        80, 84, 119, 129, 145–148, 170n48,
        174n5, 174–175n6, 175n7, 176n13,
        176n20, 176–177n23, 187n34
feminists, 16, 154
Ferguson, Michaele, 173n76, 176n12,
        188n46
Fine, Ben, 179n14
Firestone, Shulamith, 175n7
first-person experience, 9, 35, 40, 42, 48,
        50, 103, 106, 124, 126, 127, 131,
        140, 149, 155